MW01235702

Dementia With Dignity

Living Well with Alzheimer's or Dementia Using the DAWN Method®

Judy Cornish

Dementia & Alzheimer's Wellbeing Network®

ISBN: 1974027627

ISBN 13: 9781974027620

Library of Congress Control Number: 2017911956

LCCN Imprint Name: Amazon kdp.com

For my clients, each and every one—who have taught me, led me, put up with me, inspired me, and forgiven me in turn. They are my elders, my heroes, courageous trailblazers of the intuitive path.

We're all just walking each other home.

—Ram Dass

Contents

Foreword

So you admitted to yourself that a friend or loved one has dementia. With that admission comes the knowledge that the world as your loved one knows it is no longer the same. It's all changed, and soon much will be gone: logic, rational thinking, awareness of time, likes and dislikes, recognition, life-long behaviors. As a friend, lover, companion or caregiver, your sense of the world must now also change.

At the least, your journey will be taxing; at worst, it will be morally and emotionally destructive. You will need to learn how to navigate this new world, how to understand this new "other," and how to communicate in ways that may seem sneaky at times but would so benefit your companion. Your learning curve will be very steep. *Dementia With Dignity*, Judy Cornish's second book, will not necessarily make your learning curve any easier, but it will definitely make it more understandable. Judy's case studies are practical, and her interpretations of the world that is dementia are extremely accessible, relatable, and sensible.

This is not to say that your journey will only be emotionally taxing; it will be financially taxing as well. Securing dementia care for a loved one is the most expensive thing most families ever face. A year in a memory care unit is more expensive than a dream vacation, wedding, or college education—even some homes. So count yourself lucky to have discovered this book, for Judy's approach and techniques will give you the skills and knowledge to postpone the need for institutional care. It will still be extremely expensive to bring in outside help, but Judy's approach is your best way to keep expenses down.

Two-thirds of my way through *Dementia With Dignity* my main thought was, "Damn, I wish Judy had written this eight years ago." I say this for two reasons. First, at eighty-four years of age my Mom moved from Plymouth, Massachusetts, to Spokane,

Washington, so we would be closer. At that point I'd been designing aging-in-place living environments for the elderly for twelve years, and I thought I had an understanding of what aging means and how to support it. Yet, what my mother taught me during the last four years of her life was profound, not only *in spite of* her dementia, but through it. And I found her teachings echoed and reaffirmed throughout Judy's insightful writing. I'm not surprised, for Judy says that it was her clients who taught her the principles and techniques she shares in these pages—not a professor or textbook.

Second, and just as importantly, so much of what Judy shares would have contributed to a stronger me. *Dementia With Dignity* simultaneously works in two directions. It improves the life and well-being of both you as a dementia caregiver and your companion. And it goes beyond that, too. *Dementia With Dignity* is a catalyst—stimulating critical thinking and self-reflection, and leading the reader to understand not only how to become a better caregiver but also how to become a more engaged human being.

In the pages of this book, you'll discover a deeper appreciation for life—riches for both you and your loved one. Enjoy!

Bob Scarfo, PhD, Emeritus
Landscape Architecture

Introduction

It's Thanksgiving Day and a friend has invited me to join her family for dinner. I sit at a table set for twelve, with three generations of her family present. On my right sits Hazel, her mother, the oldest by several decades. With her soft white curls, gentle smile, and twinkling eyes, she's a gracious and attentive tablemate. She listens carefully to everything I say, sometimes gently touching my arm when asking a question, but she's listening to everyone else at the table too: she quickly joins in when laughter surges and watches each person's face with an attentive smile as they share anecdotes and memories of a long family history. In the center of the table is a sumptuous arrangement of pumpkins, gourds and foliage dusted with glitter and draped with strings of tiny lights, and candles flickering in tall brass holders; Hazel created this feast for the eyes with her daughter the day before. The clink of cutlery and crystal blends with barely audible strains of old ragtime tunes. The aroma of roasted turkey and the apple pies warming in the oven hangs sweet in the air. Hazel is captivated, and so am I, not just by the beauty of the table and the atmosphere, but by her multigenerational family in action.

Hazel is so interested in what is going on around her that from time to time I comment to her about how good something tastes—the hint of pepper in the mushroom relish or the sweetness of the buttery carrots—and bring her attention back to her plate. I'm beginning to wonder if Hazel is enjoying her family so much she might leave the table hungry. During a lull in the conversation, my friend suggests that we each share something we are especially thankful for; when it's Hazel's turn she looks across the table at her daughter and says, "I'm thankful for you. All of you." I knew she couldn't recall the identity of more than one or two people at the table, but I could see the gratitude in her eyes. Hazel is ninety-one, and she has dementia.

Another mother I know was not with her family that day. While we shared memories and good food with Hazel in my friend's home, this second mother sat in a care facility just a few blocks away. This mother lives in the south wing of a four-story building that is home to several hundred seniors. She's in the memory care unit, behind a key-coded door. If you had dropped by there that Thanksgiving afternoon, you would have seen her first through the metal mesh of a safety glass window, seated in a sturdy plastic chair at a white Formica table, with a plate of barely-touched food in front of her. Once the aide let you in, you would see from the scattered plates along the long table that the residents had just finished their Thanksgiving dinner. The centerpieces here are cardboard turkeys with pop-up tails made of iridescent yellow, orange and red tissue paper; they give the room a decidedly grade-school atmosphere under the harshness of the fluorescent lights. The smell of cooked food would hit your nose first, but not quite strongly enough to cover the more pungent odor of disinfectant and urine. You would see two other residents still sitting at the table with this mother, facing plates of cold sliced turkey, sweet potato casserole, green beans, and gravy on mashed potatoes. The gravy is gray and congealed; the food was cooked in a kitchen on the main floor and delivered already on plates. One aide is pressing a spoonful of mashed potatoes to a man's lips, which smears on his cheek as he turns away. The second aide is out of sight, but you can hear her talking loudly to someone in a room to the left of the main hall, while down a hall to the right someone is calling out: "*Help!* I need some *help* in here." This is a four-star memory care unit, where people with dementia are cared for.

If you are reading this book today, you are facing a life-changing decision, one that will affect not just you and your elders, but also your children, maybe even theirs. You are facing a fork in the road that will define your family's future. And yet most Americans have no idea that there is a decision to be made, or a road to be chosen, let alone the financial and emotional impact it will have on their family's lives. The choice is whether to provide care for their elders in their homes, using time-honored methods that support the dignity of aging, or to relinquish them to care facilities run by corporations and staffed with medically-trained aides. Our medical and senior care industries have long been telling us that the latter is the only logical choice; the norm in the United States now is to treat dementia as a disease requiring institutionalization and medication. But there is another way. It's the way that people cared for their family members for centuries, one we seem to have forgotten. It's an approach shaped by the knowledge that those who age before us are entering elderhood, not failing at adulthood; that they have arrived at a time meant for sharing wisdom and companionship, rather than accumulating skills and assets; and that they have reached life's final chapter—one that should be rich with *being* rather than the demands of *doing* and *having*.

I believe we have been led astray by what has become a hugely profitable medical industry. I saw the effects of it first as a psychosocial skills trainer working in a facility that housed both the mentally ill and people with dementia, then again from an entirely different perspective after I became an attorney and practiced elder law. I write this book with expertise and a very diverse background, but not with a medical degree. I stumbled upon dementia care through my concern for a neighbor, not through an educational program. But my lack of medical training has turned out to be the best preparation I could have asked for, because it allowed me to see my neighbor and all the people I've worked with since as people whose cognitive skills are changing, rather than as patients suffering from a disease. My life experience led me to see a new paradigm.

This book is about what dementia looks like when we focus on the person who is experiencing it rather than seeing a disease and its symptoms. It will open your eyes to the pattern of skills and abilities that remain available to people even though they have dementia, and how we as their companions can enrich not only their lives but our own as well. You'll find that I don't refer to people who are experiencing dementia as patients or describe their experience with dementia as *suffering*. Those words are disempowering and imply loss and disablement. They imply sickness and a subordinate role. Yet dementia isn't really a disease: it's a condition—something a person experiences—a syndrome associated with diseases such as Alzheimer's or Parkinson's in which people are living with the progressive loss of specific cognitive skills. As I'll show in the pages that follow, when we experience dementia we lose our rational thinking skills but not our intuitive skills; we lose our remembering selves but not our experiential selves; and although we lose the ability to choose to be mindful, we can continue to benefit from the tools of *mindlessness* well into dementia.

Dementia does not make us crazy. It simply forces us to interact with the world and people around us using a more limited set of skills than we have been accustomed to employing, and that in turn causes predictable emotional reactions. When families and caregivers recognize which skills are lost and which are retained— and provide truly strength-based support—distress is greatly reduced for everyone. This book provides tools and techniques that we can use when we spend time with people experiencing dementia, which will dramatically improve the emotional environment for both parties in the care relationship.

I have included many stories and anecdotes from my work with people living with dementia here in Moscow, Idaho, where I have two companies, the Dementia & Alzheimer's Wellbeing Network (DAWN®), and Palouse Dementia Care. My work since 2010 has been primarily with people whose families have supported them in continuing to live in their own homes; I've been able to see what dementia looks like before the artificial environment of a care facility is imposed. Of course, I have changed my clients' names and as many identifying details as possible. They deserve their privacy and they have my utmost respect. However, my caregivers wanted to have their real names used, so I have, because they believe in the value of the DAWN Method as much as I do.

PART ONE

How DAWN Care Came to Be

CHAPTER ONE

Dementia Care at Home

It is nine o'clock on a Monday morning. My staff and I are at work with our clients. Megan and Christie, two of my employees, are with clients elsewhere; Heike, another employee, is with me in a client's home—Jennie's.

Before we arrived, Megan picked up Jennie for their usual Monday morning excursion. They'll soon be eating breakfast in the Gritman Medical Center cafeteria in downtown Moscow, where the kitchen staff have already put aside a freshly-baked sweet roll just for Jennie. They know how important it is for Jennie to begin her week with a sweet roll and scrambled eggs. If there isn't a sweet roll for her, Jennie becomes fixated on trying to understand why it's not there and then increasingly agitated by this disruption of her routine. Jennie is eighty-one years old and in the middle stages of dementia. Her intuition quickly tells her if something is different or unfamiliar, but she is unable to understand *why* something has changed in her schedule, or why something is missing, because her rational thought processes are fading.

This morning, Jennie's sweet roll will be there waiting for her next to the cash register, as always, and Megan and Jennie will enjoy breakfast together like two good friends. They'll chat about events from Jennie's deep past (for example, early childhood memories of visiting her grandmother each summer), because Jennie's ability to recall anything from the recent past is gone. At present, Jennie lives alone in a condo that she and her late husband moved into over two decades ago, but the memories of her husband and children are fading. Megan will manage the conversation with Jennie by providing any needed facts about the past and future and returning often to what is happening around them in the present moment.

When Megan brings Jennie home, Jennie will begin the arduous task of doing a single load of laundry—a task that will take her the rest of the day. Without the ability to recall facts, Jennie will repeatedly return to the calendar on her kitchen counter to find out what day of the week it is so that she can remind herself what she should be doing. Jennie is very task-oriented and has long associated various household chores with each day of the week. On her calendar, the first six days of September will be crossed out, including Sunday. Her long-term memory will remind her that Mama said Mondays are laundry day, so she will go down the hall to her bedroom to retrieve her dirty clothes. There she will become distracted. She may notice a wrinkle in the quilt on her bed and straighten it, or realize that she needs to use the bathroom, or look out the window and see children playing in the backyard of the home next door. Eventually, she will return to the calendar to find out again what day of the week it is. She'll remember that Mondays are laundry day and the process will begin again. She will work her way through the steps by happenstance and visual cues. At some point, she will walk into the bedroom and succeed in gathering her dirty clothes; the next time she enters the room she will see the pile and go to retrieve the laundry basket from the bathroom; eventually she will succeed in putting the clothes into the basket and the basket beside the washing machine. As morning becomes afternoon and evening approaches, Jennie will complete a load of laundry. The task would be terribly frustrating for Jennie if she had memory, but, at this stage in her dementia, her memory span is so short that she exists in the present and frustration does not develop. When Megan returns at 5:30 p.m. with an evening meal to share, Jennie will have finished her laundry, and she will be tired and ready for companionship.

However, right now, it's still nine o'clock in the morning. Megan and Jennie are sharing breakfast at the hospital, and I'm standing in Jennie's kitchen with Heike. Heike is here to do her usual weekly "sneak clean." We must resort to stealth to keep Jennie's home sanitary because Jennie believes she is an expert at homemaking, even though she hasn't done any household chores other than laundry in several years. Like many people who have dementia, she is unaware of her impairments and so would be insulted if offered help to do chores she believes she does herself. She also believes that she cooks and eats a nutritious meal every evening, although we've been bringing in meals twice daily for more than a year.

After Heike finishes cleaning, she'll be off to pick up another of our clients, whom she'll take on a scenic drive and out for lunch. Heike knows that her primary duty is not to clean, cook, or help our clients maintain good hygiene, although she helps with those tasks as the need arises. Heike knows that her first responsibility is to provide dementia care—to manage our clients' moods, to direct conversations so they can successfully take part, to ensure that they receive enough social and sensory stimulation to be relaxed and ready to rest by nightfall, and to help them make sense of the world around them even as their sense of reality becomes increasingly altered by memory loss. In short, Heike will use her own rational thought and judgment to help our clients continue to live at home safely, and with as much happiness and autonomy as possible.

This is what my staff are doing, but what am I doing in my client's home early on this Monday morning? I'm here as Jennie's case manager, to join Heike in looking for clues indicating how well Jennie manages when she's at home alone. Dementia is a condition of cognitive decline that has no set rate of deterioration, so continuous reassessment is essential when providing dementia care.

Heike and I start in the kitchen. The cup, mug, plate, and cutlery in Jennie's dish drainer have been washed, so she still remembers dish soap and how to use it. In the trash, we find banana peels and apple cores, so we know that Jennie still recognizes that bananas and apples are food when she sees them in the fruit bowl on her counter. In the refrigerator, we can see that the milk bought last Friday is being used, so we know that she still knows a milk carton contains milk and that milk is something she likes to drink. We check the expiration dates on the juice cans in the freezer; the two lemonade cans have expired. The orange juice cans are still current, however, and in the refrigerator is a near-empty pitcher of orange juice. So while we know that she prefers lemonade to juice, the lemonade cans evidently no longer hold meaning for Jennie, while she must still recognize the orange juice cans as containing a beverage, remember how to mix up the juice, and see the orange-colored liquid in the pitcher as being something to drink. Several take-home containers from restaurants are untouched, and we remove them. During the past six months, Jennie has stopped recognizing cardboard or Styrofoam containers in her refrigerator as sources of food, and has not taken a can or box out of her pantry in months. It is likely that she also has forgotten the fact that cupboards are places where food is stored.

In the living room, we check the TV remote and see that it is set to turn on her favorite evening news station with a single push of the power button. Jennie is still collecting the newspaper from the front porch each morning: several are neatly stacked on the coffee table. Today's paper is on top, unopened. The older papers have been carefully refolded so we know she has looked at them. In the bedroom, we can see that Jennie has laid out clothing items on her settee, sorted into outfits that include tops and bottoms. The clothes she has laid out are clean, so we know she still distinguishes between clean and dirty clothing. In the bathroom, we look for evidence that she is using her bathtub. Heike carefully places a single hair in a fold of the bathmat so that if Jennie moves the bathmat this week we'll know. We also arrange the bar of soap so Heike will be able to tell whether it's been moved. The time will come when Jennie no longer remembers what soap is and forgets how to use it. Soon after that, she'll forget about bathing and how much she loves to soak in a tub full of hot water. When that time comes, Megan will invite Jennie to join her on a weekly outing to the local wellness center for a soak in their hot tub. Jennie will be happy to accompany her friend on such a pleasant outing—and be unaware that the real purpose of the activity is for her to take a cleansing shower before getting into the hot tub.

Christie, another DAWN caregiver, is driving on Highway 95, just north of Moscow, heading for the little farming community and lumbermill town of Potlatch, where she will pick up Rachel. Rachel has just finished spending the night with her son and daughter-in-law, as she sometimes does on weekends. She is ninety-two years old, has dementia, and has become very frail this past year. She lives alone with her dog, Ralph, in a condo in Moscow and is adamant that she be allowed to remain there until she dies. Her son and daughter-in-law are devoted to helping her continue to live in her own home as safely and independently as possible. While Rachel is willing to spend the night with them in Potlatch, she often becomes anxious and distracted the next morning. Within the hour, Christie will have her back at home, and the two of them will begin Rachel's usual morning routine: taking a shower, reading the paper, working through a crossword puzzle, having a nap, and enjoying Ralph's antics and seeing to his needs. Rachel will begin to relax. The entire time Christie will be managing their conversation—just like Megan is doing for Jennie—carefully introducing topics she knows Rachel feels comfortable talking about, and using casual chatter to interject any facts Rachel might need to know so that she can avoid feeling confused about the topic of the conversation. Rachel's memory is erratic and her ability to use rational thought is waning. She quickly becomes embarrassed and depressed when she can't follow a conversation or is unable to recall how to do a task. Christie helps her avoid this by cheerfully verbalizing her own rational thought processes as they complete tasks together.

Rachel gets great satisfaction from completing the crossword puzzle and has always enjoyed reading the morning paper. Christie will point out headlines and comment on news items in general terms; she will read a crossword clue aloud and then think out loud as she considers possible answers. Rachel will become more and more tranquil as she follows along with Christie's constant, lighthearted recitation of the relevant information. When Rachel tires and lies down for a nap, Christie will slip out to buy groceries and run other errands, such as picking up Rachel's dry cleaning or prescriptions. But just like Megan and Heike, Christie knows these tasks are not her primary responsibility. She is not with Rachel to take care of household chores and errands. Instead, her central role is to ensure that Rachel feels comfortable and secure, and is able to continue to enjoy the companionship of her cherished dog and the people she loves. That's Christie's job on this crisp, sunny September morning.

Now, having spent an hour with Heike reviewing Jennie's home, I feel comfortable about Jennie's ability to continue functioning on her own. I step outside onto her patio and look up at a cloudless blue sky, taking a deep breath of air scented with pine and wet grass. Her lawn slopes down to a creek, edged with brush and a few poplars and Ponderosa pines. Beyond the creek, I can just see a ranch house set low in the rolling hills that rise to meet the steep, wooded slopes of Moscow Mountain. On my left, at the edge of her patio, is a rosebush—one I know she started as a clipping from a climbing rose that once blossomed in her grandmother's backyard. It is once again covered in tiny yellow buds edged with pink. I take another deep breath. It is a typical Monday morning, a crisp September morning that will no doubt turn into another hot, late summer afternoon in northern Idaho. My staff and I are with, or soon to be with, people we love—our clients. We are providing dementia care for our elders, in their own homes.

The Beauty of DAWN Care

As you can see, what we do here is radically different from the usual approach to dementia care, which is medication and institutionalization. This approach is what I learned during five years spent working directly with people living with dementia in their own homes, often without family nearby; I learned it from them—my neighbors, my elders, people from all walks of life: professors, ranchers, housewives, and business owners. As we spent time together, I saw a pattern in what they could and could not do, a pattern of loss that is the opposite of one I once experienced in my own life to a lesser degree. I saw that while they were losing their rational functions, such as analysis and judgment, they retained—and in some cases seemed to be honing—their intuitive skills, such as reading other people's emotions, enjoying what their senses show them, and experiencing beauty. Recognizing this pattern made it possible for me to see how I could help them continue to live with dignity and remain independent despite having dementia. I have found that if my staff and I take care of the rational functions for our clients by providing companionable support in their daily activities, they become more relaxed and are able to enjoy life using their remaining intuitive skills.

In the language of the dementia care community, the DAWN method uses the habilitative approach, and an experiential rather than biomedical model. It represents what is called *person-centered* or *person-directed* care (we'll look at dementia care philosophies in more detail in chapter 4). Rather than offering another variation on the traditional medical approach to dementia, this approach is unique because it shifts the caregiver's attention from symptoms to emotions. In other words, I believe the problem caused by dementia is not "dementia-related behaviors," but rather the emotional distress that people experience when they undergo progressive cognitive impairment. The tools and approach that I detail in this book focus on identifying emotional needs, because I believe that if we look at emotional distress as the central problem, and the behaviors of those with dementia merely as manifestations of this distress, their behaviors become predictable and avoidable. Medical professionals think of dementia-related behaviors such as anxiety, wandering, and sundowning as being caused by failing communication skills, inability to perform tasks or cope with the environment, or compounding health issues.[1] I see them as having a single root cause: the emotional distress which people experience as they become less able to communicate or perform once-easy tasks. This focus on meeting emotional needs and recognizing retained skills, combined with support of the person's loss of rational thinking skills and memory, is what makes the DAWN approach so effective.[2]

---

[1] For an example of the conventional argument, see *Understanding Difficult Behaviors*, by Robinson, Spencer, White (2007).

[2] Wandering is a particularly difficult dementia-related behavior. The Mayo Clinic suggests that it is due to stress, fear, boredom, attempting to meet a basic need (like finding a toilet or food), searching, or following past routines. We have very little trouble with it; I believe this is because we are meeting our clients' emotional needs, and giving them adequate sensory and social stimulation each day.

The way we care for our clients here is unique, but it isn't rocket science. It requires no college education or medical training. I have watched a six-year-old intuitively use my principles in her interactions with her grandmother and, at present, I am teaching an eight-year-old to apply these techniques with his grandfather. The tools that I will outline in detail in the coming chapters are versatile. They will help families living with loved ones experiencing dementia just as surely as they help my caregivers and me with our clients, or help caregivers working with the residents of long-term care facilities. My reason for writing this volume, as well as my first book (*The Dementia Handbook – How to Provide Dementia Care at Home* (2017)), is to empower the families and caregivers of people experiencing dementia. With this book, I provide you with a set of tools for caring for your loved one in a way that will replace their distress with a sense of security and wellbeing, and lower your stress as well. It will provide you the means of accessing and creating the same joy in caring for someone who is experiencing dementia that brought my staff and me to work so happily on that sunny September morning. And it will allow you to postpone the crushing expense of long-term care.

Why We Need Home Dementia Care

We cannot put off learning how to enable people who are experiencing dementia to stay at home longer and in more safety and comfort. Dementia is the most likely health issue American families face today. In 2014, the Johns Hopkins Clinic reported that by the time we reach the age of sixty-five, we have a one in ten chance of developing dementia, while the Alzheimer's Association estimates that 14 percent of Americans seventy-one years of age and older have dementia. In 2016, there were more than 5.5 million people living with a diagnosis of Alzheimer's disease (which accounts for 60-80 percent of the dementias diagnosed), meaning that something closer to 8 million people were diagnosed with dementia. And yet, only about half the people who would meet the diagnostic criteria are diagnosed, so a conservative estimate would be that there were about 16 million families dealing with dementia in 2017. And these numbers are expected to increase at a rate of 35 percent by 2030 and 110 percent by 2050.[3]

Yet, dementia is not only the most likely health issue American families will face, but also the most expensive. On October 27, 2015, the American College of Physicians published a paper announcing something that elder law attorneys have known for years. In a study primarily funded by the National Institute on Aging, researchers found that healthcare costs for dementia were substantially larger than for other diseases (such as cancer and heart disease), and that many of the expenses were uninsurable, placing a huge burden on families.[4] Medicare does not pay for home health care or stays in facilities unless nursing care is required due to an illness or injury that first resulted in a hospital stay. Medicaid does not cover the cost of long-term care until families have used up their own resources. In many states, Medicaid doesn't cover home health care at all—forcing families to put their loved ones into institutions when they can no longer afford to pay out of pocket for assistance at home.[5]

However, according to the SCAN Foundation (an organization devoted to improving long-term care for the disabled and elderly), state Medicaid programs still bear the brunt of the cost of long-term services and supports. In 2012, Medicaid paid $134.1 billion for long-term care services and supports, which was

---

[3] For an in-depth look at the prevalence of dementia, see the Alzheimer's Associations' *2017 Alzheimer's Disease Facts and Figures*, available online at: https://www.alz.org/ri/documents/facts2017_report(1).pdf. The Alzheimer's Association updates and republishes this publication yearly.

[4] See the *New York Times* article "Costs For Dementia Care Far Exceeding Other Diseases, Study Finds," at http://www.nytimes.com/2015/10/27/health/costs-for-dementia-care-far-exceeding-other-diseases-study-finds.html?_r=0. A synopsis of the study is available on the Annals of Internal Medicine website at: http://annals.org/article.aspx?articleid=2466364.

[5] This is still true in Idaho, even though the Idaho Legislature states in its *State Plan for Alzheimer's Disease and Related Dementias*, published in March 2013, that the cost of caring for a person with dementia in a facility is three times the cost of providing in-home caregivers.

about 31 percent of all Medicaid spending.[6] Families paid an additional $49.3 billion. It is estimated that 70 percent of people aged sixty-five and older will use long-term care and that people over age eighty-five (our fastest growing population segment) are four times as likely to use long-term care as those between sixty-five and eighty-four years of age.[7] Think about the cost of long-term care versus other expenses families typically face. In 2014, the *U.S. News & World Report* republished a comparison study they originally posted in 2012 (the most recent I could find). The one-year cost of the average mortgage is under $13,000; in-state tuition at a public college averages $23,000 annually, while one year at a private college is about $45,000. An average wedding costs $28,000. Compare that with one year in a private room (not a suite, just a room with a bed) in a care facility: the average cost rose from just over $90,000 in 2014 to $97,452 in 2017.[8]

When I talk about the cost of dementia with other elder law attorneys, we agree that far too often we see the wealth of families being consumed by care facilities rather than being passed on to their children. Dementia is bankrupting both the traditionalist and baby boomer generations. When families must pay for care for a family member in a facility, many see a lifetime of savings disappear in just a few years—leaving little or no income for the healthy spouse who continues to live in the community. When spouses are able to care for each other in their own home, or family members are able to move in and provide care, they are giving a momentous gift to the person with dementia and the rest of the family.

As dire as all this is, there is presently no treatment or cure for dementia. No drug has yet been shown to consistently slow the progression of the condition. In the United States, the Alzheimer's

---

[6] See the SCAN Foundation Fact Sheet, January 2013: "Who Pays for Long-Term Care in the U.S.?" available at http://www.thescanfoundation.org/who-pays-long-term-care-us.

[7] See the Kaiser Family Foundation's publication #8617-02, "Medicaid and Long-Term Services and Supports: A Primer" (December 15, 2015).

[8] See the article titled "Compare Long Term Care Costs Across the United States" at https://www.genworth.com/about-us/industry-expertise/cost-of-care.html.

Association has been working to encourage state governments to publish plans to address the seriousness of having such a large number of individuals disabled by cognitive impairment and unable to care for themselves. However, we have spent a pittance on searching for a cure for dementia and Alzheimer's disease compared with what we have invested in other diseases. The AARP reports that for the fiscal year 2015, the federal government committed $5.4 billion to studying cancer, $3 billion to research on HIV/AIDS, and $1.2 billion to studying heart disease. Funding for Alzheimer's research, however, was set at just $566 million.[9] Finally, in September 2017, the Alzheimer's Association announced that the Senate Appropriations Committee had approved an additional $414 million increase for Alzheimer's and dementia research for the fiscal year 2018 budget, which would bring the amount allocated for research up to $1.8 billion. Yet, despite our limited investment in finding a cure, we hear more about finding a cure than we do about developing better ways to care for the huge number of people who already have dementia. I agree that we need a cure, but our more pressing need is to find a better way to live and work with the people who have dementia right now—one that is humane, one that accords them dignity and respect as our elders. The expense of institutional care in both dollars and quality of life should lead us to first focus on ways to postpone or avoid using it, then on ways to treat and cure dementia so fewer people are in need of care.

This is what I set out to do here in Moscow, Idaho, more than seven years ago. I knew I could not find a cure—I'm neither a doctor nor a scientist. But I knew I could spend time with my clients and learn what they needed from me, as a companion. I believed that, if I paid attention and persevered, I could find ways to help them be happier and safely remain in their own homes for longer. At first, I dared dream only of helping those whom I came into contact with here. Then, as I found I could train my staff and

---

[9] See the January/February 2015 AARP Bulletin for an article by T.R. Reid titled: "Where's the War on Alzheimer's?" at http://www.aarp.org/health/brain-health/info-2015/alzheimers-research.html. In this article, Reid points out not only the lack of research funding for dementia but also the stigma and financial and personal costs of the condition.

our clients' families how to use the approach I was using so successfully myself, I realized I could do more and help more people. A friend offered to guide me, and her encouragement and business acumen helped me found DAWN. Then, when Atul Gawande published his book, *Being Mortal* (2014), I saw the beginning of a much-needed conversation regarding health and aging in the United States, and I began to write this book. In *Being Mortal*, Gawande asks America to wake up to the polarity between treatment and care, between preserving life and preserving the quality of life. I believe we need to apply that same awareness to the way we respond to dementia. We cannot afford to carry on the way we have been, believing that warehousing people in long-term care facilities and quieting their distress with psychotropic drugs is appropriate. We need to turn to the great thinkers of our times and look across disciplinary borders to understand the duality of our rational and intuitive thought processes, the existence of both our experiential and remembering selves, and the joy that can be found with those who, due to dementia, now live only intuitively and in the present.

We can and should be equipping families to care for their loved ones at home, by themselves and with caregivers trained specifically in dementia care. We need to create a new support industry—actual dementia care agencies—that can be hired to provide case managers and dementia care specialists trained in working with memory loss and cognitive impairment. If the system of case managers and dementia care specialists that we use here with the DAWN method were available across the country, families that cannot care for their loved ones could bring in professionals trained to monitor and meet the changing needs that dementia creates. Dementia care will never replace senior care— there will always be seniors who are frail and need assistance at home with the tasks of daily life. Most of us will need care from time to time as we age, in facilities staffed with nurses and aides who can meet our medical needs. We will always need hospitals and skilled nursing units for providing medical and rehabilitative care, but we also need dementia care that recognizes and supports autonomy and enables us to age in place, at home. Aging in place means not only a higher quality of life but also less expense—to us, to Medicare, and to Medicaid. As a society, we cannot afford to ignore the expense of long-term care and, as a culture, we cannot ignore the distress that treating dementia as a disease is causing.

CHAPTER TWO

My Journey to Dementia Care

Looking back into my own past, I recognize two experiences—helping my father run his vocational rehabilitation business, and taking a job as a psychosocial skills trainer before starting law school—that led me to dementia care, the work that has become my vocation.

In 1994, when I was in my mid-thirties, my father was diagnosed with amyotrophic lateral sclerosis (Lou Gehrig's disease). He needed immediate help with his business, a vocational rehabilitation firm located in Vancouver, Canada. His firm assessed and retrained people who had been injured on the job and were receiving benefits from the provincial workers' compensation system. I had left Canada to marry an American fifteen years earlier, and was raising my children with my husband in southern Oregon when my father became ill. I returned temporarily to Vancouver to help him. This is where my education in working with people with cognitive impairment began.

When I took over my father's case management duties, I began arranging medical and psychological evaluations, skill and aptitude testing, and educational and vocational opportunities for his clients. We would place clients with employers to see how they functioned in the workplace and then interviewed their supervisors, coworkers, and family to see where they were successful and where they needed help. Once we had written up our findings, we presented reports to the Workers' Compensation Board and made recommendations regarding our clients' pensions and rehabilitation. Although it was analytical work, it also required a great deal of creativity; it was more like creating a work of art or writing a story than drafting a legal brief. We were looking at the whole of a person's abilities and disabilities, and coming up with new ways for him or her to function and succeed. It was the process of looking for and recognizing a pattern—a set of related facts—that would solve the problem of reemployment. I was relying heavily on intuitive thought and creativity, which I enjoyed, since as a child I had been deeply involved with art, spending most of my time in secondary school with the art teacher, and completing my academic studies at home on my own.

For me, the most interesting aspect of my father's business was working with people who had suffered traumatic brain injury (TBI). TBI usually results from a violent blow or jolt to the head or body. About one in ten of our clients was learning to live and work with cognitive deficits due to an on-the-job TBI injury. In addition to documenting their abilities and writing proposals for their futures, we also designed practical solutions to help them function more successfully at work and at home. I found devising ways to overcome a person's cognitive impairments to be creative and rewarding work. By comparison, my previous jobs as a graphic designer and a management training executive at the Hudson's Bay Company seemed unimportant and mundane. Now, in helping people cope with disabilities, I discovered the satisfaction of doing something of lasting value for others.

One of our clients, whom I'll call Bill, had intact working memory—he could repeat back to his employer exactly what he'd just been asked to do—but had no short-term or long-term memory. That meant that within a few seconds, he could no longer recall the task he'd been assigned. It was the same at home. He constantly found himself looking around a room he'd just entered, unable to recall why he had entered it. To help Bill navigate this new cognitive landscape, we created a note system for him, putting notes in each room so he would know what his next task was. For example, when his alarm rang in the morning, he would reach to turn it off and his hand would brush a note taped to his clock. The note told him to put on his slippers and go to the bathroom for more instructions. In the bathroom, notes told him to brush his teeth and shower and return to the bedroom, where notes told him to get dressed, and so on. I found outwitting memory problems and devising ways for people to live on their own and support themselves very fulfilling. At the time, I thought I'd found my life's calling.

However, within the year my father had closed his business. I returned to Oregon, enrolled in college, and earned an undergraduate degree in literature and language. I chose this area of study because it again called on my creativity and intuitive thought processes. From childhood, I had been drawn to patterns as well as to creative and intuitive activities, in comparison to which rational thought seemed limited and pedestrian. For me, creating a painting, drawing, or print had been a matter of selecting the most complementary elements in a face or scene and reproducing them on the page in a balanced and satisfying pattern. A piece of literature was just another collection of patterns—this time conceptual and verbal. Helping someone learn to speak a language, or write a language, seemed to be a matter of recognizing the patterns or systems latent in the new language and expressing them in terms of those that typically occurred in the student's native language.

In 1999, I finished my undergraduate degree. My youngest son was still living with me. I had graduated top of my class in both my major and minor, and received a scholarship from the Ford Family Foundation, which had funded my undergraduate degree, to continue studying languages in a master's program at the Monterey Institute of International Studies in Carmel, California. Attending the Monterey Institute, however, would have required a move from a small Oregon town (La Grande) to a California city, quite an adjustment for my son just as he was beginning high school. I decided to look for a local job while I considered my options. Both the Ford Family Foundation and the Monterey Institute agreed to hold my scholarships until I could use them. So my son and I stayed on in La Grande and I took a job working as a psychosocial skills trainer in a twenty-five-bed lockdown facility for the mentally ill. Once again, I was working in the world of cognitive impairment; here I began learning about mental illness. As a psychosocial skills trainer, my role was to help the residents gain the skills needed to interact better with each other and with people outside the facility. For most, possible trips out might include lunch, dinner, or a visit to a park; others needed to remain within a more controlled environment. Again, my work meant thinking about how to help people with cognitive limitations navigate daily life, and how to work with someone whose understanding of reality differed from mine. And as I considered ways to improve the lives of our residents, I was once again doing creative work that drew more upon my intuitive skills than on my analytical abilities.

Yet there was one aspect of my job that I didn't enjoy at all. In the same building, on the other side of a key-coded door, was an Alzheimer's unit with about a hundred beds. I had never encountered this disease before. At that time, I didn't know that Alzheimer's was one of many causes of dementia—the most common in the United States. From the first week on the job, what I heard coming from the other side of that door, learned from the staff working on that side, or saw when I was in the Alzheimer's unit on an errand, was heartbreaking. Sometimes I heard screams of pain, terror, or anger. Staff members on the other side of the door were exhausted and seemed hardened to the suffering. They were exasperated by their patients rather than concerned about them—cranky, not saddened. When they visited in our unit, they joked about how upset or afraid their residents were, and sometimes recounted little ways they had devised to retaliate against them for causing extra work. One morning, while going from room to room in the Alzheimer's unit looking for the nurse on duty, I walked into a room and heard an aide yelling at a resident in the bathroom. "You're not getting off that toilet until I *say* you can get off that toilet! Do you hear me? You'll sit there, and you'll stay there, until I'm good and ready to get you off, so quit pushing that help button." The aide's voice was laced with derision. She didn't even look embarrassed when she came around the corner and discovered me standing there, though we both heard the sobs coming from the bathroom.[10]

---

[10] Tom Kitwood, a pioneer in the field of dementia care, wrote about the malignant social interactions that can become standard inside care facilities in his book *Dementia Reconsidered* (1997). Allen Power, an internist, geriatrician and professor of medicine at University of Rochester, New York, who has practiced in care facilities for decades, describes how we can change the culture in our care institutions in his book *Dementia Beyond Drugs* (2010).

By the summer of 2000, I'd been working in the enhanced care facility for ten months, and I didn't think I could continue. Seeing the indignities and verbal abuses in the Alzheimer's unit was too painful, and I feared becoming inured to them, like some aides I'd met who had worked there for years. I knew that neither the residents of our unit nor those of the Alzheimer's unit were at fault for their disabilities. I believed that we should be especially careful that we treat people who struggle to make sense of the world around them with dignity and respect. I couldn't understand how an entire class of people could be locked up in such emotional pain.

I had enjoyed working with people who had cognitive impairments in both my father's business and in the enhanced care facility because I felt that I was doing something positive on their behalf. Finding the patterns in someone's thinking and behavior, and crafting a solution that made daily life better for both that person and their companions, felt like an art form: it was just as intellectually stimulating as exploring literature or learning a new language. But now my enjoyment in working with cognitive impairment was joined by a deep antipathy toward institutional care, and a sense of responsibility to do something to change the system. I had chosen my calling. I just didn't know how to go about making it into a job.

On August 10, 2000, I had a flash of insecurity, and called the Ford Family Foundation to confirm that my scholarship for graduate school was still being held. Within minutes, my advisor called back, profusely apologetic, to say that, because of recent changes in the graduate program, my sizable scholarship was about to expire. On the first day of September, in fact, a mere three weeks away, I'd lose this precious doorway to future learning. I immediately did a Web search for graduate programs in Portland, Oregon, where I knew my son could attend high school in one of Oregon's best school systems. I looked for master's programs that would allow me to work with people with disabilities, but everything medical or psychology-related required an undergraduate degree in the sciences. Somehow I stumbled on Lewis & Clark Law School. Surely, I thought, a law degree would give me a way to help people in institutions or others who were disempowered? I called their registrar's office.

By five o'clock that same afternoon, my hurried application for law school had been accepted, and I was told to report for the first day of classes on August 28. What followed was two and a half weeks of frenetic activity as I worked out my two weeks' notice at my psychosocial skills trainer job, found an apartment in Lake Oswego, arranged for my son's placement at Lake Oswego High School, and moved to Portland. On August 28, my son and I both began our new lives. Over the next three years, I took classes in disability law, elder law, wills and trusts, family law, dispute resolution, mediation—anything that might prepare me to work in institutional care for the elderly. But in so suddenly deciding to study the law, I had unwittingly uprooted myself from the world of creativity and intuition and landed myself in one that required strict analytical thought. This had quite an impact on my emotional comfort.

Law school is designed to teach people to think with unrelenting rationality. To me, thinking rationally felt like trying to play the piano with one hand, or exchanging the diversity of Legos for the uniformity of Lincoln Logs. Instead of finding patterns and thinking globally, my preferred thinking approach, I now had systematically to amass facts, analyze them, and then apply the law to arrive at a definitive result. Around that time, I read a quote on the Web attributed to Einstein: "The intuitive mind is a sacred gift and the rational mind is a faithful servant. We have created a society that honors the servant and has forgotten the gift." This statement perfectly expressed my reaction to the intensive study of the law. Relying on my rational thought processes and ignoring intuitive thought felt profoundly limiting to me, but I nevertheless complied (after all, I did want to complete my law degree). I learned to think and write using purely rational thought supported only by facts. Nevertheless, I remained determined to use these new, sharp-edged skills to help people in institutions, and others at the mercy of compassionless systems.

That determination led me to the law school's clinical program, where I worked in the tax clinic during the final two years of my degree program. One of my first clients was May, who had married a longtime friend when they were both in their seventies. In their previous marriages they had been friends, and when their respective spouses died, they believed they knew each other very well already. What May did not know was that her new husband was in the early stages of Alzheimer's disease. He had been a very successful businessman; as they lived their first years of marriage together, he seemed to be taking care of their finances. She knew he was distracted at times and a little forgetful, but he went to his office each day. When she questioned him, he told her not to worry and asked her not to interfere in their business affairs. For four successive years, he asked her to sign their tax returns. Each year May assumed that he filed them when they were completed.

One night, he awoke and tried to throw her out of the house: he no longer remembered having married her and thought she was an intruder. She called the police; he continued to be belligerent, and was taken to the emergency room for an evaluation. His Alzheimer's disease was finally diagnosed, and his wife found herself suddenly on her own. After a letter arrived from the IRS asking why no taxes had been filed or paid for the previous three years, she learned they were bankrupt. He had been pretending to go to the office, but in fact had lost his ability to make decisions and transact business. He'd lost not only his own savings but hers as well. We did succeed in demonstrating to the IRS that she was an innocent, unknowing victim of her husband's incapacity. My previous work with people who had brain injuries and mental illness helped in this process, as did my exposure to the Alzheimer's unit before I attended law school, because I could understand what she had experienced, describe his behaviors, and convincingly argue his ability to mask his condition.

Another client I worked with seemed to be manic. I overheard the director of the tax clinic telling him that the clinic's caseload was full and that we could not take his case, but I recognized his likely condition from his responses, and volunteered to work with him. He was a brilliant man, a software engineer who worked as a computer systems consultant and had a reputation for creative problem-solving that outshone his erratic behavior. He was in his early forties, with a patient and devoted wife who gave birth to their first child during the time I was working with him. True to his condition, this man had gone from one job to another, and had worked in sixteen different states over a period of five years without filing any state or federal income tax returns. Naturally, his recordkeeping was terrible, and as his advisor I had a hard time getting the same information out of him twice.

Two weeks after his son was born, he came dashing into the clinic with the baby in a carrier and two policemen right behind him. He had been rushing to be on time for the appointment, and was not being careful about how wildly he was swinging the carrier. Passersby had called the police to report child endangerment. We got him into my office so I could calm him while the staff calmed the baby and contacted his wife, and the director assured the officers we would make sure the baby was back with his mother immediately. Working with this client was always dramatic. It took very creative approaches to get him to focus on the task at hand, as well as all my analytical skills to sort out what he owed to whom, so we could deal with his tax problems. I found working with these two clients very rewarding because I was able to help them settle the tax cases against them and extricate them from their problems with the IRS. I was somewhat on track with my ideal future career: I was helping people resolve problems with an agency that had great power over them, and of which they were, in a sense, victims.

After graduation, I spent two years working at the Oregon Tax Court and the Oregon Supreme Court as a law clerk, and another year as an associate at a divorce firm. I then went into private practice and focused on elder law cases. The five years I spent working as an attorney in Oregon were not happy ones for me. I had hoped to find a way, through my role as a clerk at the tax court and state supreme court, to have a positive impact on seniors and people struggling with disabilities, but in the end I failed. My subsequent move to the divorce firm was a digression, and my elder law practice gave me no satisfaction either. I found that when a family came to me for help with a parent's estate it was usually too late to have a positive impact at a human level, because the children were often divided by misunderstandings that could have been avoided with more knowledge and better advice during their parents' final years. Final years which, as it happened, frequently seemed to have been complicated by dementia.

For example, one of my first elder law cases was to settle a small estate for Hannah, who had died and left behind two adult daughters. Both had demanding jobs; one daughter lived within ten minutes of her mother's home, and the other two states away. I could see, when I began gathering Hannah's financial records and paying her debts, that she had been buying extensively from television shopping channels and ordering from telemarketers. Most of her assets had disappeared during the past two years. Hannah had multiple subscriptions to the same magazines, and her home and garage were so packed with unopened boxes that there were only pathways from room to room. For many months, the automatic deductions she had agreed to when making purchases had been overdrawing her accounts and triggering huge fees and interest charges.

The daughter living nearby was exhausted and frustrated from trying to reason with her mother, heartbroken by her inability to help her, and angry with her sister for not helping more. The daughter living at a distance remembered their mother only as the very organized and capable parent they had grown up with, and so was convinced that her sister had been negligent with Hannah's money. Her brief visits during Hannah's final years were not lengthy enough for her to comprehend the extent of Hannah's confusion. Neither daughter understood that Hannah was experiencing dementia. No matter how much I tried to explain what must have been going on, neither would forgive the other, or even consider her sister's point of view. I wrapped up Hannah's estate with little confidence that those two women would ever be able to reconcile their differences. I wished that someone had taught them earlier about dementia, and helped them work together to provide appropriate care for their mother.

Another elder law case I worked on involved a dispute over the distribution of a large estate between a woman's seven surviving children, some of whom again lived nearby and others far away. The youngest son had moved back home with his mother when she became forgetful. At first, he lived with her as an independent adult, but as she became more confused he took over her finances. Soon he was using her accounts as his own. When he moved her into a care facility, he met and married a nurse and they both stopped working and lived as if they had retired—on his mother's money. When his mother died six years later, there was a lot of money missing from the estate. Some of his siblings thought that the "caregiver" brother deserved every penny he'd taken, because he had looked after their mother; some thought he had acted improperly. By the time it was determined that he and his wife had used up about a quarter of a million dollars on drinking, gambling, and living expenses, and once the various parties' lawyers had been paid, the family was estranged and only two siblings that I know of were still speaking to each other.

Although I was dealing with senior issues, I still didn't feel good about my work. I didn't want to become involved in the affairs of families so late in the process that I could only watch them break apart. Instead, I wanted to be involved at an earlier stage, where I could help families stay together. It was early 2008 and I was unhappily living in Portland, Oregon, liking neither my job in elder law nor the city itself. I knew my heart was still in helping those who were disempowered by cognitive impairments and living in institutions. I knew I preferred using my intuitive and creative skills over using my rational and analytical skills. My son was by this time attending university in Europe with no plans to return to Portland, so I decided to not only look for a career that I felt good about, but for a living situation I liked better as well. I stopped taking new clients, began gradually closing my practice, and started thinking about where I would like to live. I decided to look for a small city or town, still in the Pacific Northwest but with a sunnier climate than Portland, where I could use my law degree and legal skills in ways that aided the community as well as my clients. By December, my business was closed and my condo sold. I headed east, for the Rocky Mountains and the Inland Northwest, ending up in the town of Moscow—home of the University of Idaho. The rolling hills and wheat farms of the Palouse and the small-town atmosphere of Moscow immediately felt like home, so

24

I began getting to know my neighbors, making new friends, and talking to the local lawyers. Then fate intervened. A friend of my landlord dropped by, saying she needed help for her mother who lived alone across the street. Her mother had been diagnosed with Alzheimer's disease and would have to move from her home of many years into a care facility if no-one living nearby could keep an eye on her. I offered to stop in and take her on her errands and activities because, after all, I wasn't working yet. Soon another neighbor's parent needed help, and another; within three months, I was helping half a dozen seniors, and had to hire staff to help *me*.

At first, I thought that I had accidentally started a senior care business. However, I soon realized that we were not primarily working for seniors who had become physically frail and needed help with housekeeping or personal hygiene. Instead, nearly all our clients had dementia. They were becoming increasingly forgetful and confused, and needed increasing supervision and assistance with tasks like taking medications regularly, paying bills on time, keeping their homes safe and in good repair, caring for their pets, remaining involved with their usual activities, and keeping in touch with their friends.

Further, most of the seniors we were working with were unaware of their growing impairment. This made meeting their needs a delicate matter: my staff and I had to find ways to help without impacting their dignity or sense of independence. To do this, we had to make our presence in their lives seem due to our friendliness rather than their neediness. Those who understood that they were losing their ability to take care of themselves were afraid and despairing; however, the majority were offended by offers of help, even though they were increasingly frustrated and confused by simple tasks in their daily lives. All of them were becoming more isolated as they became afraid of being embarrassed in conversations, and increasingly unable to remember the people and activities they once knew well. I gradually understood that my clients needed emotional and psychological support in conversations and in maintaining their usual routines far more than someone to do tasks for them. Given the right prompts and someone to lend a hand when necessary, they could maintain their confidence and function well enough to remain in their own homes, rather than be forced to move into institutional care.

The Beginning of the DAWN Network

Now I had no time to think about what area of the law I could work in, to help people who were subjected to the indignities I had seen in the Alzheimer's unit. Instead, I was spending my days with people who were living with dementia in their own homes; I was trying to understand how to help them stay happy and safe, and pondering how to train my staff to help them accomplish these goals consistently and effectively. One morning, during that second summer, I sat at the kitchen table with a ninety-year-old man who was completely unaware that he had dementia. We were sipping tea and reading the *New York Times* aloud together. I was carefully expressing any facts his memory and rational thought failed to provide. His home was clean, his laundry folded, his refrigerator stocked—all of which had been done by my staff without his knowledge, while I was out to lunch with him the day before.[11] Without our help, this man would have continued to resist care, and would eventually have been medicated and locked away in a memory care unit. I suddenly realized I had accomplished my goal. I had found work I could feel good about. I was contributing something of value to the community I had chosen to make my home. Most importantly, one person at a time, I was now helping people with cognitive impairment avoid the indignities of institutional care.

I keep referring to the two distinct types of thought people have, rational and intuitive. Let's now take a little time to consider the properties and functions of these two very different types of thinking skills. Most of us correctly associate reason with rational thought, but not as many of us can accurately describe what it means to use our intuitive thought processes. However, as I came

---

[11] This is a good example of how, without rational thought, someone with dementia will fail to see cause and effect: it never occurred to this man that someone must be doing his household chores (although in my experience male clients are more likely than female clients to accept magically clean homes and laundry!).

to understand not long after that morning when I sipped tea and read the *Times* at my client's kitchen table, when we live or work with someone who is experiencing dementia, it is essential that we understand the attributes and benefits of each of these equally valuable, yet very different, thought systems. I have come to believe, through my work with my clients, that the behavior of people who have dementia is primarily and profoundly affected by the loss of the first type of thought, and retention of the second.

rational   *intuitive*

CHAPTER THREE

Left Brain, Right Brain?

The most beautiful thing we can experience is the mysterious.
It is the source of all true art and all science.
—Albert Einstein (1879–1955)

What do I mean when I talk about the difference between the rational and intuitive functions of the brain? Generally, we think of our intuitive and creative thought processes as being our right brain activity, with rational thought being a left-brain function. This left brain/right brain terminology comes from Roger Sperry, an American psychobiologist who wrote about the concept during the 1960s.[12] The terms have come to be widely used, although they are not accurate (our intuitive functions are not located exclusively in the right hemisphere of our brains, nor are our analytical thought processes located only in the left). We know now that the terms are simplistic and unsubstantiated, as the work of scholars such as Iain McGilchrist demonstrates.[13]

Our rational thought processes are based on logic. The English word *rational* ultimately derives from the Latin root *ratio*, and refers to that which is reasonable or logical. When we make

---

[12] See Michael Parrish's article on Sperry's life and accomplishments at http://brainconnection.brainhq.com/2001/06/26/roger-sperry-the-brains-inside-the-brain.

[13] See the TED talk by Iain McGilchrist at https://www.ted.com/talks/iain_mcgilchrist_the_divided_brain. For an in-depth discussion of why asking how our brains function is more important than determining which hemispheres does what (and how the divided brain has shaped the cultural history of the Western world), see his multi-disciplinary book, *The Master and His Emissary* (2009). McGilchrist is a psychiatrist, neurologist, philosopher, writer, and Oxford scholar.

choices or comparisons, search our memory, or consider whether we behaved appropriately in a social situation, we are using rational thought. Using rational thought takes conscious effort and attention, and can be interrupted. If I am sitting here at my desk writing this paragraph and my phone rings, my train of thought will be broken; I will find myself wondering who is calling and, likely, whether I should answer it. After I hang up, or even after simply considering whether to answer, I may not be able to recall exactly what I had been thinking or writing prior to hearing my phone ring. When I consider, or go back and reread the previous paragraph to try to recapture my train of thought, I am using rational thought, something I choose to do consciously.

Conversely, intuitive thought is unconscious (or, more accurately, something that takes place beneath the level of consciousness) and includes hunches, gut feelings, and instincts. This type of thinking doesn't occur sequentially; we just seem to know how we feel about something. This is because our intuitive thinking processes are the ones that take into account and respond to our experiences and emotions, not just knowledge we have consciously set out to learn. This type of thinking is not linear or systematic, but abstract. It's not for considering details, but for looking at the big picture and gaining a global impression. If I had answered that earlier phone call and found it was someone calling to ask about arranging care for her parents, my intuitive thought processes would unconsciously have interpreted her emotions and intentions even though our interaction was over the phone. By the time I hung up, I would have arrived at certain assumptions about her affection for her parents, and her reasons for calling, which would have been derived not from the words she'd actually spoken but from the intonation of her voice.[*]

The fact that we have two distinct types of thought has been written about in various cultures for centuries, and in modern fields of study such as neuropsychology, philosophy, religion, and law. Carl Jung, the psychologist and psychotherapist celebrated as the founder of analytical psychology, defined intuitive thought as "perception via the unconscious," explaining it as a means of arriving at ideas, possibilities, and patterns. He saw intuitive thought as the source of creativity, and creativity as a precursor to great thinking.[14]

Instinctive and Instant Thought

Have you noticed that sometimes you think slowly and carefully, and sometimes you seem to have made a decision or responded to something without thinking at all? Let's imagine that I'm at my home here in Moscow on a frosty spring morning and decide to drive downtown to have a cup of coffee. I back out of my driveway slowly, checking both directions first to make sure no one is coming. Once on the road, I accelerate slightly and head toward the corner at the end of my block, noticing as I drive by that Carmen's tulips have bloomed. *They're lovely!* I think. *What a pretty pink. Shell pink, I think that's called.* Then I spot a for-sale sign by the next house. *Moving? Already? But that young couple just moved in. What happened?* At the corner, I stop, look both ways again, and notice that where trees hang over and shade the road, it's still frosty. I drive carefully through the intersection, which takes me down a slight hill toward a blind curve. As I drive, thoughts continue to pass unbidden through my mind. *The road is slick. April and the roads are still icy. Not much snow, but lots of ice this year.* I am primarily using memory and my rational thinking skills. Then, as I come up on the blind corner, I see a young woman riding a bicycle on my side of the road. *Boy, I wouldn't want to be on a bike this morning—she's probably freezing.* I'm still thinking my unhurried thoughts as I ease closer to the center line to make sure I pass her safely, but as she and I enter the blind curve, her front tire whips out from under her and she falls to the left, her helmet on a collision course for my right front tire.

I swerve over the center line and just avoid crushing her. My next conscious thought is *I hope she's okay!* I find myself glancing from the rearview mirror to the curb, where I pull over as quickly as I can. But how did I manage to miss her? Did I swerve without thinking? No, actually: I did think, but not with a conscious,

---

[14] If you're interested in another enjoyable discussion of our intuitive and rational thought systems, turn to Daniel Kahneman's fascinating book, *Thinking, Fast and Slow* (2013). Kahneman refers to our two systems of thought as System 1 (intuitive thought) and System 2 (rational thought).

rational thought process. Instead, I employed my intuitive thought: my instantaneous and subconscious thinking. My arms didn't "decide" to turn the wheel by themselves (although it may have seemed so); my brain told them to. Yet this certainly wasn't a rational decision—if a car had been coming around the blind corner, I would have hit it head-on. The type of thought that made me swerve was one of our oldest brain functions. It was an instinctual reaction to the threat of harming a fellow human, and it allowed me to instantly respond to the indication of danger. Intuitive thought draws upon the accumulation of our varied life experiences, shapes perception, and gives us instantaneous reactions.

The pattern I began to see as I worked with my dementia clients, with their varied backgrounds and different types of dementia, was that they were all retaining—and sometimes even seemed to be developing—their intuitive functions, although their rational functions were fading away. This observation is the basis for our belief at DAWN that our clients' intuitive faculties are a strength that can be supported, and is the foundational key to this method. I can't provide a scientific explanation for why the intuitive skills seem to remain longer. I can only posit that it may be because intuitive thought includes some of our most primal skills.

Our intuitive thought system, which receives information from our senses, is also the source of much pleasure. When we look at a painting or a landscape, we immediately find it pleasing or displeasing. After this initial reaction, we might then begin using our rational thinking processes to analyze or explain to ourselves (or others)—to rationalize—why we find the piece or scene appealing, or not. Sometimes we even produce reasons that lead us or others to change our initial reactions to what we've seen. Intuitive thought is at work with our other senses as well: when we hear something melodious, taste a delicately flavored sauce, or smell roasting meat, our enjoyment comes primarily from our intuitive thought system. Even as my clients progress into the latter stages of dementia, for as long as they retain a particular sense, they retain that instantaneous response of pleasure or displeasure.

Let's suppose you and I are walking down Main Street in Moscow and we catch a whiff of something baking at Wheatberry's Bakery just down the block. Both of us will have instant responses of *Mmm!* whether we voice them or not, and even if we don't know exactly what it is that has just come out of the bakery's ovens, we will both recognize the wonderful smell and involuntarily savor it. But if we then cross the street and walk around the corner and into the alley behind the co-op, where they keep the trash cans and recycling bins, we'd probably have the opposite response, one just as instantaneous and automatic. Again, we won't know exactly what we are smelling inside those cans, but our reactions will be strong and immediate. Our senses provide us with lots of varied stimuli—sometimes enticing, sometimes repellent—that we don't need facts or additional information to enjoy (or abhor).

✗   So sensory stimulation is a key source of pleasure. If we hear a piece of music, we don't need to know the name of the song or composer, or when it was written, to be brought to tears by its beauty. One of our clients finds great enjoyment in attending classical music concerts, particularly symphonies in which someone is playing a clarinet. Her enjoyment stems from the fact that her daughter played the clarinet since childhood, and is now a professional clarinetist. She can no longer remember this daughter's name or even that she ever had children. She no longer knows what a clarinet is, and would never recognize one. But the sound of a clarinet activates feelings of love, acceptance, and pride within her.[15] All of us have associations like this. Enjoyment that comes to us via our senses can give us immediate pleasure in the present, with no need to access the past or the future, which is why people who have dementia benefit so greatly from it. Further, without the distractions provided by the intrusion of memories or

---

[15] In technical terms, this is an example of classical conditioning, famously demonstrated by Russian physiologist Ivan Pavlov and his salivating dogs. He showed that when dogs heard a sound they associated with food, they salivated (see http://www.simplypsychology.org/pavlov.html). This concept underlies behavioralism and comparative psychology, and continues to be central to modern behavior therapies.

rational thought, they are even more fully present and more able to enjoy all the stimulation and beauty their senses bring to them.

Instantaneous thinking, recognizing beauty, and enjoying the information our senses give us are all aspects of our intuitive thought system. Another skill associated with this system is our ability to sense how other people are feeling. Think of how we read the facial expressions, voices and body language of those around us. If I were to go into the bicycle shop in downtown Moscow and walk up to two salespeople talking, I might not know either person. However, when they look up at me I am likely to be able to tell instantly, from their expressions, body language or other cues, whether they are talking about something they don't want me to hear. When we know a person well, it's even easier to perceive what he or she is feeling. Suppose I walk into the kitchen and my husband is sitting at the table playing solitaire on his iPad. Even if his back is to me, if I say, "Darling, would you come for a walk with me, please?" I will know while the word "please" is still hanging in the air whether he feels willingness, ambivalence, or irritation. The more intimately we know a person, the easier it is for us to read an emotion from a posture, expression, tone or ever-so-brief pause. If you're like me, you spend a lot of time using your rational thought processes to mull over the information that your intuitive thought processes have instantaneously provided.

Some of us are better than others at reading our companions' facial expressions and body language, but people who have dementia do not lose their abilities until the very late stages of dementia, if ever.[16] In fact, as we'll discuss at length in chapter 6 when we explore how to manage a loved one or client's mood, people with dementia often pick up on our emotions and moods instantaneously—and retain them for a long time. This is a blessing if we have communicated a positive emotion, but potential trouble if we have communicated exhaustion, anger, worry or other negative emotions. Caregivers of people who have dementia need to understand and constantly remember that mood is easily read

---

[16] In *Dementia Beyond Drugs*, Allen Power reports having seen people score 0 out of 30 on the Mini-Mental State Exam, a score that demonstrates severe impairment, who can still recognize a companion's distress and offer comfort.

by their companions, and may well have a pronounced impact on them, positive or negative.

Facts, Facts, Recall

At the beginning of this chapter, I quoted Albert Einstein on the pure beauty of the mysterious. I think that with this statement, Einstein, a legendary analytical thinker, was acknowledging the essential value of our intuitive thought processes—a value even higher than rational thought. This is not to suggest, however, that we should ignore the value of our rational thinking skills, or the difficulty that comes with attempting to navigate our daily existence in the twenty-first century without these skills. Life for anyone in a first-world culture today involves dramatically more rational thought in the form of timekeeping, decision-making, and multitasking than at any other time in history. The word "multitasking" was originally coined to describe something a computer could do; it didn't become an attribute of people until the late 1990s. We make appointments and keep rigorous track of time, down to hours, by minutes and sometimes seconds. It wasn't always this way. People who are now in their eighties and nineties can remember a time when punctuality could mean showing up within the hour. Further, we now expect to be in constant communication with everyone in our lives, near and far, via telephone, voicemail, email, text messaging, and social networking. When I was a child, staying in contact with a family member living at a distance meant sitting down and writing a letter to be sent through the mail; I didn't expect a response for at least a few weeks. Now I wonder if my son is okay if I don't receive a response to my e-mail by the day's end. Keeping track of events at such a rate requires the constant exercise of memory and rational thought.

Our homes are filled with technological gadgets that require rational thought to operate, from coffeemakers to thermostats to television remotes and cell phones, and some of them require regular updates that substantially change their functioning. Using each of our devices requires that we retain and recall information, and act analytically. When people lived their entire lives in a single village or town, and their work involved caring for animals or tending gardens or crops, there was far less change. Less change meant less to relearn or remember. If someone developed dementia, but had lived in the same building or on the same farm since childhood, memories from the distant past would remain accurate, and would continue to guide them in their lives. However, when someone has moved numerous times, often from one city to another while pursing career advancement, and then from a family home into a condo or retirement community in hopes of simplifying daily life, their long-term memories are of no help to them when dementia begins to affect them. In fact, since these memories are out of sync with the present, they only increase the person's confusion about the present. Retaining the knowledge you grew up with in Northern Idaho, that when the last daffodil wilts it's time to plant vegetable seedlings, won't help you find your way home from the grocery store now that you're living at your daughter's home in Austin, Texas. You'll need recent memories and rational thought for that. If you have been moved into an assisted living facility in hopes of helping you stay safer and more socially connected, you will need memory and rational thought to cope with your new surroundings and build new relationships. Memories from the deep past are no help in learning to wake, eat, and sleep on a new schedule, or for finding your own doorway among the many doors that line the corridors. Those activities require learning. Our modern lives require constant adjustment to change, so we need intact rational thought processes to take care of ourselves and accomplish even the simplest of daily tasks.

Rational thought is focused, deliberate, and linear, and it takes effort. It allows us to accomplish an enormous range of tasks, from navigating our day-to-day world to applying systems and laws equitably and accurately, setting up and running communities, industries and nations. Our rational thought functions deal with facts, which are stored in memory. Think back to my description of driving downtown for coffee. Every conscious thought that passed through my mind was based on memory and facts: that the flowers I saw were tulips, what shade of pink they were, what my neighbor's name was, when the young couple moved in, and why the road was slippery. Each of my thoughts would be an answer to a question of who, where, what, why, when, or how. When we ask someone a question, we are asking him or her to use analytical, "left-brain" processes. We are asking the listener to pay attention to our words, decipher what information is wanted, arrange the correct facts in the relevant order, and then use language to communicate those facts back to us. This is successful when both parties have access to their rational thought processes. But if the person who is asked for information has dementia, we are asking him or her to use skills that are rapidly becoming inaccessible, if they've not already disappeared.

One of my clients, Carla, has a devoted son who lives far away. He has phoned his mother every Saturday evening for years. As Carla aged into her eighties, her son Juan noticed signs of confusion and memory loss and their weekly phone calls became more difficult. In the past, their conversation would be a chance to update each other on the events of the week—joys, concerns, visits, and happenings among family and friends. But as her dementia progressed, Carla became increasingly uncomfortable talking on the phone because her ability to recall what she had done that day or any other day was fading away. Juan and I talked about the problem; I recommended that Juan simply stop asking her about her week and what she'd done and whom she'd seen. At first it was difficult for him to do this, because he felt he was being rude and uncaring, but Juan soon found that when he focused on telling his mother about his activities rather than asking about hers, she became more relaxed. Sometimes her memory would be jogged and she could volunteer an anecdote about her own week. Juan gradually came to understand that allowing Carla to listen, letting her absorb his happiness and devotion during those minutes on the phone, were acts of kindness that adapted to his mother's changing abilities. When Juan stopped asking Carla to use the memory and rational functions that she was losing, Carla's anxiousness to get off the phone disappeared and she began to enjoy Juan's calls again. She loved listening to her son's voice, hearing about his week, and knowing that he loved her enough to call. Juan was allowing his mother to communicate with him using her intuitive functions only.

Our Durable Intuitive Functions

My clients' often make comments which demonstrate how their intuitive functions are still intact, perhaps even stronger. One of my clients, Mia, was both physically frail and experiencing dementia. Her very busy daughter could only take a few days off to help her move from her home to an assisted living facility, so the time available for this major operation of sorting and packing was limited. Mia lay on the couch in her living room and watched as her daughter sorted possessions and packed boxes as fast as she could, working faster and faster as the afternoon wore on, for the movers were scheduled to arrive in the morning. Suddenly Mia burst out, "Thank you for loving me this way!" Rather than thanking her daughter for the tasks she was performing that made the move possible, which would have been a factual statement, Mia recognized the motivations and feelings behind her daughter's actions, and expressed her appreciation for those. This was her intuitive brain at work.

Recently, a friend of mine was trying to decide whether it was time for her mother, who has Alzheimer's disease, to move from assisted living into a memory care unit. She decided it wasn't when her mother took her arm and said, "I can't think of the word, but I feel as if I'm a fifth grader and you're locking me away with kindergartners." Being unable to think of the word she wanted could have been either a failure of her memory or indicative of her fading vocabulary skills. However, my friend's mother clearly knew how she felt about the proposed move, and being able to recognize our own feelings about a matter is a function of our intuition thought processes. If we, as caregivers, can recognize this truth—that the intuitive function of *feeling* emotions remains intact despite the loss of the ability to name or express them—we can use it to help our loved ones and clients feel heard and understood, and working with them will become less difficult.

Throughout our lives, we are very accustomed to having both types of thought at our disposal. When I meet a friend for lunch, I primarily use my rational thought processes to select my meal, but my intuitive ones to enjoy it. I use my rational thought processes to follow my friend's explanation of why spending

Easter weekend with her husband's family doesn't appeal to her, but my intuitive processes to recognize that underneath her declarations of needing a quiet weekend at home is insecurity about not being as socially accomplished as they are. We routinely use both types of thought processes to get through the day. When we begin losing one set of thinking skills to dementia, and memory as well, the simplest tasks and interactions become difficult. Here in Moscow, as we spend time with our clients, no matter what activity we are engaged in, we remember that they are losing their ability to recall information and use rational thought. We take care to remind them of facts (without grilling them and making them aware of what they've forgotten), thus becoming supportive companions in their daily lives. When people experiencing dementia have companions who support their abilities and recognize the skills they are losing, they can remain safely at home for much longer, rather than be put into care facilities at great expense to their wellbeing and their families.

However, providing care that supports a person's enduring skills rather than focusing on their increasing deficits is not the typical approach. On the contrary, certain very different philosophies have shaped the way Americans typically care for people who are experiencing the progressive cognitive decline of dementia. These philosophies, which shape our assumptions about what proper dementia care is, are based on misapprehensions and inaccuracies about the human mind. They cause great and unnecessary harm and misery. A closer look at the assumptions of standard dementia care in America will allow us to recognize these deficiencies, and improve the way we care for people with dementia.

CHAPTER FOUR

Redesigning Dementia Care

Dave and Susan

A heavy thump on the ceiling overhead jarred Dave from deep sleep. He felt a jab of apprehension. Someone or something appeared to be in the attic. He reached for Susan, his wife, but discovered her side of the bed was empty. In fact, the sheets on her side of the bed felt cold, which meant she must have been gone for a long time. She must be in the attic.

Dave sat up, but a pang of pain in his shoulders and wrists forced him to stop moving until it eased. Arthritis was his constant companion, even in the heat of summer. He blinked to clear his vision and took a deep breath. Early morning light lit the wall across from him. Bracing one hand against the nightstand and the other against the bed, he pushed himself to his feet and shuffled out of the bedroom, through the hallway, living room, and kitchen, to the foot of the stairs.

Stopping there to catch his breath, his thoughts wandered over what their lives had been for the past two years. He had become concerned about Susan's memory lapses and uncharacteristic irritability two summers before, and convinced her to see their family doctor with him. Their doctor had sent them on to a neurologist, who diagnosed Susan with vascular dementia caused by her blood-pressure problems. Since then, she had become increasingly irritable, lashing out at Dave over small things like finding a fluff on the carpet or seeing water spots in the bathroom sink. She began to have periods of weepiness and depression as well. Gradually they had arrived at a workable routine, with a housekeeper coming in weekly and Dave accepting Susan's outbursts as unavoidable. Lately, however, she had started becoming increasingly difficult to look after, with daily episodes of delusions and wandering. At Susan's appointment last week, their family doctor had recommended putting her into a memory care unit, but Dave believed marriage meant caring for each other until death and was determined to keep her at home. For the past few weeks, she would sleep only an hour or two at a stretch, so Dave was becoming increasingly exhausted. Last night he had been up with her twice, the last time at three o'clock, when he had made her a mug of hot milk and tried to convince her there wasn't a nest of spiders outside the front door that had to be exterminated immediately. It had taken more than an hour to get her back to bed.

Now, as he stood at the foot of the staircase steadying himself against the handrail, it was just after six. The house was bright with long rays of sunshine, and Dave could hear goldfinches squabbling at the birdfeeder outside the kitchen window. For Dave, though, the beauty of the summer morning held nothing but the promise of another long, exhausting day of struggling with Susan. Dave looked up the stairs, hoping he wouldn't have to climb them, and saw that the half-door into the attic at the top was open. Dim light spilled out onto the landing. He couldn't hear anything, but his hearing wasn't what it used to be. *Could she really have pulled herself up into the attic?* he wondered. The attic floor was three feet above the level of the stair landing.

"Susan, darling—are you up there?" he called.

"Yes. We need the tree."

"The *tree?*"

"Yes!" She sounded irritated.

"Susan, what tree are you looking for?" Dave began to climb the stairs, gripping the handrail tightly as he mounted each step.

"Christmas! They're coming—I can't find the tree!"

"Susan, it's not Christmas. No one is coming. It's *August*, not Christmas."

"Yes, it is! Come help me. Danny and the girls. *You hid the dollhouse!*" Now Dave could hear hysteria in her voice.

He paused halfway up to catch his breath. *Dollhouse? Christmas?* Dave was groggy from lack of sleep and his joints ached. He resented having to climb the stairs. *A dollhouse?* Their son Danny and his wife had divorced a decade ago. Danny's girls were now twenty-four and twenty-seven years old—certainly not interested in dollhouses. Where on earth had she come up with dollhouses? Dave resumed climbing. When he reached the top of the stairs, he stood on the landing and looked into the attic, his breath ragged. The attic was a jumble of boxes and old furnishings extending the width of the kitchen and living room, with bare rafters, plywood flooring, and a space down the middle just wide enough to crawl along. He could see Susan on her hands and knees, past the single lightbulb that dangled from a rafter about twelve feet in. She must have found a box of winter clothes, for she seemed to be wearing a parka. When she turned and looked over her shoulder at him, her face was red and sweaty, whether from exertion or the heavy jacket Dave didn't know. He sincerely hoped he wouldn't have to climb in to get her. He didn't think his right wrist could take any more pressure that morning, and he hadn't tried to crawl that far in a long time.

Dave sighed. "Susan, come here. It's not winter. It's not Christmas. Come here. Come here *now*."

"*No!* No, no, *no*—I won't! Leave me alone. Leave me! Go away!"

"Susan—I—it's not Christmas. Susan—"

"Go away! Christmas! *Go!*" she cried. Her face was now very red, and she turned and crawled as fast as she could toward the farthest corner of the attic.

■ ■ ■

Poor Dave. It wasn't even breakfast time, yet he'd been dealing with Susan's delusions off and on all night, he'd had little sleep, and there was a long day ahead of him. There is no question that he loved her and was trying to care for her in the best way he could. His intentions were to be a loving and responsible husband, and to keep Susan safe in her home—*their* home. Yet his beliefs about how he should respond to her altered view of reality and

43

changing needs as her dementia progressed were increasing her confusion and misery rather than helping her feel more comfortable. Dave was not only becoming physically exhausted and emotionally drained, but also becoming frail as he tried to keep up with her. Dave and Susan are rapidly approaching a crisis.

The Appropriate Care Approach and Reality Orientation

Dave's approach to caring for Susan is typical of how most of us respond to dementia. Whether we are looking after someone in a home setting, or working with residents in a care facility, our knee-jerk reaction when people are confused about reality is to correct them. We want them to understand what is *really* happening. We do this because we treasure truth and integrity.

Historically, in our care facilities, medical staff and aides have been taught that enforcing acceptance of reality, of what is actual and true, is the proper way to provide dementia care. It is the default approach in the United States; we call it *appropriate care*, which loosely defined means care in which the expected clinical benefits outweigh the expected negative side effects. *Reality orientation* refers to the correction of someone's confused beliefs about time, place, or events. It is the default approach that many well-meaning families and caregivers use with their loved ones and clients at home as well. However, when we attempt to convince people who are experiencing dementia to accept that what their brains are telling them is false, and what we say is true, we produce profound emotional unease.[17] When Dave, faithfully following reality orientation, reminded Susan that it wasn't Christmas, so no children were coming over, and that it was summertime, he jarred Susan's world view and humiliated her. As often happens, this brutal, head-on approach failed miserably. Susan didn't accept Dave's version of reality, accurate though it was. She did not believe his assertion that it was August, and crawl back out of the attic. In fact, decades of experience with dementia-related behavior

---

[17] For a poignant depiction of the potential pitfalls of reality orientation, see this post: https://local.theonion.com/dementia-patient-s-family-keeps-ripping-her-away-from-i-1819578494. *The Onion* is an online newspaper that uses satire and humor to draw attention to important social and political issues.

in our care facilities have shown us that correcting the realities of people with dementia seldom results in compliance and acceptance of the caregiver's explanation. More often, the result is anger and belligerence from the person experiencing dementia (who cannot use reasoning to consider the validity of someone else's version of reality), and then behaviors that put the person and others at risk, followed by use of psychotropic medications to calm and control those behaviors.

I used reality orientation with my traumatic brain injury clients in my father's vocational rehabilitation business, and with my mentally ill residents in the enhanced care facility. I had learned it in Canada because, in Canada as in the United States, it was the dominant theory of care for working with those populations, and for people with dementia as well. However, it failed to help my dementia clients, much as it failed to help Susan. I believe this is because people with dementia are, by definition, losing their ability to employ rational thought. During the first year that I worked with people who had dementia, I realized that when I attempted to correct a client's perception about what was true or real, I would get one of two responses. If I was successful in convincing my client that what I believed to be true was actually true, and that what he or she believed to be true was not, I then found myself dealing with a person who had lost faith in his or her own ability to perceive reality. The result of that deeply unsettling realization was withdrawal, depression, fear and insecurity. More often, however, I would be unable to convince my clients they were wrong about whatever it was they believed to be true. I then often found myself dealing with someone who was angry, belligerent, and determined to continue doing what he or she *knew* was right.

One thing that didn't occur to me was to assume that my clients' behaviors were simply random symptoms of a diseased brain, even though my colleagues in senior care seemed to think so. While studying language and grammar, I'd read a book by Mina Shaughnessy called *Errors & Expectations* (1977). The premise of her book is that our errors in learning to speak or write a language are neither random nor illogical, but rather the result of our previous experiences with language. Having read that book, when

I tutored students in the language or writing labs during my undergraduate studies, I expected to find patterns in their errors just as I had seen patterns in literature and art. This proved true. There were patterns in my tutees' errors that reflected, among other things, their native languages, early socialization, and degree of exposure to written English. Later, when I found myself faced with difficult behaviors from my dementia clients, I again expected there to be a pattern I could discover and a way to avoid their negative behaviors. Behaviors, I reasoned, were logical expressions of our brains at work. They would be influenced by past experiences and emotions, just like errors. And the primary and most overwhelming pattern that appeared in my clients was their altered sense of reality.

This first pattern seemed obvious: our version of reality is necessarily based upon what we remember, so someone who is losing the ability to remember will have a sense of reality that is different from someone whose memories and memory skills are intact. I already knew that if I tried to reinstate my clients' memories, even gently, by reminding them of what they should already know, I would succeed—at best—in proving to them that their brains were impaired, without supplying any way of remedying this impairment—hardly a reassuring or desirable result. After a few months of working with my dementia clients, I had concluded that it was pointless to try to make someone who has lost memory and rational thought rejoin me in my reality, or at least my highly rational version of reality.[18] It would be the same as explaining to someone who has lost a foot the mechanics of walking and how she had previously walked, and then expecting her to join me on a hike. Since dementia actively erodes our loved ones' and clients' ability to join us in *our* reality, I thought why shouldn't we accept their version of reality, at least in our

---

[18] In this book, I speak of "reality" as being something singular and shared by all who have healthy brains, even though advances in neuropsychology have shown reality to be individualized and subjective. I do this to keep our focus on the changes to the perception of reality caused by dementia. It would be more accurate to think of our individual realities as being like a flock of birds swirling and flowing in synchronized flight, no bird colliding with another, until dementia takes away the ability to stay in formation.

interactions with them, and attempt to make the world they inhabit safe and comfortable? Early in my work with my dementia clients, I stopped trying to correct their rational "errors," and instead began supporting and working with their beliefs about what was real.

The Habilitative Approach

In her book *Learning to Speak Alzheimer's* (2003), Joanne Koenig Coste explains the vital need for caregivers to work with their loved ones' or clients' altered sense of reality. Coste coined her approach *habilitation*, which she explains as providing care in ways that make people who have dementia more capable. She developed this approach in the same way I did: by loving and caring for someone who had dementia—in her case, her husband—and being determined to find a way of making care at home possible. "If I can reach him on an emotional level," she writes, "instead of on a verbal or cognitive one, maybe life can be less threatening and frustrating for him." She goes on to explain that when we as caregivers use the habilitative approach, we do not ask people who have dementia to join us in our reality, nor do we expect them to function in their homes as they have always done, or learn new ways to cope. Instead, we care for them by altering their environments to meet their changing needs and diminishing abilities. We now talk about habilitative care as being person-centered or person-directed, and as being *strength-based* (focusing on the person's abilities rather than disabilities). With the DAWN method, we use the habilitative approach to make our clients more capable in three very specific ways. We alter our clients' physical environments as necessary for safety, enrich their lives with appropriate stimulation, and communicate with them by supporting their loss of memory and rational thought. In other words, we support their strengths.

With the DAWN method, we never correct the misapprehensions of our clients. I cannot overstress the importance of this rule. If you want to keep your loved one at home and care for him or her yourself, or if you are a caregiver working with people who have dementia, the most important step you can take toward decreasing the number of stressful interactions you experience is to stop expecting someone who is losing memory to join you in your reality, which is informed by so many crystal-clear, short-term memories. When progressive cognitive impairment causes people to experience an increasingly altered sense of reality, their inaccurate beliefs are clearly not the result of their own dishonesty. Therefore, we are not being dishonest if we accept the alterations to reality which they cannot avoid. Our loved ones and clients are no more able to use memory and perceive our version of reality than someone who has lost a leg in a car crash is able to grow another.

Anyone who has spent time with someone experiencing dementia knows that dealing with dementia-related behaviors can cause extreme stress for caregivers. Being the caregiver of a loved one at home is particularly debilitating because of the frequently round-the-clock demands of the person, and the difficulty of finding someone who can step in to give the primary caregiver a break. Behaviors such as exit-seeking, pacing, excessive talking, combativeness, hallucinations, and repetitive actions can reduce even the most skilled and devoted caregiver to tears even before breakfast is over. Not surprisingly, when I look at books on caring for someone with dementia, I find entire sections devoted to behaviors and how to deal with them. This advice is organized by situation, or task, such as how to deal with behaviors that occur when bathing, eating, dressing, or using the toilet. The consensus in the medical community seems to be that behaviors have multiple causes and are difficult to address.

I agree with the former statement, but not the latter. I agree that behaviors have multiple causes—specifically, emotional causes. When we look at them as symptoms of underlying emotional needs, rather than as random responses to various situations, the pattern becomes plain and the behaviors far easier to deal with. A person's refusal to take a shower and his desire to leave a room could be prompted by fear. Or the same two behaviors could be caused by a need to express autonomy, or by the desire to feel in control. They could also be the outcome of the need to resolve confusion. I found that when I looked at my clients' behaviors as symptoms of their emotional needs, rather than as random expressions of a diseased brain, I was able to identify effective responses.

This approach was also the result of a context I imported from the law. In the law, we gather facts, look for the underlying issues, identify and apply rules, and reach conclusions. The facts were my clients' widely varied behaviors, and the stress my staff and I experienced as we tried to preserve both their safety and their autonomy. Although at first their behaviors appeared unrelated or even random, in the law we expect that facts may look unrelated until an underlying issue is identified, so I looked deeper. The three issues that became apparent with all my clients were: loss of memory and rational thought processes, emotional distress due to this loss, and the almost paradoxical retention of intuitive thought processes despite their other cognitive losses. The rule I applied was threefold: support their cognitive losses, meet their emotional needs, and recognize the skills they retained. When I applied this rule, my clients became happy and relaxed, and their behaviors ceased to be problematic. I had identified a solution.

The seven DAWN tools are, in effect, an organized system of providing support for the loss of rational thought and memory, as well as specific emotional needs that arise from the progressive cognitive impairment of dementia. These tools were shaped by my dismay at my first experience with an Alzheimer's facility, my love and respect for my dementia clients, and my desire to help them continue to enjoy life. When we focus on our loved ones' and clients' emotions, we are paying attention to *them*, not merely to their behaviors. This shift in focus changes the caregiving model, from treating symptoms to helping the person—the whole person. We move from understanding dementia as a disease requiring medical and pharmacological treatment—a model that is causing such distress to residents of countless memory care facilities today—to concentrating our attention on the very individual needs and experiences of the people who have dementia. This is the essence of strength-based dementia care, and the purpose of this book.

The DAWN method is predicated on this new understanding of dementia and its treatment, which is espoused by a handful of leading dementia experts. Coste said that while many experts concentrate on treating the negative behaviors of dementia, she finds it vastly more helpful to her clients when she concentrates on dementia's negative impacts on their emotions. Likewise, in *Dementia Beyond Drugs*, Allen Power states that if we define dementia as a disease, our response to those who have it will be protective rather than empowering, and our focus will remain on diagnosis, prevention and cure, so that we cannot help but see medications as the appropriate vehicle for dealing with behaviors (which appear as symptoms of the disease). This conventional biomedical model may be appropriate for doctors, researchers and scientists, who are engaged in finding cures for dementia. But it is a poor model for families and caregivers—for those of us who are living and working with dementia. We need to focus on what our loved ones and clients are experiencing, and identify their feelings and needs. In other words, we need to provide care rather than treatment.[19] When we define dementia as ongoing cognitive impairment that gradually changes perception and function, but not personhood, we are being respectful of those who are experiencing it and recognizing their station in life as our elders. Our focus will then be on maintaining autonomy, maximizing wellbeing, and changing the environment to minimize the effects of their growing detachment from the "normal," rational world. The best model for caregivers to provide humane, dignified lifestyles for their loved ones or clients is the experiential model, which concentrates on the emotional needs of the people who are *experiencing* dementia.

My diverse background, not medical but legal and experience-driven, led me to expect to find logical patterns in the behaviors of my dementia clients. Paradoxically, my legal training and expectation of finding a pattern is a good example of what Harvard professor and founder of the Langer Mindfulness Institute, Ellen Langer, describes as context. We often understand

---

[19] Yet the biomedical model exemplifies America's current approach to not only dementia, but to aging as well. Atul Gawande's book *Being Mortal* (2014) provides a sobering and eloquent discussion of aging and dying in America today, where the response to aging is one of treatment rather than care.

and solve problems within predetermined frameworks, which can either limit or expand our overall grasp of them. Yet seeing a problem in a radically different context can be beneficial. When we think of heroin as a street drug, for example, we may forget that it can be beneficial when used as a painkiller for end-of-life care.[20] My assumption that dementia-related behaviors would be logical, which I'd borrowed from both my language studies and legal training, came from outside the usual context of dementia care, and was helpful. It prompted me to search for meaningful patterns and deeper causes, and to define the problem of caring for those with dementia differently than a medical professional.

As caregivers, we need to recognize that very early in caring for someone with dementia we will come to a fork in the road: we must choose whether to use reality orientation, where we attempt to correct our companion's misunderstandings, or accept these misunderstandings as inevitable, and instead allow them to be comfortable with their impaired sense of reality. In my work with people experiencing dementia, I have come to believe that the former is a losing battle, which inevitably demoralizes and disturbs them, and that the latter—accepting the person as they are, rational impairment and all—is the only sensible and humane option. With this in mind, I have developed the DAWN approach to provide caregivers with the tools they need to turn philosophy into action—to see a behavior and understand its cause, respond quickly, and avoid unpleasant or dangerous outcomes.

To illustrate why the assistance traditionally offered in the senior care industry is inadequate, and why a new approach is called for, let's consider a few case studies. First, let's meet Edna.

Edna

A cat's purring woke her. When she opened her eyes, the rumble intensified and a raspy tongue swiped her cheek close to her nose. *Dear Bandit.* Edna didn't move, for Bandit lay in his usual

---

[20] See Langer's book *Mindfulness* (1989). Her book has an inspiring section on the positive effects of mindfulness on aging. And for an entertaining and visual depiction of the effect of context, take a look at this animation of the social model of disability at www.youtube.com/watch?v=9s3NZaLhcc4.

position, sprawled on her pillow and leaning heavily against her head. Bandit was a big tabby. She reached up to caress his ears and felt another weight shift by her feet, followed by a plaintive meow. Edna tucked her chin to glance down at the end of the bed. She could see a fluffy cat head silhouetted against the window. "You, too, Jinx. You know I'd never forget you, Jinxy dear."

Edna lay back and stared up at the ceiling, where shadows played. It was brighter outside than in the room; she listened carefully for sounds that would tell her more. *Daytime.* She could hear children playing at some distance and the faint whine of a lawn mower. *Summertime.* Bandit purred again and batted her cheek with his paw. Jinx meowed loudly. She looked back toward Jinx and began to orient herself. It was her bedroom. She recognized the sheer white curtains on the window at the foot of the bed, the pale yellow walls, the yellow and gold rose-patterned comforter, and the black-and-white wedding photo over the dresser to her left. Her eyes rested on the faded photo. *Gil. Oh, yes, Gil left me. Well, died. That was quite a while back,* she thought. *Years? He just collapsed one morning in the living room. Gone before the paramedics arrived.*

Edna began the process of getting out of bed. She turned onto her side, pushed herself upright, and slowly lowered her feet to the floor. Bandit rolled off the pillow when she moved, and stretched out in the center of the comforter, staring unblinkingly at Jinx. Jinx ignored him and sat watching Edna quietly. Edna carefully arranged her feet on the floor, still thinking about Gil. *Left me alone. Just when I really needed him.* She half rose to test her weight and then sank back down on the edge of the bed. She turned to look at the clock radio on the nightstand beside her. The numbers lit in red on its face read "11:20." *It must be morning—wouldn't be light at night. But what morning? Ah, my Day-Timer on the bathroom counter,* she thought. *That will tell me.* Edna pulled herself upright slowly, shifting her weight tentatively from one foot to the other and back again, and then edged carefully around the bed. *A little creaky, but not bad for old joints. This getting old thing isn't for sissies!*

"If Gil was here, we'd have a good laugh about how much effort it just took me to get out of bed," she said to the cats.

Once around the bed, Edna stopped next to the dresser and leaned against it. A memory as clear as if it were happening that very moment overtook her: she and Gil waking together on a sunny morning, right there in that same room. A stab of grief, of loss realized afresh, gave Edna an almost physical pain. For a moment, she thought she could smell the familiar scent of his hair cream, feel the softness of his hand against her cheek. Then Bandit jumped to the floor with a thump and stalked out of the room. *Now what was I doing? What day is it?* Edna blinked and rubbed her forehead. *Ah, my Day-Timer. That will tell me.*

As she rounded the corner into her bathroom, Edna saw a bathing suit hanging from the shower head, dripping slowly. *Oh, yes, it must have been a swimming morning.* On the counter, she saw her Day-Timer lying open. The left-hand page, dated Tuesday, June 21st, was crossed out. "Senior Lunch: leave at 11:15" was written squarely in the middle of the page, with a checkmark carefully inked beside it. The right-hand page, for Wednesday, June 22nd, was not crossed out. At the top of that page was written: "Radio on 6:00. Out of bed 6:15. In the car 6:25. In the pool 6:45." The first two entries had checkmarks beside them; the last two did not. Edna glanced back at the damp bathing suit, then carefully placed a checkmark after "In the pool 6:45." *I must have gone to the pool. In the car? My little red car? No. Debra sold it. That Debra, always meddling.*

Edna felt a stab of annoyance. *Always taking over, even though I'm really just fine.* A memory filled her mind of her daughter, Debra, standing beside the kitchen table, clutching Edna's keys and saying, "No more driving, Ma!" Indignation welled up just as strongly as it had that day. *I've been driving since before she was born!* Edna thought. *Ridiculous to be telling me what to do!* She took a deep breath and set the pen back beside the Day-Timer and then turned and walked slowly out to the living room. *Now Judy takes me on errands and swimming. Judy,* Edna reminded herself. *She sits and reads and I swim. At least no one has to escort me up and down the lanes. Well, not yet.*

Edna paused in the middle of the room, one hand to her forehead, trying to remember what had brought her there. She could no longer recall why she felt so angry either. She heard the cats in the kitchen—a demanding meow from Jinx, wanting food no doubt, and a short hiss from Bandit. "Bandit, you leave him alone!" Edna called. *Feed the cats,* she told herself. She headed into the kitchen and paused at the counter. It was covered with rows of sticky notes and piles of scrap paper. She ignored the sticky notes and picked up the top piece of paper from the nearest pile, on which was written "Tuesday" in her careful handwriting. Below that was a list: "cats out 1:20, cats in 1:55, cats out 4:11, cats in." After the last entry, there was no time.

Where are those cats? Edna felt a stab of concern. She looked up at the clock and saw that it was 11:32; then she looked back down at the last notation of 4:11. *I'd better go out and find them!* But just then, Jinx meowed again more loudly, at her feet, and twined between her legs.

"Oh, Jinxy, you're in! I'd better write that down before I forget," Edna said and picked up the pen. She turned to look up at the clock over the wall telephone. Its hands pointed to 11:32. *I wonder what day it is,* she thought. *I'd better go check my Day-Timer.*

■ ■ ■

Although Edna could remember her anger at having her car taken away, she couldn't remember the many times she'd driven to the grocery store and walked home without it, or driven around town for hours, unable to recall what errand she'd set out to do. Edna's memory was unreliable, allowing her to remember me, her new neighbor, and the fact that I regularly took her swimming, but not what day of the week it was, or that we had been at the swimming pool just hours earlier. Edna had become aware that her memory was going not long after her husband had died, five years earlier. She'd been diagnosed with dementia a year later. She began writing what she planned to do in a Day-Timer, checking off each item as she did it. Now she was only able to copy her regularly scheduled activities from the previous week, and then look for clues and check off anything she could find proof of having done. Two months earlier, when the police contacted Debra to report that her mother's car had been abandoned in the Safeway parking lot, Debra knew it was time to intervene. She came from Boise for an extended visit and talked with Edna's friends and neighbors.

Debra learned that Edna's memory had become worse, and that her attention span and ability to make decisions were becoming dangerously impaired as well. Those around her could see that she now needed someone to keep an eye on her—to make sure she wouldn't leave the stove on or become lost on her way home from Safeway. Accordingly, Debra took away Edna's car keys, bought her a microwave, tried to convince her to move into a facility and, when that was adamantly refused, introduced her to me.

Edna, however, did not perceive her impairments. She refused to accept that she was frail or at risk of falling, that she needed help with cooking or housekeeping. As a result, she responded to Debra's interventions with indignation and resentment. If I hadn't been living across the street from Edna that summer, and offered to help, Debra would have sought assistance from a senior care agency or forced Edna to move into a care facility. The result would, I believe, have been bad for Edna. Refusing to accept her actual condition, she would have resisted the kind of care that a senior agency would have offered her, and deeply resented being moved out of her home of fifty-plus years. Yet though Edna did not need senior care, she did need *some* care. She was quite able to feed her cats but, only minutes later, unable to recall whether she had done so. She could write a check for items at the store, but could no longer read her bank statements or reconcile her checkbook. She could put potatoes and green beans in a pot on the stove to cook for supper, but, when she left the kitchen to use the bathroom, she'd forget that the stove was on. Without someone to remind her of facts and help her make safe decisions, the loss of her rational thought and judgment would eventually have led to a serious crisis.

Had Debra called a senior care agency for help, she would have been assigned a certified nursing assistant (CNA), someone who has been trained and certified to help people with "activities of daily living," or ADLs—tasks that we must be able to perform in order to live on our own. Senior care agencies are designed to provide assistance for elderly people who need help with ADLs. The six essential ADLs are:

- Transferring (helping someone reposition safely)

- Bathing
- Dressing
- Feeding
- Personal hygiene
- Toilet hygiene

If someone needs help with at least two ADLs, they are officially considered disabled, and qualify for support through programs such as Medicaid or Social Security Disability.

However, when people have dementia, with impairments or disabilities that are cognitive rather than physical, they frequently don't need assistance in the above areas for years after they've first been diagnosed. Instead, people with dementia require help with the "instrumental activities of daily living" (iADLs)—in essence, the cognitive abilities required to know that ADLs should be performed. The nine officially-recognized iADLs are as follows:

- Taking medications consistently
- Using communication devices
- Responding to emergency alerts such as fire alarms
- Managing money
- Getting around the community
- Shopping for groceries or clothes
- Preparing and cleaning up after meals
- Maintaining a safe and sanitary living space
- Taking care of pets

People with dementia are often unaware of their cognitive or physical impairments, a condition known as *anosognosia*. The term was coined in 1914 by a French neurologist, Joseph Babinski, who noted that people who had suffered strokes and became paralyzed on one side were sometimes unaware of their disability.[21] I first encountered anosognosia when I was working with my vocational rehabilitation clients who had traumatic brain injuries,

---

[21] For a concise discussion of anosognosia in dementia, see the article by Leilani Doty, Director of the University of Florida Cognitive and Memory Disorder Clinics, at http://alzonline.phhp.ufl.edu/en/reading/anosognosia. pdf. For an entertaining discussion of anosognosia throughout history, see the scholarpedia.org article at http://www.scholarpedia.org/article/Anosognosia.

and again when I worked with the mentally ill. (One of the most extraordinary cases of anosognosia I've witnessed was a man with dementia who had no teeth but was unable to comprehend that this meant his ability to chew was impaired. He would order steak and then be outraged that the restaurant had served him meat too tough to chew!) With my background, I wasn't surprised when many of my dementia clients exhibited anosognosia, though often in unpredictable ways. Someone like Edna might recognize one impairment, such as forgetfulness, yet remain completely unaware of more dangerous impairments like faulty judgment or short attention span. Dementia patients with anosognosia routinely deny their need for assistance with iADLs, and refuse care. Edna, for example, knows that she needs her Day-Timer to tell her what is scheduled for the day, and that she needs notes to remember whether her cats are indoors or outside. But she also believes she would be able to successfully drive downtown to her pharmacy, find a parking spot for her car, walk to the store, refill her prescription, remember that she'd driven downtown, recall where she had parked her car, return to it, and drive home. In addition, she lacks the analytical skill of seeing cause and effect. For example, if asked, she will admit that she has lost her sense of smell as well as her memory. However, she is not able to conclude that having those two impairments makes it likely that she could put a pot of potatoes on the stove, then leave the room, and not be alerted that it had boiled dry by the smell of the burning pot—or the burning kitchen! The more areas in which people lack awareness of their own impairments, the more complicated it becomes to get them to accept necessary care.

One of the first assessments we do when taking on new clients is to evaluate their level of anosognosia. Our clients who are not experiencing anosognosia are aware that they need help and welcome it. They are grateful for anything and everything we do, recognizing that it is only with our assistance that they can continue living independently. They realize that in providing them with professional caregivers, their families are supporting their autonomy and desire to remain at home—and they perceive this as an expression of love. If they have already moved from their homes, they are very appreciative of our presence in the care facility, where we can take them to outside activities and provide more social interaction than the facility's staff typically can. People who know they are cognitively impaired, or recognize that they are losing the ability to take care of themselves, are often saddened and fearful—a sensible response to realizing they are becoming less able to make sense of the world. For these anosognosia-free people, our help eases their anxiety.

For clients like Edna with partial anosognosia, in contrast, their condition creates more tension. They tend to be angry with their children for interfering, and they may seem paranoid or secretive as they attempt to conceal their disabilities, striving to retain their former level of independence. These are the people who decide to drive to a family reunion one thousand miles away, even though they cannot recognize their own car in the church parking lot. People in this category, through forgetfulness and the inability to concentrate, may call a friend to find out where toilet paper is sold or how to mail a letter. They can burn up an entire set of cookware on the stove, one by one, and think they've solved the problem by buying more pots.

Because of their partial anosognosia, however, it's both pointless and distressing to confront these clients with their inabilities. Instead, once again, it's better to accept their inaccurate sense of reality. With these clients, for example, we might pretend to agree with them that they are quite capable and their children are overreacting, while stressing that their children only interfere out of love for them. We always assure them that we'll help them stay as independent as possible, and often begin our work together merely by offering transportation to do errands. By offering our support to help them preserve what they most desire— independence—we can gradually build a trusting relationship, and unobtrusively provide assistance they can accept without sacrificing their dignity or self-respect. We find that these clients, with partial anosognosia, gradually accept our help and direction when we support their sense of dignity and independence.

When someone has complete anosognosia, and is unaware of any impairment, we employ what we call *caregiving by stealth*: we ensure safety and provide for the needs of these clients indirectly, under cover of beneficial fictions. We devise a way to introduce the caregiver to the patient as a potential friend—someone who enjoys the same activities as they do and often drops by to see if they might enjoy running an errand with company. We might then send in a second caregiver while the senior is out with his or her new friend, so that we can keep the home sanitary and stocked with food.

Someone who has complete anosognosia, and considerably impaired rational thought, isn't able to use analysis to question such daily miracles as laundry that washes itself or a new friend who enjoys running errands with them. For example, one prospective client had three small dogs. My caregiver Heike also had a small dog. Heike knocked on the client's door, introduced herself, and asked if the client would like to join her in taking the dogs for a walk. Our new client didn't question the appearance of a stranger at her door, and happily joined her for a walk. Subsequently we were able to put a regular schedule of in-home visits in place with the client remaining unaware that her new friend was actually her caregiver. We took the same *caregiving by stealth* approach with the man in this next case study, who also had complete anosognosia:

John

John had denied his children access to the family home after their mother had died. They knew John would not be able to care for himself properly without her, and frequently tried to convince him to accept a housekeeper or some other form of help. After several years of inadequate care, John had a car accident. He needed a brief hospital stay, and his car was towed and his license suspended. His children were finally able to really look at conditions in the home and, as they'd suspected, found it to be filthy. The cupboards were bare, the laundry unwashed, the kitchen and bathrooms grimy. Distressed by his inability to deal with his mail, he'd been pushing the envelopes under the cushions of the couches and chairs in the living room, and then covering the cushions with blankets. Yet until the car wreck, John had adamantly refused assistance, and insisted that he was functioning in the same capable way in which he had lived his entire adult life.

When John's chidren contacted me and told me about his situation, I recommended that they introduce me as a friend rather than a potential caregiver. At John's birthday party the following week, one of his sons introduced me as a friend. I engaged John in conversation several times. The following day, I began dropping by his home and ringing his doorbell around lunchtime. If he came to the door, I would remind him that we'd met at his birthday party and invite him to join me for lunch. The first week he angrily sent me away, telling me not to bother him. I persisted, however, and during the second week hunger evidently overrode his pride (or perhaps his desire for solitude), because he agreed to join me for lunch at his favorite restaurant, the café at a local hotel. He offered to drive, forgetting he'd lost his license, but I suggested we take my car instead, because I'd parked my car behind his in the driveway. (This, incidentally, is a good tactic for redirecting someone who shouldn't be driving.) Soon that meal out with John became a weekly event, then daily. As we drove off each time, I would surreptitiously send a text to Sarah, a DAWN caregiver, who would be waiting nearby with groceries and cleaning supplies. While we were at lunch, Sarah would throw in a load of laundry, restock the refrigerator, and quickly sanitize the bathroom and kitchen.

Using caregiving by stealth, we were able to keep this man safe for more than a year without him meeting anyone but me face-to-face. John's refrigerator remained miraculously full and his clothes clean and folded, but he never noticed. Finally, during our second year of providing care, John agreed to allow "a young friend of mine" to begin cleaning and doing laundry for him, but only because I had suggested that he could help her pay for college. In this way, he came to welcome Sarah's presence, and continued to believe *he* was helping *her*, although he had long since lost the concept of payment and never actually wrote her a check. Until the day he died, bedridden, on a liquid diet, and cared for round the clock, John remained convinced that he was able-bodied and needed no assistance of any kind.

Suffering as he did from complete anosognosia, John would have rejected conventional elder care, and was disoriented and deeply unhappy the short while he stayed in a facility. His resistance to care there would inevitably have led to psychotropic medications, and misery for him and his family. Instead, by putting in place a series of carefully crafted physical and psychological supports at home that recognized and accommodated John's emotional needs, caring for him was more joyful than stressful. He died peacefully in his own home, with his dignity and sense of security intact. He died as an elder of his family, not as an invalid.

Designing Home Dementia Care

Caring for someone who is experiencing a decline in cognitive ability is never easy, whether the loss is due to a traumatic brain injury, mental illness, or dementia. Because of this, dementia care is a task best shared, yet I often see a spouse or a child trying to be the sole caregiver, believing they know best or that it's their responsibility alone. At other times, it's not possible to put together a care team due to isolation in a rural area, scarcity of family and friends, or limited finances. If you find that you must provide care on your own, these DAWN tools and techniques are designed to help you preserve your own energy through decreasing the number of situations in which you and your loved one experience conflict. They will enhance companionship for both of you.

Here at DAWN, our clients don't have just one caregiver: before full-time care becomes necessary, we want them to have come to trust several caregivers. Then when full-time care is necessary, one moves into the role of overnight caregiver and the others continue providing daytime care. When we do this, each caregiver is off duty for at least a ten-hour shift and can emotionally recharge. If we didn't, our clients would sense and be affected by the caregivers' exhaustion and less positive moods.[22]

Keep this in mind if you are caring for a spouse or partner, a parent, or any other loved one. Caregiving is exhausting and will deplete your emotional and physical health, no matter how much you love your family member or desire to care for them optimally.

---

[22] Having a team of caregivers sounds like an enormously expensive undertaking, and yet hiring caregivers for part-time hours at home allows families to postpone far more expensive full-time care plus room and board in a facility, often for years.

If you are up twice during the night, like Dave was, you'll have less patience when awakened at sunrise with the next incident. By the end of the day, you'll be in desperate need of a good night's sleep, yet your loved one may not give you even an hour's respite. Further, no matter how resourceful the caregiver, care from just one person is limited to the resources that that one person can bring to the client. I am constantly impressed by my staff's ingenuity. Christie is adept at finding back roads and scenic overlooks, where she and a client can sip mochas and enjoy the beauty of the rolling hills and wheat fields of the Palouse. Heike is a master at turning personal hygiene issues into girl time and transforming the disability lift at the swimming pool from a symbol of disablement to one of fun. Megan can turn a power outage into a candlelit treasure hunt through the pages of old photo albums, and Erica managed to get a client to join her for a pedicure when no one else could even get her shoes off. Dementia raises diverse issues; responding to them successfully will overwhelm the resources of a single person. We are wise to seek help wherever and whenever possible.

We also need to think carefully about what *type* of care our loved ones and clients need when dementia strikes. For someone like Edna or John, each day brings another *tabula rasa*—a blank slate filled with moments that lengthen into minutes and hours spent in unrelenting confusion. They repeatedly face another task they've performed countless times before but that is suddenly difficult, or another voice on the phone that they just can't place even though they sense the person is someone they love. People with dementia need emotional support—to have us cheerfully offer information when needed, not impatiently take over a task or conversation. They need us to recognize the fear and frustration that accompany progressive cognitive impairment, not to expect passive acceptance of their encroaching helplessness. It is time to recognize what decades of using the appropriate care method and reality orientation in care facilities has demonstrated—that offering dementia care as if we are responding to the symptoms of a disease results in difficult behaviors, costly drugs, and ultimately a form of care that is demoralizing and disempowering. Instead, we can use the habilitative approach: accepting the altered sense of reality that dementia causes, responding to the emotional needs that result, and nurturing the cognitive skills it does not take away.

Let's consider the types of professionals you can enlist when creating the best possible care team for a loved one with dementia. Here, we provide services in the three capacities listed below and then coordinate care with all available family members. The best care plans take advantage of not only professional services, but any supports available from the clients' families, friends and community resources as well.

Geriatric Care Managers. Often, the first call we receive is from a spouse or child who is concerned about a loved one and doesn't know what to do or where to turn. Unless you work in the senior care industry, you are not likely to know what is available for someone who has dementia, or how those services might be paid for. A geriatric care manager has personal knowledge regarding the types of services available in the area, and can guide families to the services or organizations that will best meet their loved ones' needs. The term *geriatric care manager* and the role associated with it is becoming more widely recognized. The need for coordinated care for seniors who have dementia is increasing dramatically as the huge baby-boomer generation enters their senior years, and dementia becomes more prevalent. (This prevalence is due to the size of our aging population, but it has also been tied to consumption of processed foods and fats, as well as sedentary lifestyles.) A geriatric care manager's background is usually in nursing, social work, gerontology, or psychology; however, elder law attorneys are now combining their skills in end of life management with organizing care for their clients. My role here in Moscow, after eight years spent helping seniors and their families find the right resources and care in this area, is that of a geriatric care manager. I educate families about the services available locally, and guide them toward the ones that would be most beneficial—such as to lawyers who specialize in Medicaid planning, daytime health services, housing options, and senior or dementia care.

If you are wondering how to organize supportive care for a loved one who has dementia, I would recommend that you look for a geriatric care manager in your region before making any other calls. An hour spent with one of these professionals will save you a great deal of time and expense in finding your own way through the senior care or dementia care world by trial and error.

Case Managers. A case manager, also typically someone with a background in nursing or social work, usually coordinates, oversees, and evaluates care for children and adults who have developmental disabilities, mental illnesses, or brain injuries. Case managers are not yet common in senior care or dementia care. At present, senior care agencies tend to employ aides and nurses who are individually assigned to work with numerous clients and provide ADL care. Usually, an office manager will oversee and supervise the care staff, sending them out according to availability rather than assigning them to specific clients in designated care teams. This focus on meeting scheduling requirements results in a constant stream of ever-changing caregivers in and out of clients' homes. Although consistency in care is not crucial for seniors who do not have cognitive impairments, it is critical for people who have dementia, because they lack the rational thinking processes that would allow them to learn and adapt to the changing faces and schedules they are forced to encounter. With this in mind, we assign a case manager to each of our clients so that we can ensure consistency and continuity of care. The case manager coordinates and oversees the care plan, and ensures that the family and care team are well-informed and working together.

Case managers can be certified. The National Academy of Certified Care Managers has been in operation since 1995, and most states have a credentialing system for ensuring that case managers are skilled in overseeing care plans. However, rather than hiring an independent case manager who may or may not have experience with seniors and the senior services available in your area, the better approach is to ask your geriatric care manager for not only research and advice, but also to act as your case manager—supervising the various agencies and types of care needed, coordinating the care team, and monitoring the condition of your loved one. In my own extended family, we have a senior who had a stroke and needed rehabilitative and supportive care in Portland, Oregon. Because I no longer work in Portland, nor know the services available there, our first step was to contact a local geriatric care manager. This geriatric care manager was able to make recommendations regarding services, and she also agreed to become the case manager. She began attending doctors' appointments, overseeing services, and reporting our loved one's progress and needs back to us. Because this professional knew the local rehabilitative and senior care services, and had a good working relationship with the best, we could feel secure knowing that she had put together an optimum care team for our loved one, even though we couldn't be there to oversee what was happening on a day-to-day basis.

If your loved one has dementia, having a case manager who is present and providing supervision is very important. The case manager ensures that oversight and coordination of care occurs, and that the care plan is constantly tailored to your loved one's changing needs.

Dementia Care Specialists. For day-to-day care, it is important that you put together a team of dementia care specialists. What should you look for and expect from the people you hire or delegate to spend time with your loved one? Dementia care is a specialized skill. Someone caring for a person with dementia should understand that it is emotional distress that causes difficult behaviors, and that rational thinking processes are being lost while the intuitive thinking functions remain sound. Dementia caregivers should understand that it is crucial to maintain skills and independence for as long as possible, and that it is necessary to weigh a person's need for safety against his or her need for having a sense of control over self and life. Dementia caregivers should recognize that having dementia means needing help locating food in the kitchen long before they need to have their meals prepared for them. People with dementia need help managing the calendar, deciphering mail, and remembering to take medications long before needing help in the bathroom. In other words, dementia caregivers must understand that higher-level abilities will be lost before more basic abilities, and that these losses will cause feelings of confusion, shame, fear and distress. Dementia caregivers need to understand that emotional support is imperative, because those aware of their failing abilities will be afraid and grieving, and those with anosognosia will be frustrated and angry. In short, you need caregivers trained in the DAWN method.

Here at DAWN, we train both our case managers and caregivers in the emotional support tools that help our clients develop a sense of security and wellbeing. We've found that the more people there are in the client's life who use the DAWN tools, the more comfortable the client becomes with the loss of memory and rational thinking skills. The behaviors that institutions have so much trouble with—and often resort to treating with expensive and detrimental psychotropic medications—are not a problem for us. Our clients are able to stay home much longer. They enjoy spending time with their caregivers, and continue to be active in their communities, because their abilities are being recognized even as their disabilities are being accommodated. And, we help them stay healthier with exercise, good nutrition, and social and sensory stimulation.

Working with Family and Friends

Given compassion and a basic understanding of the cognitive losses and emotional needs that dementia causes, any of us can provide dementia care that is truly supportive. It is not always possible to hire professionals (nor necessary). Even if a family does have the financial means and trained people are available in the area, care should be provided in a way that supports familial relationships and friendships. One of the greatest treasures we accumulate in life is our relationships. However, as we age and become less able to get out and be active, we lose contact with the people who are important to us and who have played valuable roles in our lives. Having dementia exacerbates this isolation. Good dementia care involves helping a person keep his or her friendships and family relationships intact for as long as possible. Good dementia care should provide enough support so that family members and friends can continue their relationships on the basis of love rather than duty or guilt. Not all their time together should be spent meeting the demands of caregiving.

Very often, having known the person with dementia for a long time, or on a more intimate level, makes it harder to provide compassionate care. This happens because when we have known someone very well, we have deeply imbedded expectations of how he or she will behave. But dementia can affect a person's personality, not just his or her mental abilities—sometimes gradually, sometimes abruptly. This makes adjusting very difficult for those closest. And yet, when they develop dementia, our loved ones need us more than ever. What I've found in working with my clients and their families is that it is hardest for a spouse to care for a loved one with dementia, and next hardest for a child, because of the degree of intimacy. It is least difficult for an unattached third party. For families, there is nothing more grueling than caring for a loved one who is continuously losing cognitive ability. This constant but varying rate of loss in mental status is one of the things that makes caring for someone with dementia so demanding, preserving relationships so difficult, and coordinating care so essential.

Coordination of care is complicated even further when the family is fragmented by divorces or distance. Often it is only the person's friends who live nearby who know that dementia is becoming a problem. How does a neighbor or friend contact a person's adult children living elsewhere, or know which child would be most able to provide care? How do you help a friend whom you can see is becoming more confused each day, especially if he or she seems completely unaware of what's happening? It is heartbreaking to watch someone descend into dementia, especially when you don't know how to reach the family and have no legal power to do anything. Several times I have sat with the friends of someone who is experiencing dementia and counseled them on how to reach family members or what to do when the family cannot be convinced that care is needed. In some cases, the only recourse for a concerned friend is to call the state adult services agency and report a situation of self-endangerment or neglect.

Sometimes it is the spouse who believes no additional care is needed. Other times a family member has visited, but still does not believe that there is a problem. Family members often will admit later that they knew something was not right, but just couldn't bring themselves to face the possibility of dementia. This is understandable—it is hard to face a situation which seems to have no solution—but the longer we avoid facing dementia, the bigger the problems associated with it become. The sooner proper emotional supports can be put into place, the better the person with dementia will cope with its progression.

Here are a few statements I typically hear from spouses and family members who fail to realize that dementia care is needed:

"I stayed for the weekend. He's okay, just a little forgetful." When I worked in the tax clinic during law school and represented the woman whose husband had failed to file their tax returns, I learned of a behavior called *masking*. Her husband had been going to the office as usual, but had been only pretending to conduct business and take care of things such as their taxes. It wasn't until the IRS sent a collections letter that she realized what had been happening. He had been masking his cognitive decline. Masking is something we are all good at to some degree. When we are sick yet must attend a business or social event, we mask how poorly we feel so that we can meet our obligations. We are able to rise to the occasion for a limited time, but once home, we might head straight to bed for the rest of the day. When we are feeling embarrassed or out of place in a social situation, we hide our insecurity and smile instead. This is masking. When people realize that they are developing dementia, they become masters at using this skill to protect themselves from embarrassment and to avoid having care forced upon them. Some can successfully mask their confusion and inability to use rational thought for years, even from someone living with them.

It is important to understand masking and keep the phenomenon in mind. If you were to visit someone who has dementia for only a few days, he or she would be doing everything possible to hide the degree of confusion and impairment being experienced. I have found that most people can succeed in appearing close to normal for about three days. However, by the fourth day they seem to have used up their emotional reserves and the facade begins to slip. So, if you think your parent or a loved one might have dementia, plan to stay in the home for at least four days, or plan to interact for no fewer than four days in a row. Some people are more confused in the mornings while others are fine until late afternoon or evening, so be sure to arrange visits at different times of the day. And, while you are visiting, seek out local friends and family members and listen carefully to what they say regarding your loved one's behavior.

"Oh, she's fine. She still goes to the gym every day." This is masking again. Yes, he may have gone to the office every day for the past forty years and may still be leaving at the same time each morning. But if dementia is now in the picture, it is questionable whether he is actually arriving at his office and not likely that he is engaging in the usual way while there. Or, as each day passes, the likelihood that she can remember how to use her favorite exercise machine at the gym once she gets there is diminishing. She may be merely sitting on a bench outside the gym door, as we discovered one woman was doing. We cannot assume that a loved one is continuing to function normally. We need to look for and plan on the imminent loss of ability. We need to expect it to happen—if not today, then tomorrow, the next day, or next week.

It is very good for someone who has dementia to stay involved in his or her usual activities (keeping involved with exercise and social contacts and hobbies is exactly what we strive for with our clients), but families and caregivers need to realize that for the activity to be continued successfully, impairment must be assumed. We need to provide gradually increasing support so that failure and embarrassment can be avoided. When a family member or friend says that their loved one is fine (that is, still functioning normally), I suggest it is time to provide a friend who will accompany the person who has dementia and unobtrusively provide cues as needed so that, whatever the activity is, he or she will be more likely to be able to continue it.

"We're doing alright—things will get better." This is a statement I hear from almost every spouse who calls me with concerns about his or her partner. For some, I think it's more a prayer than a belief. Others truly believe it out of wishful thinking or the desire to avoid facing an awful reality. No, dementia never improves. Dementia never goes away spontaneously. There is presently no cure and, if you have dementia today, any cure we might find will come too late for you. Once someone is showing signs of dementia, cognitive loss has already occurred, and further decline is inevitable and unavoidable. If your loved one is okay today, it is only for today. Today is your chance to prepare for tomorrow.

The other unavoidable truth is that no one can provide optimum care around the clock for the duration of this condition. This is not a matter of pride, or duty, or avoidance of being a burden on our families or friends. This is the reality of caring for someone whose brain is becoming more and more impaired. Truly optimal care takes a team. Even if you are managing to provide all the care needed today, you will not be able to in the future because your loved one's needs are increasing and will eventually overwhelm the resources one person can provide. You will not be able to do as good a job in the future as you're doing now because today and tomorrow and the next day will take a steady toll on you. The demands on your emotional and physical stamina will be relentless; there will be no chance for respite unless you plan for and schedule help beforehand.

If you truly love your partner, the kindest gift you can give them is to design a care team and begin enlisting help that will supplement your efforts—before you become overwhelmed. And if you cannot implement a team, due to geographic isolation or financial constraints, learning the techniques in this book will save you stress, exhaustion and heartache while accompanying your loved one on this unavoidable path.

There is another comment that I hear very often from the primary caregiver of someone who has dementia:

"I help him more than anyone else, yet he says terrible things about me." This statement voices a truth I learned as a divorce attorney. In a divorce, when children are feeling insecure and learning to live between two households, they act out and are the unkindest to the parent they feel safest with. The same seems to be true when someone develops dementia. I often hear the above statement when one family member lives nearby and provides most of the care and support. It is usually the most giving child who is targeted with unfair complaints and accusations that couldn't possibly be true. One parent whom I work with tells the siblings living at a distance that the daughter living nearby steals his car. If you are the child who lives at a distance, don't assume it's true if your parent complains to you that your sibling who lives nearby telephones in the middle of the night, withholds food, or mistreats the dog. And if your parent has dementia, and you find yourself the recipient of his or her worst behavior, I can only give you the same dismal advice I gave my clients going through a divorce: try to take solace in knowing that you must be the one your loved one feels the most secure with. We dare to express our deepest insecurities when we are with the ones we love the most.

When someone has dementia, we need to provide coordinated care—hopefully with all family members working together, along with friends and trained professionals where appropriate and available. Over the past eight years, our clients here in Moscow have shown us over and over that given a united effort between family and caregivers, they can thrive at home indefinitely.

Moving People Who Have Dementia

Moving someone who has dementia out of the home is expected and the norm at present. Often the first move for seniors experiencing dementia is from their own homes into an assisted care facility; then when the person's cognitive skills further deteriorate, a second move into a memory care unit is necessary. Moving someone who has dementia is costly, though, both financially and emotionally. Institutional care is expensive, and the move negatively impacts the person's ability to function, since coping with new surroundings requires the ability to learn. To optimize and prolong our clients' coping skills, we work with the families of our clients to put off any move for as long as possible.

Think of Edna, the swimmer earlier in this chapter. She was using long-term memory to operate within the familiarity of her home and daily routines. She was performing most tasks on autopilot. When I began working with Edna, she was no longer able to learn consistently, so she could not cope well with change. If Debra had given her kitchen a good cleaning and happened to move the napkins from the top drawer of the sideboard to the next drawer down, Edna would never again have been able to find them—even if Debra showed her the new location one, ten, or a hundred times. If Debra had moved Edna's bed to the other wall in the bedroom so she could get out of bed and walk straight into the bathroom at night, Edna would have gotten out of bed, walked around it in the same direction as she always had, and become disoriented when she found herself facing a wall. Moving people who have dementia out of their homes makes the tool of long-term memory useless and requires them to use a tool they don't have— rational thought—to try to learn new ways and cope with change. The result of this will always be increased confusion and distress, and decreased functioning.

People experiencing dementia are also using another tool, one Ellen Langer writes about in her book *Mindfulness*. When we can use rational thought and our brains are healthy, to rearrange furniture, reorganize drawers, or experiment with a better way to make gravy is wise. We are being mindful and could improve the way that we perform the task. However, in the context of dementia—when someone is losing or already missing rational thought and memory—being able to function *mindlessly* becomes a valuable tool. One type of mindlessness is automatic thinking: when performing a task has become so routine that we are unconsciously following a script. Automatic thinking is described as instantaneous, habitual, and unconscious (which sounds suspiciously like our intuitive thought processes). Another example is muscle memory—which is what we are using when we have repeated a motor task so often that our muscles seem to follow the series of movements without conscious direction. We are wise to support our loved ones' and clients' use of the mindlessness tools for routine tasks, and for living in the homes they have lived in for years. Mindlessness enhances their ability to function.

During my first year working with people experiencing dementia, I had a client who lived alone in a drafty old house near downtown. Jim could function adequately within his home. He would routinely put his coat in the hall closet, his wallet and house key on the sideboard in the dining room, his socks and underwear in the top dresser drawer, and his pajamas in the second one down. Jim's orderliness had been instilled by his wife, who had died just a few years earlier. The kitchen was large enough for two entire walls of cupboards and a full-sized table with six chairs. Jim was still able to heat a one-dish dinner in the microwave, help himself to a bowl of cereal, make a cup of instant coffee, and find the ice cream in the freezer for an evening treat.

He was beginning to hesitate, though, when looking for things in the large kitchen—such as the bowl for his cereal or sugar for his coffee. Thinking I was being a good caregiver, I took his mugs out of the cupboard, lined them up on the counter by the sink, and put the instant coffee and sugar packets in dishes beside them. But rather than being helpful, moving those items was harmful: I had turned his familiar kitchen into a strange new place and interrupted both his muscle memory and automatic thinking scripts. When I saw his confusion the next day, I put everything back, but Jim wasn't able to recapture his previous unconscious following of scripts when in the kitchen. I learned from that experience to offer assistance to my clients when they began to falter at a familiar task—to partner with them—rather than interrupt their use of the mindlessness tools. Jim taught me that if I preserved their routines and habits they could function independently for a longer time.

So often a family member has said to me, "But doesn't she belong in an institution?" I have never understood this assumption. Our elders are vulnerable and belong in their own homes for as long as their homes can be kept safe. And the most vulnerable are those who have dementia, those who are relying heavily on long-term memory and automatic thinking. To believe that they *should* be removed from their homes and everything familiar is at best misguided, but actually cruel. Yes, the time may come when someone's medical or physical needs are too great for a family to manage at home without round-the-clock nursing care, or when the family's financial resources have been depleted and Medicaid coverage becomes necessary. However, even if the time may come when institutional care is necessary, the longer we can delay it, the happier and more comfortable the person with dementia will be.

■ ■ ■

We have a senior care system. We've been using it to provide dementia care, but not adequately. If we add the services and skilled professionals I've described in this chapter, however, we will have created an excellent dementia care system. We really could provide better care at home for our loved ones who are experiencing dementia if we equipped professional case managers and caregivers in recognizing and meeting the *emotional needs* caused by dementia. I hope to see more and more people who, despite having dementia, are permitted to stay home and helped to live active lives. My clients here in Moscow have shown me that this is possible. Let's now look at the tools of the DAWN method, and at how they can help you provide truly supportive and strength-based dementia care at home.

CHAPTER FIVE

The DAWN Toolbox

My purpose in developing (and writing about) the tools of the DAWN method is to enable us, the companions of people who are experiencing dementia, to be kinder—by recognizing and supporting their changing needs, and helping them continue to live the most dignified and autonomous lives possible. So these tools are diagnostic and prescriptive. They are meant to help you evaluate your loved one's or client's mood or behavior, and then respond quickly and successfully to the emotional need driving it. When someone's emotional needs are met consistently, he or she becomes more comfortable and less prone to acting in ways that cause stress or disrupt the daily routine. The more consistently these tools are used, and the earlier they are put to use, the more effective they will be. However, if only one caregiver in a person's life is using the tools, and only for a few hours a week, the person who has dementia will not be able to develop a sense of security or regain a sense of wellbeing as quickly or reliably as when everyone in his or her life is using the same approach and delivering the same messages.

I will present the DAWN tools in what I have found to be the optimum order—first, three tools for helping people with dementia develop a sense of security, and then four that will enhance their sense of happiness or wellbeing.[23] Helping your loved one or client develop a sense of security will take longer than helping him or her experience wellbeing or happiness, because feeling secure comes from *repeated* instances of finding oneself

---

[23] Abraham Maslow pointed out that we cannot focus on self-actualization or wellbeing needs when we feel at risk or lack a sense of security (see *A Theory of Human Motivation* (1943)). Maslow was best known for his lifelong research and writing about mental health and human potential. Although we now know that a feedback loop model is more accurate than his human needs pyramid, his premises still warrant recognition.

safe—it's something we learn through experience. Experiential learning is a function of our intuitive thought processes, not our rational ones, and is referred to as *classical conditioning* (remember Pavlov and his dogs). People who are experiencing dementia are always learning one of two things from their companions: either that they are safe when with that person, or that they are unsafe. So it's important that we as caregivers begin using the security tools early and use them continuously. When we do this, our loved ones or clients will begin to feel at ease on a subconscious level and become more emotionally comfortable.

The last four tools, which are designed to enhance wellbeing, can be implemented in seconds and will have immediate results. They are like the petals of a flower—they add beauty—but they are secondary to the essential need of helping those experiencing dementia regain a sense of peace and security. Giving someone a moment of happiness is something we can do in seconds, although something might happen in the next moment to destroy it. We can then just as quickly replace it. We do this in our relationships all the time—for our children, friends, and family members—so some of you, as caregivers, will already be using some of these wellbeing techniques. Understanding how to use them specifically when your companion is experiencing dementia will make you more aware of why they are working and when best to apply them.

In any case, here, when we are able to be the primary influencers in our clients' lives—when they consistently experience care in which all of their companions are teaching them they are safe and bringing them moments of happiness daily—the change in their moods and behaviors is remarkable. Instead of descending further into an inner world shaped by fear, anger and frustration, our clients become increasingly relaxed, and remain engaged with the outer world in an intuitive way, using faculties unimpaired, or possibly even heightened, by dementia. The following diagram shows how I picture the tools of the DAWN method in relation to one another:

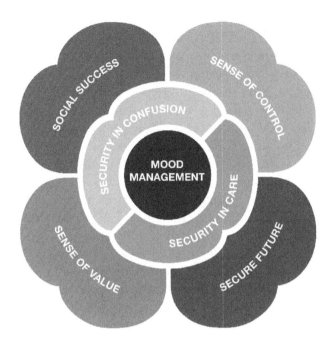

The first tool, mood management, is central. It is the core, the heart—the constant and renewable energy source around which we design our care plans. Without enabling our clients to live with a generally positive outlook on life, our efforts in the other six areas will be doomed to failure. Once we know how to establish and maintain a positive mood, we can begin creating an enduring sense of security in the two areas most vital to someone undergoing progressive cognitive impairment: living with confusion and being cared for by others. After establishing security in these two areas, which are founded on positive moods, we can enhance our loved ones' and clients' lives with the four components of wellbeing: social success, sense of control, sense of value, and secure future. When all seven of these human needs are met, the relationship between the caregiver and the person experiencing dementia can become a thing of beauty.

Let's consider the tools one by one, examining the foundational tools for security and those that enhance a sense of wellbeing when people are experiencing dementia, and consider how to employ them.

Three Tools for Developing a Sense of Security

The first tool, *mood management*, provides more power to avoid the behaviors associated with dementia than any other tool, and will have a more profound effect on your relationship with your loved one or clients—and on their quality of life—than anything else you do. First, we as caregivers need to recognize that it is essential for us to consciously manage our own moods, since whether we realize it or not, our own demeanor and visible expressions of our emotions strongly influence the moods of our companions who have dementia. Since their intuitive powers are intact, they are quite able to pick up on their caregivers' subtler feelings. And although people with healthy brains can employ their rational faculties to free themselves from the moods of others (analyzing these moods to comprehend them and dissociate themselves, and drawing on memories of better times to avoid being negatively affected by them) people who are losing their rational thought and memory to dementia cannot. Because of this, it is very important that we are aware of what we are conveying with our intonation and body language.

In addition, we must actively manage the moods of our loved ones and clients. To experience dementia means to repeatedly fail at tasks and conversations. People with dementia constantly find themselves unable to understand where they are, why they are there, and even who they are with. These repeated failures and confusion frequently trigger negative feelings. As caregivers, we will find the greatest success in decreasing unhappiness and stress for both ourselves and our companions if we realize that we can proactively create positive moods by presenting a positive mood ourselves, helping our companions succeed in conversations, and acting as their partners in accomplishing tasks. The good news is that it is much easier to manage the mood of someone who has dementia than it is to manage that of a healthy adult or even a child, because of that same lack of rational abilities. Keep in mind, however, that a single moment of reality orientation will negate a positive mood, just like any other unpleasant experience.

The second tool, *security in confusion*, helps our loved ones and clients feel safe even though they are losing thinking skills, memory skills, and actual memories. We cannot take away the cause of their increasing confusion; we can only help them learn to feel comfortable living with it. When they learn that they are always welcome to ask questions, whether they are seeking information or reassurance—and that no matter when or how often they ask, they will never be penalized by us—we are teaching them that it's safe to be confused. All too often, their frequently-repeated questions, a symptom of their confusion, can irritate or frustrate their caregivers, though, which in turn negatively affects the mood and behavior of the person with dementia. (People with anosognosia typically feel more frustrated and angry, while those who are aware of their impairments are more likely to feel afraid, embarrassed or guilty, but negative behaviors result in both cases.) We as caregivers must ensure that we communicate only patience and acceptance, and avoid giving any indication that we have heard the question before. The beauty of doing this effectively and consistently is that, once our loved ones or clients have learned that they can ask for information whenever they want, they will begin to feel more comfortable with confusion and ask less often.

The third tool, *security in care*, helps people with dementia feel secure even though they need to be cared for—it helps them understand that they can trust others to care for them as their own ability to do so diminishes and ultimately disappears. However, in American culture, independence is not only respected but admired, which makes accepting losses in self-sufficiency very difficult when dementia strikes. To help someone who is experiencing dementia begin to feel safe despite their reliance on others is a tremendous gift. Without it, their sense of security will be increasingly weakened by the advance of dementia. We are helping our loved ones retain a sense of security in this area when we avoid testing their failing memory skills, become nonjudgmental partners in completing tasks of every kind, and accept their increasingly altered beliefs about what's true, not only regarding the present but also the past and future. This allows them to grow to trust us about whatever is occurring in the moment.

One of our clients is getting very close to needing an overnight caregiver, and soon after that will need full-time care. Gerald still enjoys running an errand with his caregivers, going for a scenic drive, eating lunch at the local senior center, or taking a walk in the mall. However, he no longer feels completely at ease when he's out in the community, even when with his caregivers. Although he used to be quite independent, even reserved and standoffish, now he often wants to feel a guiding hand on his elbow when outside his home, or even to hold his caregiver's arm. Without this physical contact with a caregiver, he can become belligerent and demanding: his nervousness and fear of what he cannot understand becomes overwhelming, because of his diminishing ability to make sense of what is happening around him. Is this any different from how children—or we ourselves—might act when feeling threatened? An insignificant event for someone who feels secure can cause someone who feels at risk to react strongly, often to become obstinate or angry.

In fact, many dementia-related behaviors are expressions of insecurity. Gerald is close to needing overnight care, as I said, but he gives clear indications that he's not yet ready. When his caregiver drives him home and pulls up in front of his garage door, he invariably exclaims, "Oh, good! Back to *real* life!" He quickly gets out of the car and heads up the walk to his front door. Gerald has lived in this home for more than twenty years and finds it a haven of familiarity and routine. As we walk inside, he relaxes visibly, and no longer wants a hand on his elbow for reassurance. His relief at finding himself back in familiar surroundings is clear in his brighter eyes, bigger smile, and straighter posture. When Gerald begins to ask for direction inside his home, to look for the same reassurance he already requires when out in the community, we will add the next level of care—someone to stay overnight with him—so that his need for security will again be met, and he can continue to function without the behaviors associated with insecurity. Feeling secure is essential, a universal and foundational need common to all of us.

When people are experiencing dementia, we, as their companions, need to recognize that they are losing skills they have always had at their disposal, and are becoming unable to manage their own moods or feel secure in ways they took for granted until dementia comes into the picture. Only their companions can help them regain the sense that all is well, and that they are safe. If you are caring for someone who has dementia, putting these three tools into effect—managing mood, making it safe to be confused or forgetful, and making it safe to trust others—will change your life and theirs.

Four Tools for Developing Wellbeing

The final four tools of the DAWN method help people with dementia feel happy and enjoy a sense of wellbeing—that feeling of completeness, that *all is well* sense—in their day-to-day interactions with those around them. It took several years of consideration, and daily interactions with my clients, for me to conclude that there are *four* wellbeing needs in dementia (the fourth sounds suspiciously like a security need). But I finally came to agree with Oliver James, who wrote *Contented Dementia* (2008), that people experiencing dementia need fulfillment in the following areas:

- Feeling socially successful
- Feeling some degree of control over self and life
- Feeling valued and respected
- Feeling that the future is secure

If you can ensure that a person who has dementia has a positive experience in these four areas at least once every day, he or she will be able to relax and feel more comfortable. The DAWN approach provides specific tools for reliably creating and recreating this sense of fulfillment.

First, our loved ones and clients need to experience *social success*. The first step toward social success is to keep people from becoming isolated in their homes or care facilities. We are deeply social beings. Even those of us who are more introverted than extroverted benefit from daily interactions with other people. Here, we sometimes see our clients' degree of confusion lessen when they have been spending successive days alone, then begin to have daily conversations and activities with a caregiver. Not only do we need human interaction, we also need to be able to interact without becoming embarrassed, and succeed in contributing something of value in conversation. Having dementia predisposes people to embarrassment and a diminished sense of self-worth, as their declining rational abilities cause them ever more frequently to misunderstand what has been said and repeat themselves. The DAWN method prescribes what we call "cheerful chatter" by dementia caregivers—a steady, unthreatening flow of conversation that supplies the relevant facts so that our clients can join in successfully despite lacking memory.

Secondly, everyone needs to have some *sense of control* over his or her self and life in order to feel comfortable. The increasing sense of cognitive impairment caused by dementia, which makes good decisions and sound judgment ever more elusive, threatens this sense of control. A caregiver can compensate for this by carefully framing choices to reduce the need for a rational response, verbalizing the next step in tasks as they perform them together, and identifying activities where his or her companion can successfully be in charge. As caregivers, we should always be looking for ways to enable people with dementia to retain as much control as possible, for as long as possible. We should always be balancing the competing needs for safety and autonomy—and not simply adopt the widespread institutional approach of elimination of risk at any cost to individuality. Life is risky. Autonomy and individuality are priceless, the foundation of dignity. Truly, would a completely safe life, one in which our every choice and activity was measured against risk, be worth living?

The third wellbeing tool of the DAWN method, *sense of value*, provides techniques for giving back to our loved ones and clients their sense of self-worth and ability to contribute to their relationships. Feeling valued comes from being respected and being able to offer something useful to those around us. It is vital that we as caregivers give our loved ones and clients opportunities to be gracious, to forgive, and to be the one who has the upper hand socially. Here, we regularly tell our clients about our own forgetfulness or tendency to lose things, thus reassuring them that they are not the only ones who do. By destigmatizing memory loss, and showing our clients that we love, respect, and admire them, we help them maintain their own sense of self-worth.

The fourth and final tool for achieving wellbeing in dementia is to reassure the person with dementia that his or her *future is secure.* As dementia progresses, our clients' perceptions seem to grow simpler, as if they were creating a shorthand version of their beliefs. We can cement the sense of wellbeing for our loved ones or clients by identifying the symbol that embodies their own personal sense of future security—such as having enough money in the bank— and then regularly reaffirming it to them.

So, in sum, here are the seven tools of the DAWN method of dementia care:

1. Mood Management
2. Security in Confusion
3. Security in Care
4. Social Success
5. Sense of Control
6. Sense of Value
7. Secure Future

In the next seven chapters, we will examine each of these seven foundational tools of the DAWN method in detail. While reading about these tools, which have worked so well with my clients over the years, you might keep the following three concepts in mind. First, intuition is a gift. If Einstein, one of the most respected rational thinkers of the twentieth century, could call intuition "the source of all true art and all science" and consider it a sacred gift, intuitive thought deserves more of our attention and respect. Iain McGilchrist, in his book *The Master and His Emissary*, says:

> "I believe that the relationship between the [brain's] hemispheres is not equal, and that while both contribute to our knowledge of the world, which therefore needs to be synthesized, one hemisphere, the right hemisphere, has precedence, in that it underwrites the knowledge that the other comes to have, and is alone able to synthesize what *both* know into a usable whole."

Like Einstein and McGilchrist, we should recognize the critical role that intuitive thought plays, and encourage our loved ones and clients to recognize their remarkable, perhaps even growing, intuition and creativity, while at the same time downplaying the importance of the decline in their rational processes. Intuitive thought gives us access to two of the most valuable things in life: enjoying beauty, and recognizing the feelings of people around us.

Secondly, consider that memory loss changes reality (often for the good, if we go with it). One of the most important realizations for us to be successful dementia caregivers is that the gulf between our perception of reality and that of our loved ones or clients is ever widening, and, because our companions are losing such rational thinking skills as cause and effect, we cannot expect them to grasp that their reality might differ from ours. As caregivers, bridging these discordant visions of reality is our job. When we respect our loved ones' and clients' personal and distinct world views, we can help them develop and retain a sense of safety and wellbeing. When we do that, their behaviors become more manageable and their stress levels drop, and ours as well. I cannot overemphasize the importance, when spending time with people who are experiencing dementia, of not correcting or criticizing their interpretations of reality.

Third and finally, remember that dementia is not hopeless. When I worked with my first dementia clients and grew to love them, I grieved for their cognitive losses, and often felt that their lives were becoming bleak and meaningless, even unbearable. However, as I spent more time with them and found ways to help them continue to enjoy life, I discovered that we both benefited from experiencing the world on an intuitive level, and that by my joining them in that experience, both of us benefitted immensely, even into the latter stages of dementia. As Ellen Langer points out in *Mindfulness*, by reassessing how we define and categorize things, we may discover that nothing is intrinsically bad or good. For me, this meant discovering that dementia brings losses, but that within those losses there are gifts—not only for those who experience having dementia, but also for their caregivers.[24]

---

[24] In *Dementia Beyond Drugs*, Power recounts a conversation with an Inuit woman who told him that in her culture, having dementia is considered to be a gift.

PART TWO

DAWN Tools to Build Security

CHAPTER SIX

Mood Management

Martha

Martha had been dreaming. She'd slept heavily during the first part of the night, but now woke with a sense of unease. It was just after two o'clock. She clambered out of bed and stood for a moment beside it, looking at the tangle of sheets, and then turned and went out to the hallway. *What's wrong? What have I lost? I feel like I've lost something important.* She walked slowly down the darkened hall and into the living room, which was lit by moonlight that spilled through the open curtains. *I'm alone; no one is here. That's right—I moved here after Roger died,* she thought. *Alone. That's right,* she reassured herself, taking a deep breath. She paused beside a wingback chair and fingered a sweater draped over the back. The softness of the wool was comforting. *My favorite sweater. Should last as long as I do,* she thought. Her gaze wandered around the room and caught momentarily on a few familiar objects: her reading glasses on the coffee table, the photo albums piled on the end table, and her old pink slippers looking gray and tattered in the moonlight. Around the corner in the dining room, a Murano glass bowl stood in its place of honor in the center of the table. She and Roger had brought it home from Venice on their honeymoon trip to Europe. *Venice. Oh, Roger. The times we had!*

Martha's feeling of loss was replaced by a swirl of memories of Roger and Venice. She went to the table, sat down, and took the bowl in her hands. As she ran her fingers over its fluted edges, a memory came back to her as clearly as a scene in a movie: drizzle, slippery cobblestones, she and Roger huddled together under an umbrella, her arm tight in his, threading their way through crowded streets and sidewalks to a restaurant their hotel manager had recommended. For a moment, she could almost smell the dank reek of the canal mud exposed by the tide. She shivered and pulled her elbows close as she remembered how cold the wind had been while they headed toward the café. Soon the drizzle had become rain, and they stopped in dismay at the intersection of two streets.

Where the hotel manager's directions had led them to expect a blue-painted balcony overhanging a narrow canal, where they were to make a right turn, they instead found a row of shops with wrought-iron grillwork, some with wooden doors so ancient they looked like they couldn't have been opened for business since the previous century. The door to one shop was slightly ajar, and warm light spilled welcomingly onto the sidewalk; the shop's display window was brightly lit and filled with Venetian glassware. They ducked inside the shop to escape the rain and ask the proprietor for directions. He smiled kindly at Roger's attempt at Italian. He then led them outside, closed and locked his shop door, and took them around the corner to a tiny café where the owner seemed to be the shopkeeper's mother and the waitress his wife. Martha had no idea whether it was the café they had been looking for or another. The shopkeeper disappeared into the kitchen. The waitress motioned for Roger and Martha to sit, but gave them no menus. Before long, steaming plates were brought, heaped with pasta and seafood. Crisp, tiny octopi no bigger than cherry tomatoes, tuna with celery and capers, white fish in a sauce heavy with cream and curry—all tasting so fresh it must have been caught that morning. Afterward, they had gone back to the shop with the shopkeeper and bought the Murano glass bowl. Ever since, it had been a reminder of their first shared adventure as a married couple, of being lost and receiving kindness from a stranger.

Reliving the memory had tired Martha. She stood, went down the hall, got back into bed, and fell into a fitful sleep filled with images of winding Venetian canals and streets as narrow and dark as alleys. In her dream, she was again with Roger, searching for the café that was down the alley past the blue balcony. In her dream, she turned away for a moment, the crowd surged between them, and Roger was gone. She caught only a brief glimpse of Roger's mouth open in an *Oh!* of surprise before she lost sight of him completely.

Martha awoke with a cry, knowing she had to find Roger quickly before the crowd separated them further. She scrambled out of bed and stood steadying herself beside it. The furnishings of her bedroom were lit with the dimness of early morning light, but their familiar shapes had no impact on her dreamlike state. She remained convinced that Roger was still lost on crowded streets. "Roger! Oh, Roger!" she cried. "I'm coming—I'm coming as fast as I can!" She stumbled down the hall and hurried out the front door, not even shutting it behind her. Her nightgown tangling about her ankles, she rushed down the driveway and turned right at the sidewalk. *It was an alley; there were two larger streets and then an alley,* Martha thought. *And a blue balcony at the corner!* She heard the sound of traffic. *Traffic. It was crowded. I remember that. Cars and crowds. I must find that blue balcony.* "Oh, Roger, I'm coming!"

■ ■ ■

Due to the loss of memory, attention span, and rational thinking skills, which impact even the simplest activity, dementia causes negative emotions. The first tool of DAWN dementia care—and the most essential skill we can develop if we spend time with people who have dementia—is the ability to manage moods, both theirs and our own. Without attention span and rational thought, people are faced constantly with tasks they can no longer complete; without memory, they become embarrassed in conversations they cannot follow. And, without these same cognitive skills, they lack the very tools we normally use to manage our own moods—and to interpret the moods of those around us. This means that, as caregivers, we are impacting the mood every time we are with our loved ones and clients.

I became aware of the pervasive effects of mood early in my work with people experiencing dementia. When I would drop in to check on one of my clients, he might greet me with a quick smile but his expression and demeanor would rapidly betray worry, concern, or frustration. He might lead me to the kitchen to show me a coffeemaker or microwave he had been using for years but was suddenly unable to turn on. Another client might show me an electric bill she could not decipher, or need help finding her address book in her desk drawer where it had always been kept. Once, a client could not figure out how to replace a toilet paper roll; I suspect she had been working at it for most of the morning. She had done none of her usual activities—her newspaper lay unopened on the table beside a bowl of soggy cereal and she was still in pajamas. Other times I would find my clients struggling to resolve problems based upon events that could only have been dreamed—a report that needed to be completed for a deadline, a dinner that must be delivered to a family member now living in another state, or a long-dead spouse who needed to be picked up from a nonexistent subway station. As happened with Martha, I found that images from dreams were often imported into waking life, where they had just as much effect on behavior and mood as failure at an actual task or conversation.

I came to understand that people experiencing cognitive decline are frequently confronted with reminders of their growing inability to cope with the tasks of day-to-day life, so they are naturally in an unhappy state of mind, and experiencing normal and appropriate emotional responses: frustration, anger, fear and distress. And, even when help arrives or the problem is resolved, they remained unable to rid themselves of those feelings. I soon realized that my clients needed two things from me. First, they needed assistance in solving an immediate problem. Second, and more importantly, they needed my help to change their moods for the better. Of course, reasoning with them—telling them the problem was nonexistent or had been fixed, and everything was now resolved—had no effect. They couldn't follow my reasoning, and the negativity resulting from the cognitive impairments of dementia remained and would be exacerbated by yet another failure—their inability to follow my explanation.

Having Dementia Means Being a Sponge

Eventually I saw a more fundamental and ultimately more problematic truth about their ability to deal with emotional states. Not only were my clients at the mercy of the negativity that their dementia created, but they also seemed to have no defenses against *my* moods. I might be worried about whether my son's new living situation was working out, or irritated by a driver who had just cut me off in traffic. If I arrived at my client's door in such a state, she would invariably, and within seconds, begin asking me what was wrong, and assume there was a reason for her to be worried as well. If my client was already in a negative mood, that mood would worsen. For the rest of the visit, I might well have to deal with her agitation or temper.

A recent occurrence illustrates how this works. One afternoon I sat for over an hour with a client, Maria, in her doctor's waiting room, while she waited for her appointment. It is very hard for a person with dementia to wait for something to happen: without the ability to read a clock or track the passage of time, time becomes infinite. Finally, the nurse appeared, and said the doctor had gotten too far behind and we needed to reschedule the appointment. I replied that it wasn't a problem—that I would call to reschedule—and I escorted Maria out. Of course, she wanted to know why we were leaving, and I answered her questions by framing the incident entirely in positive terms:

> "Oh, isn't this nice? They've gotten too far behind, so instead of having a doctor's appointment, we can go for coffee. Your appointment was just a checkup. We've got lots of time to go next week. Would you like to drop in at the Café? They have wonderful lattes."

We had a pleasant interlude in the coffee shop, followed by a stroll through the antique store next door. All was well. Maria's mood was not an issue that day, nor was mine.

The next day I called and scheduled an early morning appointment for the following week, thinking that having the second appointment of the day would ensure that Maria wouldn't have to endure a lengthy wait. We arrived fifteen minutes before her scheduled appointment time. However, five minutes later the nurse again appeared to say the doctor had fallen behind and suggested that we reschedule. This time my patience failed me. "How could the doctor possibly have fallen behind after having seen only one patient?" I asked. My irritation was palpable, and Maria herself became agitated. She quickly internalized my irritation and the blame I was directing at the nurse. "Oh my, what have I done wrong?" she began to ask. "Did I forget to bring something?" She had absorbed the blame I was directing at the nurse like a sponge. Because of her personality, belief system, and inability to follow conversations—in addition to her ability to read the emotions of those around her with her undiminished intuitive skills—she instantly convinced herself that she was at fault for the clash between me and the nurse. Her conviction persisted for some time; I spent more than a week helping Maria get over the negative feeling. Each morning, she seemed to awake believing that she had committed a social gaffe or failed in some manner, and I had to use mood management techniques to transform her mood into something more positive.

People who have dementia seem to pick up the moods of their companions and hold them for a long time. One client's daughter, Jessie, recently described to me how true this is for her mother. Jessie is a busy woman who runs her own business, manages her household and family, and takes care of her mother, Julia, who has dementia and lives alone in a nearby town. Jessie prepares meals for her mom and delivers them each day, carefully wrapped and ready to reheat. On one particularly frantic day when she delivered Julia's dinner, she discovered yesterday's carefully prepared meal still untouched in the fridge. She couldn't help but sound irritated as she exclaimed, "Mom, you haven't even *touched* that dinner I made for you yesterday!" Julia promptly became irritated, too, and remained petulant and difficult for the rest of the visit. Before long, Jessie realized that her mother would intuit and adopt her own moods immediately after she arrived for a visit. If she had a positive mood and maintained it, Julia would remain happy and relaxed all afternoon, despite the frustrations typically posed by dementia.

Recognizing this truth—that our loved ones and clients have no defense against the moods of those around them—is one of the most important realizations we can come to as caregivers. And, as we become more aware of our own moods, if we begin to see how much we are affected by the baggage we carry around in our own subconscious minds from one minute to the next, our companions will reap enormous benefits, just as surely as we will ourselves. It is a wonderful thing to experience the lift in mood that comes from separating ourselves from our worries. If you are caring for a partner or parent, managing this mood transference will be particularly difficult, because in lengthy or intimate relationships we become attuned to the body language of our loved ones. As anyone who has been married long knows, something as insignificant as a fraction of a second added to the length of a pause can be loaded with meaning. Yet the lift that comes from separating ourselves from our own worries will be augmented when we protect our loved ones with dementia from "borrowed" anxieties.

Having Dementia Means Being at the Mercy of Your Dreams

As we saw in Martha's story at the beginning of this chapter, people with dementia often lose their ability to differentiate between dreaming and waking. Remember when you last awoke suddenly from a particularly vivid dream, and realized that you weren't teetering at the top of a cliff—or that you weren't at work without your clothes, or greeting a houseful of guests and realizing that you've forgotten to cook dinner. Remember that feeling of intense relief that washes over you? That relief is frequently lost in dementia. Imagine how exhausting and frightening it would be to awaken and remain convinced that whatever strange scenario your subconscious has dredged up and assembled is perfectly real. This phenomenon affects the mood of people experiencing dementia dramatically, and requires that their caregivers work with the dreamed images they cannot escape, to help them resolve and get beyond the emotional distress.

The fact that we as caregivers have the ability to transform the moods that our companions experience when they have dementia is a benefit, a responsibility, and a godsend. It is a benefit for both parties in the care relationship, because both can exchange negative moods for positive ones. It is a responsibility for us as caregivers, because we should bring only good and positive emotions into the presence of our loved ones and clients, and we alone are able to change the atmosphere when they are trapped in negative emotions. The godsend—the treasure we should recognize and appreciate—is that our loved ones and clients are just as defenseless against the gift of a good mood as they are against the negativity that is inherent in dementia. A recent study demonstrated this remarkably well.

In 2014, researchers at the University of Iowa performed a study involving two groups: people with healthy brains and people diagnosed with Alzheimer's disease. They wanted to investigate whether, for people who had Alzheimer's, emotions would persist beyond the ability to recall the event that precipitated them.[25] The researchers did this by showing individuals from each group happy and sad movies. Afterward, they asked the participants to rate how they felt (i.e. very happy, happy, sad, very sad) at intervals over the course of thirty minutes. Both groups retained feelings of sadness longer than they retained feelings of happiness; however, those with Alzheimer's disease had feelings of sadness that persisted throughout the full thirty-minute interval, while the healthy group's sad feelings persisted only a few minutes. Further, the data showed that the less the person with Alzheimer's disease remembered about the film, the longer his or her sadness lasted. The results were similar with the happy movies, but the effects didn't appear to last quite as long. Even when the Alzheimer's test subject could not remember having seen a movie at all, the feelings generated by the movie lingered.

The research team concluded that people who have Alzheimer's disease experience prolonged states of emotion—that is, states that extended beyond their ability to recall the causes of the emotion. Such results are consistent with our experience as caregivers, and support what we have found with our clients here at DAWN. We are usually with our clients for extended periods of time, and we find that when we create positive moods they can last for hours. We have also found that something negative, as with Maria's conviction that she'd committed a faux pas at the doctor's office, often remains in a person's subconscious and might affect their behavior for as long as a week.

Become the Mood Manager

If we are going to spend time with or care for people who have dementia, we must take charge of managing both our own moods and those of our companions. When we are healthy, we manage our moods continuously, using our memory and rational thought processes. We may feel a spark of irritation at a rude driver

---

[25] See "In Alzheimer's, Emotions May Linger After Memories Vanish," *Journal of Cognitive & Behavioral Neurology* (September 2014). The online version is available at http://journals.lww.com/cogbehavneurol/Fulltext/2014/09000/Feelings_Without_Memory_in_Alzheimer_Disease.1.aspx.

but escape the feeling when we recall the pleasure we just experienced over lunch with a friend. We may feel down after not getting a promotion or after an unpleasant interaction, but stop and pick up a pint of Ben & Jerry's New York Super Chunk Fudge ice cream on the way home from work. If you lose your temper with a family member and then recall your outbreak after the emotion has subsided, and realize the pain you've caused, you are using not only recall but also your ability to analyze the earlier interaction. Your memory and rational thinking skills give you the opportunity to feel contrite, and go back with hugs and apologies.

For someone with dementia, it's not so easy. If I have dementia, my short-term memory loss will prevent me from thinking back a few minutes or hours and recalling something that makes me feel good. If I have lost my ability to imagine how much time is passing—to comprehend the length of an hour or assess how much can be done in an afternoon—I will likely be unable to envision anything more than the task I'm stymied by, and become stuck in a loop of failure and frustration that I cannot step away from. If I've lost my ability to analyze or use judgment, I won't be able to reason myself out of my irritation or suggest to myself that I stop a task and try again later. Where should dementia caregivers start?

Since our own moods will be quickly picked up by the person with dementia, clearing our own minds is the first step. But how do I put aside my own problems, sense of urgency, irritations, and emotional needs? Life is full of concerns, all the more for those of us providing care—when our spouse is descending into dementia, or we are helplessly watching a friend succumb to increasing confusion. The first thing we do, when using the DAWN method, is to take a page from our clients' book: we lose our own memory.

Live in the Moment

Think about your problems for a moment. If you're like me, they usually fall into one of three categories: (1) things that have occurred and are ongoing, (2) things that have occurred and reached a resolution I cannot seem to accept, and (3) things I worry might happen in the future which I have no idea how to resolve.[26]

Let's imagine that at this moment I'm a caregiver spouse. I'm standing in the kitchen and I can hear my husband, who has dementia, beginning to stir in the other room. He's been napping in his recliner and now I can hear him getting up. I need to do a quick mental inventory and make sure my own mood is in a positive place. Let's see. I'm worrying about the puddle I found by the hot water heater this morning; the water heater will probably have to be replaced, an expense we can't afford right now. Can I solve this problem this very moment? No. I called a plumber earlier; now I'm waiting for him to call back. This is a problem that has occurred and resolution is pending. Right now, there's nothing for me to do about it. I cannot let it affect my present mood without affecting my husband's as well. So I picture a box, put my concern into it, close the lid, and imagine putting the box on a high shelf in a closet.

I am also worrying about our son. He graduated with such promise six years ago but has no ambition. He says he likes being a bartender and is living with roommates as lackadaisical as he is. Can I accept this as his life? Not yet. Can I change it in any way at this very moment? No. It is his decision, not mine. He has chosen his lifestyle, although not to my liking. I picture a box, put my worry in it, close the lid, and shelve it for later.

Now, my most consuming worry of all. I am haunted with concerns for the future. I know my husband will need more care, but when, where, and from whom? How will I handle such huge expenses, and how will I know what's best? Yet this isn't my problem today. Today my husband is okay at home with me. When I worry and fret, I'm borrowing from the future, and not taking

_____

[26] Living in the present moment, often called "mindfulness," is a popular technique for reducing stress, anxiety and depression. Its roots lie in Buddhism and meditation; Jon Kabat-Zinn is credited with its current popularity in the West, and Ellen Langer has been writing about the benefits of mindfulness for thirty-five years. If you'd like to delve deeper, you might take a look at Langer's book *Mindfulness* (2014), Eckhart Tolle's book *The Power of Now* (1997), and Dan Harris's book *10% Happier* (2014). The choices are endless, but these three would give you a good start.

anything good. The time will come to think about this, but the time is not now. So I just set it aside for later, and look around the kitchen. My husband wanders in.

What is happening right now? What could I do with the next minutes? This is where my husband lives: in this minute and the next few minutes. He is having more and more trouble recalling what's happened; he is no longer able to imagine or anticipate the future. I consciously choose to give myself a break and stay there with him, in the moment, just for now. When I make this choice, I am giving myself a vacation from the concerns and worries that I cannot resolve in the present. There is no reason not to. If I am willing, I can tune into the moment along with my husband and do what I can do: look for beauty and happiness in the present.

What do I have right now? Well, I have me. I can turn to him and see the man I fell in love with, the man who proposed to me eight times before I finally said yes at sunrise in a hotel room overlooking Diamond Head in Honolulu. I was groggy and short on sleep from coming in on a late flight to join him at a conference. He was right—he did surprise me even after all those times, and I finally had said yes. Now, in the present, I can smile and hug him with that same commitment and acceptance, and tell him our memory as a story I know he'll love to hear.

And I have coffee, as well as the cookies my neighbor dropped by with yesterday. My husband and I can sit together like we have so many times at the kitchen table and watch the finches at the feeders outside the window. As we enjoy our snack, I can tell him more of our memories—of his memories—in bedtime story fashion:

> "Darling, I remember you telling me a story of when you were a boy in Roseburg and you and your older brother, Grant, decided to drive into town after your parents were asleep and serenade his girlfriend under her bedroom window. Remember Grant? You were fifteen, I think, and he was seventeen. Her name was Emily. It was just before graduation for Grant and Emily, a hot June night…"

When we, as caregivers, are able to pause—to truly stop in our tracks, and look at what is around us—we will find that within each moment lies a multitude of options, entire arrays of opportunities. If the laundry needs to be done, it would make my loved one feel so useful to be able to carry the loaded basket to the washer, or it will give my client a sense of accomplishment to fold and refold the clean towels and socks. Caregiver and companion will accomplish a useful task together, and in doing so will preserve their respective moods.

Empathize

All of us have found ourselves in situations that require more empathy than we have the energy or capacity to give. In the case of dementia, life sometimes just tags us "it"—we discover we've become the family member providing care for a loved one with dementia because there is no one else to do it. In addition to giving ourselves breaks by living in the present, we can maintain perspective and a more positive outlook by reminding ourselves what someone with dementia is experiencing. Even if we're naturally very empathetic, we will find it challenging to remain so when we are caring for someone who has a different version of reality than ours, someone who becomes perversely focused on accomplishing tasks alone that we could have done in three seconds, but it can help to remind ourselves that our companions didn't bring about the loss of their rational functions knowingly. We are now learning that poor dietary habits and lack of exercise can predispose people to dementia, but none of this was known at a time when those who now have dementia could have exercised more consistently or eaten more healthily. Now, with no forewarning, they are experiencing something irreversible, and they deserve our compassion. Imagine the fear you would feel if you realized that you gradually were losing your ability to make sense out of your surroundings. Or imagine finding yourself constantly at odds with your loved ones, because of this loss. Remember Edna and her dear cats, Bandit and Jinx? As her memory worsened, rather than forget that she had cats, she lived in constant anxiety about their whereabouts. Her kitchen counter was littered with scraps of paper with her carefully written notes: "Cats in 7:05 pm"; "Cats out 8:15 pm"; "Cats in 9:20 pm." No matter how many notes she wrote, she could not give herself the comfort of knowing where her beloved pets were unless she could see them. Imagine living with this level of constant trepidation.

Another of our clients, Sean, was someone whose idea of relaxation meant enjoying a strong cup of well-sugared tea. Sitting down with his "cuppa" was how he solved problems, relaxed, woke up, and prepared to sleep. Very early in his dementia, Sean forgot how to put the kettle to boil and how many spoonfuls of his favorite imported Earl Grey tea leaves to put in his porcelain teapot. When we were first with him, we could help him make tea, and then out of habit he would wait for it to steep before pouring himself a cup and adding milk and two lumps of sugar. But he soon lost all knowledge of how to make his tea taste the way he preferred. Imagine living without the ability to give yourself the simple comfort of a cup of tea. We as caregivers need to remind ourselves often how powerless our loved ones and clients really are, in order to find our way to the acts that give them the most solace. They are not trying to be difficult. They are doing their best to get along as they have always done, but the memory and rational thinking skills they once took for granted are fading away or already gone.

Can we pretend to be in a good mood? Sometimes my caregivers will ask me this when I first start teaching them about mood management. The answer is yes: if you can't muster genuine happiness, it's still better to simulate it. However, you'll soon find that to successfully fool someone with dementia about your mood, you will have to be a gifted pretender. In other words, you will need to make every expression, gesture, and inflection communicate a relaxed and happy demeanor, because your loved one or client will be tuned in to your body language with often remarkably sharp intuition. The good news is that you won't have to pretend for long, because when we "put on a happy face" we really do begin to feel happier. Daniel Kahneman describes this phenomenon in detail, pointing out that being amused tends to make us smile, while smiling predisposes us to being amused. He recounts studies in which test subjects who held a pencil crosswise in their mouths (simulating smiling) found cartoons funnier than those who pursed their lips around the end of the pencil (simulating frowning). So yes, if necessary, pretending to be in a good mood is a very good way to begin spending time with a loved one or client who has dementia, and it's a very good technique for improving your own mood as well.

Be Person-Centered, Not Task-Centered

As caregivers, we can manage our own moods through focusing on the immediate present and empathizing with our loved one's or client's predicament, but often we must accomplish something on a deadline, which can be very difficult to do when we're with someone who is experiencing dementia. If you are a professional caregiver with multiple clients, you will have tasks assigned and duties to be checked off on a roster for each person, so you well know the frustrations of providing care on a schedule. If you are a spouse, child, or friend helping someone living at home with dementia, it is just as often a trial. Sometimes you can say to yourself, "Well, it doesn't look like this is the day to go to the grocery store. I can see that getting dressed and into the car won't be happening this afternoon. I guess we can make eggs and toast for dinner again." At other times, someone does need to be cleaned up, helped into clean clothes, or taken to an appointment. We find that, invariably, our clients seem to become the most intractable when there is a deadline that must be met or something essential is looming. We've begun calling this phenomenon *dementia time*. Somehow, coming up with a humorous name for something that can cause a lot of anguish has made it a little easier to deal with.

Dementia time happens like this: Let's imagine that Vicki, who has dementia, begins complaining of pain in her left lower abdomen. Megan, her caregiver, watches and notes Vicki's complaints for a few days, to see whether the pain is something temporary, but it persists. A call to her doctor gets an appointment three days later, but this very busy doctor has a firm rule of turning away patients who are even five minutes late. Megan helps Vicki mark the appointment on her calendar in ink, in large letters, so it cannot be erased or written over. She reminds her several times each day and writes two large notes—one for the kitchen counter and one for the bathroom mirror. Megan calls first thing that morning and reminds Vicki that she's coming to pick her up shortly. She arrives an hour early, but Vicki is not dressed, hasn't eaten, is incredulous that she could have a doctor's appointment that day—and insists that she needs to stay home because her long-dead aunt is coming to visit. Dementia time is in effect.

The most reliable way to eliminate the phenomenon is to be sure to ensure that your focus is on your loved one or client, not the deadline or task. If we decide that our goal is to make a positive, personal connection with our companion *right now*, right here, in this moment, we will find that our schedule and deadlines will be more attainable and that the dementia time effect is reduced. In other words, our focus needs to be person-centered—our goal should be to create a positive mood in our companion by having a pleasant interaction with them and giving them the gift of acceptance, peace of mind, laughter, or love. When we have a goal that puts them in a positive frame of mind, we will encounter less resistance from their strongly-felt but imaginary concern.

In the scenario above, Megan needs to focus on Vicki's immediate needs—helping her get dressed and prepared for the day—and change her goal from getting to the doctor's appointment to having a good interaction with Vicki. To do this, she should adapt to Vicki's version of reality, perhaps using her imaginary visit from "Auntie" to get Vicki ready for the actual appointment with the doctor. She should repeatedly agree with Vicki about how nice it is going to be to see Auntie again. While Vicki is performing her usual morning tasks, Megan can talk about not only getting ready to meet Auntie, but also remind Vicki that Auntie couldn't possibly arrive until after lunch, because during winter the only daytime flights coming into the Moscow airport arrive at 12:35 p.m. By cheerfully supporting Vicki's version of reality and adding a new fact, Megan will probably be able to get Vicki to her doctor's appointment. By the time they return, the distraction of new stimuli at the doctor's office will have erased the images Vicki most likely dreamed just before waking that morning.

In sum, as caregivers, clearing our minds of what we cannot effectively do in the present, in addition to improving our empathy and ensuring that our interactions with our loved one or client are pleasant, enables us to improve our own moods so that we can effectively manage theirs. Once we have made sure that our own moods are positive, it's time to learn how to redirect our companions' moods. Remember the default emotional states for someone with dementia: fear, sorrow, frustration and anger. If the person with dementia has been alone for any length of time, he or she will likely be experiencing one of these negative emotions when you appear, so our first task will be to intentionally change these emotions. How do we, as caregivers, have a positive effect on someone else's mood? As mentioned previously, we need to become very aware of our intonation and body language.

Use Nonverbal Communication Purposefully

When we work with people who have dementia, we must keep in mind that the *way* we say something will communicate more than our choice of words. Eventually, someone who has dementia will not gain meaning from words at all, for language skills are part of what is lost, and he or she will understand only the speaker's emotions, which can be read intuitively from intonation and body language. Attaching meaning to a word is a fact-driven process, whereas the ability to understand nonverbal communication is an intuitive one.

One day I was with a client, Sherri, and we were just leaving her home to do errands. She suddenly noticed that one of her cats had used the litterbox next to the back door. "Just a minute," Sherri said. She reached down, picked up the gooey dropping, and took it over to an open trash container in the kitchen where she dropped it in. She then looked at her smeared and gravelly fingers, paused, wiped them on her pants, and said, "Now I'm ready."

All my professional reserve and politeness disappeared in a nanosecond, and I began to rant about germs and the danger of disease and infection, with a great deal of intonation and emphasis. I often had difficulty getting Sherri to wash her hands; however, after listening to my horrified outburst for about thirty seconds regarding the need to wash her hands and change her pants, Sherri calmly replied, "Well, if it makes *you* feel better, I will."

For me, it was a moment of revelation. Being quick on my feet, I replied, "Oh, it *really* does. *Thank* you! I *really* appreciate that. I know I'm a little over the top about cleanliness, but I just *hate* messes and sticky hands. I *really appreciate* you doing this for me."

I had just learned two very important truths. First, that I should give my clients the opportunity to be gracious and forgiving (which we'll talk about in detail in chapter 11). Second—and more importantly for mood management—that strong intonation (in this case, authentic alarm and revulsion) would get a strong response. I have no doubt that the rational concerns I had imbedded in my rant about the danger of germs went right over Sherri's head; what she did hear loud and clear was my feeling of disgust, which she intuited without ambiguity from my animated delivery. There was no change in her positive mood that afternoon because I took responsibility for the incident by claiming to be overly fastidious, rather than accusing her of being dirty, and because I was so very appreciative of her cooperation. She washed and changed, we went off and did errands, and then we relaxed with smoothies in a downtown café. At dinnertime, when I took her home, her mood remained positive, for she retained only the sense of having spent a pleasant afternoon together. In fact, her memory of my words and the litterbox episode itself had disappeared within minutes of their occurrence.

Gestures and posture can also have a marked effect on the moods of people experiencing dementia. If I hadn't said anything to Sherri about my revulsion, she would have picked up my reluctance to give her a hug, touch her hands, or have her sitting in my car in soiled pants. Her mood would have plummeted and remained negative no matter how hard I tried to be upbeat, because I would be delivering an underlying message of withdrawal and avoidance. I was lucky to have lost my reserve and used intonation to such good effect at the beginning of our interaction that day. Posture and gesture are loaded with messages just as much as intonation. Whether we cringe slightly or pause momentarily, turn to face someone when we are speaking, stand over someone in a wheelchair or crouch down to eye level, or stand with our arms folded or relaxed at our side, each posture delivers a very clear message to people who have dementia. Each will have a prolonged effect on mood.

One of the quickest ways to improve, or ruin, the mood of someone with dementia, is with eye contact during the initial moments of an encounter. Here, I teach my caregivers that when they arrive and first see a client, they need to look into the client's eyes and, for just a few seconds, hold eye contact and deliver the message that something good is about to happen, and that they are glad to be there. With this initial eye contact, they should also be communicating acceptance—that the client has their respect, and admiration for their courage and perseverance in their increasingly confusing world.

We see our clients, as they move deeper into dementia and become reliant on their intuitive thought processes alone, begin to crave touch. Touch, even if it's brief, can deliver positive or negative messages just as surely and powerfully as eye contact. As someone loses memory and rational thought, receiving expressions of acceptance and reassurance in sensory ways becomes ever more important. Whether a hand clasp, squeeze of the arm, or a hug—such gestures, or their omission, can have profound effects. Even those who were standoffish and reserved earlier in life come to need reassurance through touch.

We will look at nonverbal communication again in chapter 7, in more detail, as we consider its effect on communicating safety to people with dementia. Becoming more aware of what we communicate nonverbally is a good start for influencing the moods of our companions, but we also need to consider what may have caused their negative moods in the first place—causes which they themselves often do not understand. Someone with dementia might be fearful or frustrated and not know why, or might be embarrassed or afraid after failing at a task or conversation, or they may simply be experiencing a vague sense of loss from having forgotten something, as Martha was when she woke from her dream at the beginning of this chapter. So our next step is to think about whether we are dealing with a mood that is a response to a specific task or situation, or a generalized unease.

When Mood Is a Reaction

Dementia often creates frustrating and frightening situations, because people lose the ability to understand both information and events. As you read this book, you are receiving information and sorting it into many overlapping categories: familiar, unfamiliar; known, unknown; like, unlike; what you agree with and disagree with; what applies, what does not; etc. Essentially, you are creating a framework or filing system in your mind into which you are organizing what you are reading. When you fall asleep tonight, your brain will continue this sorting process and create even more order (which is why it is often a good idea to "sleep on" important decisions before making them). We perform these functions all the time—cataloging and categorizing what we see and hear, recalling sequences of events or steps in a task so we can understand the present and function successfully.

However, with dementia, even getting a morning cup of coffee becomes complex. Making coffee requires remembering what items to use (pot, water, grounds, scoop, cup, stove) and where to find each item, how much to use and where each is put, how to use the stove or coffeemaker, how long to wait, what sound the pot or coffeemaker will make when the coffee is ready—many facts to be recalled and retained at once, as well as the ability to pay attention and avoid becoming distracted during the process. If a mistake is made, or an item mislaid, a whole new set of problems arise.[27] So negative moods accompany dementia because of its cognitive losses, which impact even the simplest activity.

I had a client, Chuck, who would put the kettle on the stove to boil water for coffee, turn aside to reach for a cup, and immediately become distracted. Off he would go, leaving another kettle to melt onto the burner. He would have been safer if he could have forgotten what a stove was for, but even after several pots were melted, he didn't. We tried unplugging the stove and hiding the remaining pots and pans, hoping he would resort to using the microwave. No luck—Chuck just pulled out the stove, saw the cord unplugged, and solved this obvious problem. Back in the plug went, back through the cluttered kitchen cupboards he would rummage, and another pot we had tried to hide was melted onto the burner. We solved the problem by cutting the cord off the stove. Then he would pull out the stove, see no reason for the

---

[27] This emphasizes how important automatic thinking and muscle memory (the tools of mindlessness) are in dementia. As long as people are in a familiar place, they can use those skills to mindlessly go through the steps of routine tasks. A different kitchen, however, requires mindfulness—thinking through the necessary steps.

stove to not be working, push it back in, and continue waiting for the unheated pot to boil until he turned away to look for a cup and became distracted. The safety issue was averted, but poor Chuck still needed his caffeine jolt, and now had the added frustration of failing at a task he was sure should be a simple one. His most persistent mood was one of distracted annoyance.

Here at DAWN, our first step when we want to change the mood of someone who has been frustrated by failure at a task is to cheerfully chatter about the relevant facts needed to perform the task, so that he or she can follow along. This amounts to verbalizing the chatter that a healthy brain produces internally. Here's a sample of my narrative with Chuck:

> "Hi, Chuck, how are you? It's lovely outside today—so sunny and bright. I can see your cherry tree is beginning to blossom. See that—all those tiny white flowers. Right outside your kitchen window. How pretty! So how about a cup of coffee? Let's see, where are the mugs…here they are, and here's the coffee pot. Now we just need the coffee. It's in the freezer. Do you want to grab it? That's right. That's the canister. Here's a spoon. What do you think, shall we use four scoops today?"

My narrative of cheerful chatter will continue as we prepare mugs of coffee for the two of us and lay out breakfast. While we eat, I'll be reading one section of the paper while he looks at another, and I'll be pointing out headlines about topics that I know he will be able to comment on. When I chat with Chuck like this, he becomes more relaxed, for I am performing the functions his brain is failing to do for him. (If I were to do this with my husband, on the other hand, it would have the opposite effect, for my husband has a healthy brain with its own chatter, and my verbosity would be an irritating and continual interruption to his own thought processes!)

In each activity or task with your client or loved one, try thinking out loud. If it's lunchtime, chatter as you go about deciding what to have and how to prepare it. Verbalize the steps to making a sandwich or heating up soup as you perform them so that your loved one or client can follow along and feel the sense of accomplishment that comes from checking off a list, and the sense of security that comes from knowing what will happen next. Do you need to get groceries? Voice your thoughts as you draft a list and talk out loud as you gather what is needed to make a trip to the store. When we do this with our loved ones and clients, they can relax and feel safe from embarrassment and confusion, and we will be able to keep the mood positive and upbeat.

When Mood Is General Unease

At other times, people experiencing dementia are not reacting to something specific. Feelings of confusion and failure from trying to recall something and being unable to do so, or from worrying about the future and not being able to plan or act, result in a vague sense of loss or foreboding. Our response should be to help them focus on the present. What we do is the same as what a parent would do for a child who is unhappy or in need of a behavior change: we distract and redirect. To distract a client, we think about what kind of sensory or social stimulation he or she would find pleasing. We can then redirect their attention to whatever it is they would find enjoyable and watch their mood improve.

When I first begin working with someone, one of my initial considerations is whether the person is more of an introvert or an extrovert. This helps me predict whether he or she has a greater need for sensory stimulation or social stimulation, so I can introduce the right balance of stimulus during the day to be sure that my new client will be able to feel relaxed at day's end. People who tend toward introversion need quiet and time to be alone; if we fill their days with conversation and group activities, they will become exhausted and cranky. People who are more extroverted and don't get enough social interaction in their days become restless and are more likely to exit-seek toward the end of the day or during the night. Knowing what types of stimulation work best for your loved one or client will take some careful watching and trial and error, because although someone may have been particularly introverted or extroverted during earlier years, dementia can alter personality and lifelong tendencies.

What qualifies as appropriate social stimulation varies from one person to another. Our more introverted clients are most comfortable in one-on-one conversations; they get ample social stimulation while sitting on a bench in the park with a caregiver, and watching children playing on the swings nearby. Going to the theater to watch a movie about families or animals is another good way to let them enjoy the companionship of their caregiver and be a spectator of human interactions. Conversely, our more extroverted clients benefit from being in crowded coffee shops and restaurants with the din of mealtime surrounding them. They need to interact with waitresses and clerks, pass the time of day with the mothers at the park, have their caregivers join them at the book club they have belonged to for years, or accompany them to the bowling alley or a service club meeting. When these clients move to a care facility, it is essential that they attend the activities and organized outings so that their need for conversation and social interaction can be met.

Regardless of where people fall on the scale of introversion and extroversion, however, everyone needs sensory stimulation, whether they have dementia or not. When using the DAWN method, we are careful to provide stimulation for all five senses: sight, sound, scent, taste and touch. We are fortunate here on the Palouse to have so much natural beauty around us. We can take a half-hour drive through rolling hills in any direction from Moscow and end up in a small town with an antique store, an art gallery or a coffee shop. And because we have two universities nearby, the town offers symphonies, concerts, plays and dance productions year-round. We have swimming pools, movie theaters and great destinations for walking or hiking. These venues offer ample and varied sensory stimulation, and we take our clients to all of them. Whatever your location, if it is possible to get your loved one or client out of the building he or she lives in, even just for a car ride, the extra stimulation will result in less restlessness and anxiety. And if you cannot, look for ways inside the building to trigger all five senses.

One of our clients, Verna, is a devoted chocolate lover. So distraction or improving her mood is never a problem. I simply say, "Verna, do you feel like getting hot chocolate? Let's go get one." Another client, Marge, who had been an avid quilter, is always cheered by meandering through the JoAnn Fabrics store at the mall, where she can feel the textures of tweeds, chiffons, silks, and upholstery fabrics, and revel in the colors and patterns in florals, plaids, stripes and paisleys. The mood of another client can be changed by a short walk and some fresh air. All we need to provide distraction successfully is to make use of our clients' favorite activities, foods or places.

When I worked with the mentally ill at an enhanced care facility, one of our residents' favorite activities was a jelly bean game. We'd take turns closing our eyes and trying to identify the flavor of a jelly bean without knowing its color, or looking at the colors and trying to guess the flavors. Just a few jelly beans provide great mental exercise as well as elicit memories from childhood. A handful of jelly beans can provide color, taste, and mental stimulation—a lot of fun and stimulation for little cost. We also use smells to provide stimulation. Every neighborhood, city and small town has much to offer. Hardware stores and lumberyards are filled with the scents of paint, birdseed and fresh-cut wood. Even the bins of nails have a smell. Grocery stores not only have bakeries and cut flowers but also herbs in the produce section and fish in the meat department. Nurseries have greenery throughout the growing season, and car dealerships provide access to that distinctive new car smell, if you can cajole a salesman into letting you sit in a car for a moment. A client and I once went to the grand opening of a hotel. The smells of new carpeting and fresh paint awoke her long-dormant memories of having had a home built decades earlier.

Music is a very important means of changing someone's mood. In 2008, a retired social worker named Dan Cohen, who knew he would want to be able to listen to the music of his youth if he ended up in a care facility, began personalizing iPod Shuffles for residents of care facilities in New York. He discovered something amazing: even when residents had been unable to communicate for a long time, when headphones were put on their ears with music they had loved earlier in life, they became conversational and interactive again. Music seems to unlock the parts of the brain which allowed someone with dementia to begin communicating again. I have always appreciated the power of music in my work here, and seen its positive effect, for the intuitive part of thinking is activated when we listen to music. I find that music, like all sensory stimulation, is energizing and captivating for my clients.

In sum, when we as caregivers provide an appropriate level and blend of sensory and social stimulation, we will see positive and often lasting changes in our loved ones' and clients' moods.

Accept Altered Versions of Reality

Once again, accepting the altered sense of reality that comes with dementia is critical. One moment of reality orientation will negatively alter mood as surely as does asking your partner rhetorically whether their comment at a dinner party was wise, or telling a toddler he doesn't need the dish of ice cream the waiter has just offered. Being asked to question our own behavior, desire, or version of events requires us to agree or disagree with the speaker. With dementia, the unavoidable result is either fear or anger. A recent exchange between my client, Rosa, and her husband Manuel helps to illustrate this:

> Manuel looked across the kitchen table at Rosa with profound irritation. He said, "Darling, we *did*. We had dinner last night with Jack and Anna. Don't tell me we didn't. You ate Anna's pecan pie, so now you have an upset stomach. Don't complain."
>
> Rosa was floored. "We didn't go *anywhere* last night!" she replied. "Why do you always have to be so difficult? Now my stomach feels worse." She put down her mug of coffee and stared down at the scrambled eggs on her plate. *Why did he do this? Jack and Anna's last night?* Rosa thought hard but couldn't recall anything about dinner last night.
>
> "Rosa, please think. Jack has been ill. We hadn't seen them in quite a while. Anna was so pleased to have us come. She made that salmon dish—the one with the lemon caper sauce. Remember?"
>
> Rosa tried again to recall going out the evening before; once more no memories surfaced. Now she had had enough. She pulled herself to her feet, grabbed her mug, and stomped over to the sink to dump her coffee.

Then she stood there a moment, so angry at Manuel that she couldn't think of what she'd meant to do. Her stomach cramped again. She decided to call Dr. Tang's office and talk to his nurse. She looked over at Manuel, wishing he'd leave—go for a walk, go out back to work in his shop. He was calmly taking a bite of toast, crumbs dropping on the table and in his lap, a smear of jam on his chin. When he turned to look at her, her feelings of injustice and resentment flared anew.

"They told us that Ned and Carmen would be coming this weekend," he began again, "from Boston. Remember talking about all the snow they've had in Boston this winter and how they had to buy a new stroller with bigger wheels so she could get out with the baby? Can't you remember tha—?"

Rosa's mug smashed into the wall just above his head. She had aimed at his jam-smeared chin, but missed.

Our sense of what is real and true is greatly affected by what we remember to have already occurred. When people have dementia and their memories are declining, their individual versions of reality will diverge more and more from those around them. Instead of trying to reason with people who are losing or have lost reasoning, we should accept their versions of reality and, if that reality is unpleasant, introduce new facts or distractions to help make it pleasant. In the above scenario, Manuel didn't succeed in convincing Rosa that her stomachache was due to eating pie at their friends' the night before; he only succeeded in angering her to the point of throwing a mug, because Rosa believed he was being argumentative. He would have done better to accept Rosa's faulty memory of the night before, and express sympathy for her discomfort. His demand that Rosa accept his memory of the facts was counterproductive.

One resident I worked with at the enhanced care unit for the mentally ill, Melanie, had very erratic behavior. She couldn't leave the unit even with a worker, because we never knew when she might become upset. One day, as I sat talking with her and trying to understand her turmoil, she looked at me and said:

"I don't understand why they won't just let me watch the evening news. If I can watch those commercials, the little green men tell me what to do. But someone's always standing in the way or turning off the sound, and then I don't know what I'm supposed to do the next day."

She was calm, but I could feel the intensity of the frustration behind her words. I think she shared her secret with me because, even though reality orientation was the accepted practice in the unit, I had always listened respectfully to what she had to say. At that moment, I saw with new clarity that although her reality included things I could not believe, they were utterly real for her, and had a marked effect on her behavior. In addition, her perception of what was true and real was something she could not choose to change. We arranged for Melanie to be able to watch the evening news uninterrupted; she gradually became less volatile and was able to move out of the enhanced care unit and into community housing. I learned from that encounter with Melanie that no matter how strange someone else's version of reality might seem to me, it will be present, real, and believable for him or her.

Another example of how critical it is to avoid using reality orientation with someone experiencing dementia would be a client we'll call Nathaniel. He and his wife had lived together in their home for twenty-five years, until her death a few years before we began working with him. In the night, Nathaniel would wake up, reach across their bed, and find that Angie was gone. He began calling the local sheriff department in a panic; when they attempted to convince him that she hadn't gone missing or been kidnapped, Nathaniel would become more frantic and volatile, because his memory of the recent past (his lonely years after Angie's death) had been wiped away by dementia. Once notified by Nathaniel's family that I was working with him, the sheriffs would call me and I would call Nathaniel for a chat. After picking up the phone, Nathaniel would immediately explode about Angie's disappearance and the authorities' lack of concern.

Trying to convince him that she was dead would have been pointless. Instead, I expressed concern, and asked him to look out the front window to see whether Angie's car was there. Of course it wasn't—it had been sold years earlier. Then I asked him to look in the closet to see if her purse and coat were gone too, which of course they were, having also been disposed of years earlier. Next, I asked Nathaniel about the dear friends in Oregon whom he and Angie had visited so often and had enjoyed many happy times with. Those long-term memories were very comforting to Nathaniel and, while we talked about his dear friends, his mind would leap to the assumption that Angie was there visiting them. Within minutes he would be calmly talking about how much she must be enjoying her visit there in Oregon.

Without my intervention and gentle shaping of his sense of reality, his nighttime calls to the sheriff department would have resulted in a visit from two sheriffs and probable transport to the emergency room for medication and observation, followed by a permanent move into a care facility. Instead, I was able to help dissolve his confusion and fear during a pleasant phone call with a friend, which sent him back to bed with happy thoughts. Nathaniel eventually stopped waking up in a panic, and he was able to continue living at home for months longer.

In other countries, using the habilitative approach and supporting the altered views of reality of people experiencing dementia has long been the norm, even in institutions.[28] In Germany, care facilities are routinely built with fake bus stops, after the staff at a care facility in Dusseldorf realized that if one of their residents escaped, they invariably headed straight for a bus stop, and used long-term memory to try to find a way back to a former home. More and more European care facilities now include bus stops right out front, where residents are encouraged to wait for a bus whenever they wish to leave. No buses ever arrive, though, and they soon return to the facility due to short-term memory loss and lack of attention span.[29]

An even more delightful account of using the habilitative approach is Hogewey, on the outskirts of Amsterdam, a

---

[28] Keep in mind that the concepts of "appropriate care" and "reality orientation" are American in origin. Atul Gawande traces the development of our senior care industry in his book *Being Mortal* (2014).

[29] See the article at www.iacp.org/Fake-Bus-Stops-For-Alzheimers-patients-in-Germany.

community that CNN dubbed the *dementia village*. Hogewey has 152 inhabitants, all of whom have dementia and think they are living normal lives. The village is outfitted with secured access and video monitoring, however, and caregivers are playing the roles of shopkeepers, policeman, gardeners, and waitresses. A similar village has been created in Penetanguishene, Ontario, Canada.[30] The result is the same any time the habilitative approach is taken: happier residents and less stress for staff members.

However, some would argue that the use of fake bus stops at care facilities, or the way I led Nathaniel to think his wife was alive and visiting friends in Oregon, is dishonest. To tell a lie is to say something we know to be untrue with the deliberate intent to deceive. So yes, strictly defined, I was lying to Nathaniel, and a staff member at a European care facility who encouraged a resident to wait for an imaginary bus would be lying, too. However, when we decide whether we want to be completely honest with someone, we take into account more than the veracity of the statement. We consider not only kindness and courtesy, but the hearer's cognitive development. We respond to a six-year-old's question about terrorism or where babies come from differently than we do to the same question from a twelve-year-old. We do this as a kindness, and with respect for our companion's cognitive development, because a six-year-old is not able to understand and process information in the same way an older child can. In my view, I was exercising the same kindness and respect when I evoked happy memories for Nathaniel so he could relax and go back to bed. Nathaniel did not have the cognitive ability to process and retain the information that his wife had died and would not be there when he awoke in the night.

One of our clients, Jacob, who was still functioning well enough to take a short flight alone, needed to fly to Seattle to attend his older brother's funeral. When Jacob returned from his weekend away, however, his reality did not include attending a funeral. He returned thrilled and energized by his weekend at the

---

[30] See "The Dutch Village Where Everyone Has Dementia" at http://www.theatlantic.com/health/archive/2014/11/the-dutch-village-where-everyone-has-dementia/382195/ and a story about the Canadian version at www.aplaceformom.com/blog/7-2-15-canadian-dementia-village.

"family reunion"—having spent time with his "brother," who had flown from the East Coast just to be with him. None of this was, strictly speaking, true. Jacob had been there at the graveside with the rest of his family and seen his brother laid to rest. A family member had come from the East Coast, but it was Jacob's son that he had spent time with, not his brother.

If we had insisted on a more accurate account of the events, Jacob would not have benefitted. Instead, he would have been infuriated by the suggestion that he'd mischaracterized his weekend away, all the more since none of us had been there with him. He had stored away memories of the weekend as a time during which he and his brother had enjoyed each other's company in mutual admiration and respect. The kindest way we could respond to Jacob was simply to go along with his version of reality.

■ ■ ■

At DAWN, the management of our clients' moods is our every-day, every-visit task, almost as automatic as saying hello when we arrive at a client's home. We assume that if a client has been alone for any amount of time, he or she needs a mood change. We expect that when our clients wake up, they are likely to think that what they just dreamed is real and still happening, as Martha did, or that they will be confused about the present, like Nathaniel. Because we respond by actively creating a positive mood of acceptance and enjoyment, our clients welcome our company. They become increasingly relaxed and at peace as time goes on, developing confidence that we will help to ensure that all is well in their worlds. As one of my first clients used to tell me with a hug, "You and I *always* have a good time together."

When we realize what an impact actively managing mood will have on our caregiving experience, it becomes both natural and effortless. It is not hard to transform the mood of someone who has limited memory and no ability to analyze why he or she is being offered a distraction. The tools and techniques I've described in this chapter will help both the caregiver and the person experiencing dementia gain reliable relief from the negative moods that usually accompany dementia. Now let's look at how we can help our loved ones and clients develop a sense of security, even in the face of their increasing confusion about the world around them.

CHAPTER SEVEN

Security in Confusion

People will forget what you said; people will forget what you did;
but people will never forget how you made them feel.

—Maya Angelou (1928–2014)

Raymond

The doorbell rang. *Who can that be?* thought Raymond. He pulled himself to his feet, using the kitchen table for support. *Have I forgotten something? Did I call someone?* The doorbell rang again. He smoothed his hair and rubbed the stubble on his cheek. *Haven't shaved. Am I dressed? Yes, slippers, pants, t-shirt, robe…. Good enough.*

The doorbell rang yet again, twice as long this time. As Raymond left the kitchen and shuffled down the hall, his irritation grew. He didn't like surprises. A retired college dean, he was used to knowing what was going on—or rather, to being the person who *decided* what was going on. As he reached the front room, he straightened his back and his shuffle became more purposeful. He was annoyed because he didn't know who was at the door and because the caller's heavy thumb on the doorbell made him feel like he was being summoned. "All right. All *right*, I'm coming!"

Again it rang, two short bursts. Raymond opened the door to find a young man in a blue workman's shirt, carrying a box of tools.

"Who are you?" Raymond said, his frown deepening as he leaned down to peer at the name and logo on the badge sewn to the repairman's shirt.

The young man paused, then straightened, and half shrugged before he said in a low voice. "I'm the repairman you called to fix your fireplace damper. Can I come in?" Raymond only caught half of what the man said, and his irritation grew.

"What? Speak up. What do you want?" He had an intense dislike for mutterers.

"I'm the repairman from the hardware store. You called and asked for someone to come fix your damper!" the repairman responded with much more volume.

"My what? My damper? I called? I don't remember calling anyone." Flustered, Raymond leaned forward and peered at his visitor's face more closely. The repairman shifted his weight from one foot to the other and looked away. "Oh well, you'd better come in then, but I don't think there's anything wrong with my damper. My fireplace works just fine."

Raymond moved aside to let the repairman pass and then turned back to the front door to shut it. As he did so, he noticed a moving van driving by slowly, as if looking for an address. *Wonder who that's for?* Raymond squinted at the van, trying to see the state insignia on the license plate. *People are so transient these days, always moving. No one has a sense of place anymore,* he thought. *Except me. I've been here longer than that tree.* Raymond straightened to admire the graceful birch tree he and Ellen had planted in a corner of the front yard. *My, it's grown!*

"Mr. Morrison, I need to get started. *Mr. Morrison!*"

Raymond turned to find a young man wearing a blue workman's shirt standing just behind him in the foyer, a box of tools at his feet.

"*Who* are *you*? What are you doing here?"

Why Do We Need to Know?

Why does anyone ask a question? Why do we seek information? We ask because our brains need data just as our bodies need fuel in the form of proteins, carbohydrates, and fats. Our brains are designed to take in information via our senses so that we can assess our circumstances and decide what action to take. Tinnitus is an example of how much our brains need information: if my ears become unable to process a single soundwave frequency, my brain will become discomforted by the lack of data on that frequency and fill in the gap with that inescapable phantom ringing.

In addition to helping us make decisions and understand what's happening around us, having information meets an emotional need. It helps us to feel confident, safe, and in control. We've all felt that surge of anticipation and delight when we are presented with a wrapped gift, or read a gripping story, or hear the phone ring when we're expecting a call from a loved one. We all know burning curiosity as well as the persistent dull ache of trying to figure out why something troubling has happened. We take in what we see, hear, smell, taste and touch; we assemble the data and organize it into patterns that make sense to us. From these arrangements of information, we create stories about what has happened, is happening, and will happen in the future.

Imagine suddenly waking up in the night. You are quite sure you heard a sound. You search your memory for what type of sound it was that woke you. *I think that was a thump,* you decide. Then you go through the things you know of that might cause thumps in your home during the night. *The furnace turning on? No. The dog wagging his tail in his sleep? No. My husband using the bathroom? No. The paper being thrown at the front door?* At the same time your brain is also giving you a list of things you don't want it to be. *A burglar! Someone breaking in! An earthquake!* Some are possible, others quite unlikely. But while you're sorting through the possibilities, you're also considering potential courses of action. And all this is happening in milliseconds.

These are your rational thought processes at work, sifting through previously stored information and grading it in various ways to make sense of the present. If you were to jump out of bed and make a run for the back door, that would be your intuitive thinking at work—your instincts telling you that immediate action is the surest means of survival. Instead, you remain under the covers, calmly recalling, sorting, organizing, and creating sequences out of new and stored facts. As you read these words, your rational mind is performing this same process.

But what if your rational thought processes were becoming impaired? What if you were losing the ability to recall? What if you could only bring to mind one or two facts at a time? You would find yourself constantly surprised, much like Raymond, who forgot he had let the repairman into his home after he turned his back and was distracted by new thoughts. For Raymond, the repairman's visit was intensely unsettling. Being surprised by the visit made him feel out of control. Being unable to remember what had just been said left him feeling embarrassed and inept. Without recall, he simply could not access information long enough to make sense of having a stranger standing in his front room. Raymond needed to remember that his fireplace leaked smoke when he built a fire each evening (the fact that he could not be deterred from building fires is another tale of dementia care, described in chapter 11). He also needed to remember that a repairman had been called and an appointment had been made for that specific day. And he needed to be able to recall that this stranger was the repairman, and that the reason for his presence was to repair the damper. However, because Raymond could not recall for more than a few moments that his living room became smoky when he lit a fire—let alone these many other facts—he could not make sense of the repairman's presence.

I arrived at Raymond's home just a few minutes after the repairman. By the time I walked into the living room, there were two very angry men standing chest to chest and shouting. Raymond's hearing loss wasn't helping the situation. He felt indignant, embarrassed, confused, and invaded. I'm sure the young repairman was wishing he had waited in his truck until I arrived, as I'd suggested when I made the appointment. He was feeling attacked and trapped in a nonsensical interchange. He was experiencing anger primarily because Raymond's repetition of the same questions over and over made no sense in the story his own healthy brain was attempting to write about what was going on between him and this homeowner. He had probably never encountered someone with severe memory loss before.

My response was to begin cheerfully supplying information to Raymond, as often as he needed it, which was on a moment-by-moment basis. As I continuously provided my client with facts regarding the repairman and his reason for being there, he calmed. Each time I did so, his sense of control and safety increased. Soon he became a most gracious host and began telling and retelling a story, with the regularity of a metronome, about how his father had once fixed the damper in his childhood home. This went on for the rest of the repairman's visit, for more than an hour. I had plenty of time to demonstrate to the repairman that although Raymond was unable to retain information, when supplied with facts as he needed them, he could communicate without problem, and a conversation—albeit repetitive—could take place. The repairman very quickly understood this and began following my lead. In fact, he caught on so well and became so gracious himself that he is now our first choice when we need a repairman to do work for a client.

Raymond's lack of recall made him unable to move forward in *conversation* or allow the repairman to proceed. At other times, we see the inability to retain information trap our clients within repetitive or circular behaviors.

Jeanette

Laura knocked loudly, opened the back door, then stuck her head in and called out a hello. Her mom was usually in the living room in the morning, sitting in her easy chair and looking at the newspaper or doing Sudoku. Her little dachshund, Missy, would be in her lap. The back door opened into the laundry room, and the kitchen was between it and the living room. Laura always felt guilty when she dropped in on her mom. Even though she called ahead every time, Jeanette couldn't retain even for a minute the memory of having been called, and was always shocked by Laura's "unannounced" visits. She would even be a little miffed that Laura hadn't called first. Laura had started calling Jeanette from her cell phone as she turned the corner onto Jeanette's block, but Jeanette was still surprised when Laura called out a hello from the back door a minute later.

"Hi, Mom, it's me!" Laura stomped the snow off her boots and stood for a moment in the laundry room before heading through the kitchen to see if her mom was in her chair in the living room. She was, with Missy in her lap.

"Oh! Hello, darling—what a surprise!"

"I called to tell you I was coming. I really did. Are you ready? Let's go to the grocery store." Laura felt a familiar sinking feeling at seeing her mother's expression of surprise melt briefly into disapproval before it was replaced by a smile. She could almost hear her mother saying, "I thought I raised you better than to drop in on someone unannounced."

"Go for groceries? Do I need anything?" Jeanette's smile turned thoughtful.

"Yes, Mom. You called me. You need milk. I need a few things too. Let's go." Laura sighed. She knew getting out of the house was going to be a process.

Jeanette set Missy on the floor and pulled herself to her feet. Missy shook herself and looked up at Laura. Her expression was clear: reproach at having her nap interrupted. Jeanette headed down the hall and was back in the doorway moments later with a tattered blue vinyl purse in her hands. "I'd better make sure I've got some money—in case we go to the grocery store."

"Mom, you've got money. We went to the bank yesterday," Laura said. "You have five twenties in your purse. Let's go."

But Jeanette pushed past Laura, headed for a kitchen chair, and sat down. Laura watched her mother as she pulled out her wallet and began carefully counting out the five twenties. With a deep sigh, Laura sat down too. Jeanette was now pushing the bills back into her wallet. She jammed her wallet back into the front pocket of her purse. Jeanette looked across at Laura and smiled with relief. Laura stood, helped Jeanette to her feet, and gave her a hug. "I love you, Mom," she said.

"Oh honey, I love you, too!" Jeanette looked up at her with an affectionate smile. "Now, where are we going?"

"Groceries, Mom."

"Oh, just a minute. I need to look to see if I've got any money."

"Mom! It's *okay*," said Laura, her hands still on Jeanette's shoulders. She caught Jeanette's gaze and held it. "Mom, you just looked in your wallet. We went to the bank yesterday and you have money in your wallet. We just checked."

"Well, okay, honey, but I need to make sure. I don't want to end up at the checkout counter without money."

Jeanette sank back into the chair, opened her purse, pulled out her wallet, and painstakingly counted out the five twenty-dollar bills inside. Laura took a deep, slow breath and exhaled just as slowly. She closed her eyes, opened them, squared her shoulders, and looked down at her mother with eyebrows raised and a carefully blank expression on her face. Jeanette pushed the bills back into her wallet, wedged it back into place inside her purse, snapped the flap, and began to pull herself to her feet. She straightened her sweater and smiled at her daughter. Laura took her arm and they headed for the back door. Jeanette paused to check her reflection in the little mirror that hung over the coat hooks, patted her white curls, and turned to her daughter.

"Just a sec, honey. I'd better go sit down. I need to see if I have any money. I sure don't want to go out without money."

"Mom—no! I told you—we went to the bank yesterday. You have money! You've already checked twice. For goodness' sake, Mom. Let's *go!*"

■ ■ ■

Losing the ability to retain and recall information means losing the sense of being secure. We cannot feel safe if we do not know what is going on. If we, as dementia caregivers, want to be able to help our companions feel safe and stay comfortable, we need to help them retain and learn a sense of security even though they cannot regain their memory or rational functions. This means that we need to take care of those functions for them. If people experiencing dementia find that their companions are consistently and readily providing them with the information they need, they begin to relax and feel safer.

For someone experiencing dementia to remain in a positive mood and feel comfortable despite the lack of recall and constant feelings of confusion, he or she needs to develop an ingrained sense that information will always be available when needed, and that there will not be a price to pay for asking. This sense can only be learned intuitively, through experience. However, when we are taking care of someone who is losing the ability to retain information, it is easy to be overcome with frustration and anger at having to supply the same information over and over. This is a normal reaction. Yet if we recognize that knowing what is going on is driven by an essential human need, due to the way our brains function, it becomes easier to be patient and helpful. Voicing relevant facts and verbalizing our rational thought processes is important when caring for people experiencing dementia. It is as central to providing care for the person with dementia as physical supports are when providing care for the person who has just had a hip replacement. When we consistently and happily supply information as it is needed, we will find that our companions become more comfortable and relaxed, and that they will act out less due to fewer feelings of confusion and insecurity.

Chatter, Chatter, Chatter

When our rational thought processes are operating normally, they supply a steady stream of chatter that goes on in the back of our minds. This inner dialogue can be distracting, at times preventing us from being able to relax or fall asleep. I notice my brain chatter most when I'm doing a task or following directions— I find my inner monologue talking me through the process with a series of questions and statements about what comes next: "Hmm, the screw for my glasses is loose. I need a tiny straight screwdriver. Where'd I put that? Kitchen junk drawer? No, no, desk drawer. Yes—here it is." This recitation is automatic and unavoidable. Sometimes I catch myself saying it out loud. However, people with dementia lack an inner monologue that operates consistently and effectively. Often, my clients will be unable to recall a step just taken or identify the next step, due to this missing inner dialogue, and as a result feel frustration or confusion. Remember how I chattered to Chuck, in the previous chapter, as I made coffee and laid out breakfast? Chatter can be used to create security in confusion too. When we provide a narration for people who are experiencing dementia, we help them direct their thoughts so they can complete tasks and feel secure about having done what they need or want to do. For someone whose rational thought processes are faltering, this chatter is as comforting as it can be irritating to those whose rational thought is intact.

In the story at the beginning of this chapter, Raymond's primary need was for information—for someone to give him the facts continuously. He needed to be able to make sense out of the presence of the young man in his living room and, with my cheerful conversation, he was able to stay informed and regain a positive mood. However, in Jeanette's case, her primary need was emotional. Her fear of arriving at a checkout stand without enough money to make her purchases was deeply rooted. Most likely, she had found herself in a store without money or checks several times during the early stages of her dementia. Her caregiver and daughter, Laura, needed to address her fear—not just supply the facts as needed—before she could resolve the compulsive and cyclical wallet-checking behavior that Jeanette had developed. Behaviors due to an underlying fear can become crippling. One of our clients had locked herself out of her home several times during the early stages of her dementia and, by the time I began working with her, she had become fearful of leaving the house. It was essential to help her begin to feel secure when we left the house, so I made a ritual out of us both having keys in our hands as we went out the door and locked it. After a few weeks, the relief of feeling keys securely in her hand replaced the dread of finding herself locked out, and we could walk out without needing to stop and deal with fear-based behavior.

These types of behaviors—searching for keys or money, needing to verify repeatedly what day it is—are common for those with dementia. They often begin as irritating hitches in the performance of some task, and then escalate into inexplicable refusals to cooperate with some benign but necessary activity. Edna, from chapter 3, was constantly searching for her cats. Here, we are careful to respond to these behaviors as an expression of an emotional need, and to help our clients develop a comfortable path through the behavior. The trick is to begin providing the information before the behavior starts, framed in a manner that will dispel the fear or insecurity that prompts it.

With Jeanette, the most effective response would be to anticipate her need for reassurance and voice the information before she needs it. Laura should tell Jeanette that she has money in her purse *before* Jeanette begins to feel the fear of being in a store without money. As Jeanette goes to get her purse, Laura might begin to say:

> "I sure am glad we went to the bank yesterday, Mom, and took out that money! Now you've got five twenties in your purse and we won't have to worry about not having money at the checkout stand. That was good thinking. It's *so* nice to know you have the money you need when you're leaving home on errands."

Laura should repeat some version of this cheerful monologue as she helps Jeanette put on her coat, as they walk through the kitchen, as they arrive at the back door, and as they get into the car. If Laura does this each time they prepare to leave home, Jeanette will begin to feel a sense of safety and comfort when preparing to do errands with her daughter, rather than fall prey to her habitual fear of having no money. Jeanette will intuitively (experientially) learn that she is safe leaving home with Laura. It's vital that we, as caregivers, meet our clients' need for reassurance consistently and as early as possible. If we don't, something that might be only a little troublesome today can quickly grow into an entrenched behavior that will be difficult to dislodge in the future.

How do I know that reassurance is needed, not just knowledge of what's happening? Several clues suggest that fear or the need for reassurance are the root cause of our loved one's or client's repeated requests for information. The most obvious indicators are in their expressions and body language. Emotions such as worry, concern or anxiety in a person's face or posture are easy for most of us to recognize (e.g., hunched shoulders, clenched hands, widened eyes). However, I also pay attention to the extent to which my clients vary the wording of their repeated questions. I don't know why this holds true, but when my clients change their wording, I assume they need more than just information, and I tailor my responses to provide emotional support as well as facts. To provide reassurance, I begin to chatter about what has just happened and what is about to happen, giving them more and more details to draw reassurance from.

Here's how the conversation went one evening when I took a client to a social gathering in the home of mutual friends. Dana and I had just gotten into the car. I backed out of her driveway and we headed toward the stop sign at the foot of her street:

"Where are we going?" Dana asked.

"We're going to your friends' home for poetry night," I responded as I slowed down and put on the turn signal.

"Oh. Okay," she said. We both looked left, then right, and then left again. The turn signal clicked; we watched as a car approached and passed in front of us.

"Why are we in the car?" Ronda asked.

"It's Thursday night, and we're headed to poetry night," I said as I turned right and accelerated. "You've been going to poetry night for years. Tonight, it's at Becka and Lawrence's. They're such good friends of yours."

Dana sat very still, looking straight ahead as we drove two short blocks to the next stop sign. "Becka and Lawrence? I don't remember Becka and Lawrence," she said quietly.

"No, but they're your dear friends. Mine, too," I said.

I wanted her to feel natural going with me, that we were doing something fun together rather than that she was simply being delivered somewhere, but I was also sensing that she was uncomfortable about something. We went through the second stop sign, drove another block, and stopped at the stoplight where we would make a left turn onto the highway. I said:

"I really like them and I can see they really *love* you. You've been getting together for poetry night for years. We're driving to their home now."

129

"We're going *where?*" Dana asked. Her tone was more insistent, with a hint of worry, though not frustration.

"To Becka and Lawrence's. They're your dear friends. They love having you over to their house."

"Becka and Lawrence. Well, those names don't mean anything to me, but they do give me a warm feeling inside."

Often I find that a client is unable to recall a fact but able to recall a feeling or association that she once associated with the word or phrase. Once I realized that the phrase "Becka and Lawrence" was attached to old memories of companionship and gave Dana a feeling of familiarity, I continued to use it as I drove her to their home. This helped me meet the need for reassurance and security that lay behind her repeated questions. Without making her feel like a nuisance, I freely answered her questions and recounted past events and described what was about to happen, which restored Dana's feeling of security.

One afternoon another client, who at the time was in his final months of life, bedridden and frail, turned to Heike and said, "I bet you think you're the boss!" Heike wisely chose not to answer factually, that yes, she was the caregiver in charge that day. Rather, she responded to the emotional need that she suspected had prompted him to ask the question in the first place. She responded, "Oh no, Dr. Warner. You're the boss. You're always the boss here." Even though he was completely incapable of making decisions or caring for himself, this man needed to feel in control. Heike's affirmation that he, not she, was in charge met his true need. He had been an extremely capable and accomplished scientist, a man of both national and international influence, so how could he feel comfortable being out of control now that he was so vulnerable? Once reassured, Dr. Warner smiled and relaxed back against his pillow, feeling safe, comfortable, and in control.

At other times, we ask questions simply because we want the answers. In such cases, the person with dementia is less likely to vary the wording of his or her questions and will tend to remain focused on one subject. Ronda was a client who had been with us for several years and had developed a sense of security in us as her caregivers. One morning, she and I were in the car together, heading for her dental appointment. We had been driving long enough to get out of the neighborhood and onto the highway. Here's a snippet of our conversation, which actually continued with very little variation throughout the entire twenty-five-minute car ride.

"So, where are we going?" Ronda asked.

"We're going to the dentist. You're going to have some work done," I said, turning to give her a quick smile.

"Me? What kind of work?" Ronda's tone was one of incredulity. (We find that many of our clients have a default belief that any appointment with a dentist or doctor is for the caregiver, likely because they cannot remember anything being wrong with themselves.)

"The dentist is going to fill a cavity for you. He's a great dentist. You and I both go to him because he's such a good dentist," I responded brightly.

"Oh." Ronda looked out the passenger door window at a cyclist, who went by in the other direction on the bike path that ran parallel to the road. She turned back and looked straight ahead for about three seconds.

Ronda turned to me and asked, "So where are we going?"

"We're going to the dentist. You really *like* this dentist. He's a good one," I responded with enthusiasm.

"Oh. *Who* are you again?" Ronda looked at me closely as if realizing for the first time that she didn't recognize me.

"I'm Judy. We haven't been able to be together for a while because I've been out of town. But we used to do lots of things together." I flashed her another quick smile, looking to see if she was anxious. Her face was relaxed. She was looking at the car ahead of us without concern.

"Well, I'm not going to remember your name, because I'm really good at being forgetful. But I'm Ronda," she offered with a laugh and toss of her chin. I chuckled with her. Less than a minute passed. Her attention was focused on a log truck we were passing.

"So, tell me. Where are we going?" Ronda asked with an interested smile.

As you can tell, Ronda's sense of safety despite confusion was well developed. She experienced no distress at all about being forgetful; further, she was comfortable being in the car with me for quite some time before she felt the need to know who I was. Ronda is an example of someone who has learned that she will be safe even if she is confused—and that she can ask for information whenever she might want it without upsetting the people around her.

So, when someone wants information, rather than reassurance, I have found that he or she will usually ask the same question, in the same words, over and over. As dementia progresses, the length of time a person can retain information decreases. If your loved one or client is in the early stages of dementia now and you are finding yourself frustrated by constant questioning, you will need to get beyond your sense of irritation and the idea that you are dealing with an unreasonable behavior. Needing information is both reasonable and necessary, whether we have dementia or not, and someone experiencing dementia will never become better at recalling or retaining information, only worse. I know this sounds like the exercise of superhuman patience, but we actually can decrease our companions' need to ask questions if we are careful always to provide information when asked—and always do so without making them feel embarrassed, foolish, or guilty for asking. If we do this, they develop the sense that information is readily available, and become more comfortable with not only asking but also with *putting off asking*. I don't think of myself as a very patient person. What I began to do, however, was to tell myself that I would only answer questions happily for the next hour or two—not forever. And, without intending to develop patience, or be patient, I found that I had increased my tolerance gradually through exposure and, in a sense, through self-preservation.

What They See Is What They Hear

Whether our loved ones or clients learn to feel safe asking for information or remaining without it depends largely upon which emotions they pick up from us when they do ask. As we discussed in the previous chapter, people who have dementia retain their ability to interpret nonverbal communication. They may even become more adept at it: when our rational thought processes begin to fade, and distract us less with constant processing, evaluating and planning, our minds are increasingly free to focus on what can be intuitively picked up from the intonation, expression, gesture and posture of the people we're with. Let's explore nonverbal communication further.

Maya Angelou said that although people forget what we say or do, they never forget how we make them feel. This is never truer than when we are with people experiencing dementia. Like the adage that our actions speak louder than our words, this underlines the importance of being careful about *how* we say things, not just what we say.

One of the easiest ways to deliver positive emotions with your voice is simply to smile while you speak. You don't even have to feel happy; just use your facial muscles to make a smile. Research has shown that smiling when speaking communicates happiness even when our faces cannot be seen.[31] There's an easy way to verify how well this works: try smiling when talking on the telephone with customer service workers and you'll find they warm up and become more helpful. We do a lot of smiling with our clients, whether we are with them or on the phone, and we see their uncertainty and distress begin to melt away.

We also look for reasons to laugh out loud, wholeheartedly, when we are with our clients. With my client who was anxious about leaving home and forgetting her keys, I began making a joke about whether we were prepared or not: "Let's see, I've got my

---

[31] See University of Portsmouth, "Smile—And The World Can Hear You, Even If You Hide," ScienceDaily: www.sciencedaily.com/releases/2008/01/080111224745.htm. See also "Speech Communication," Science Direct, Volume 50, Issue 4, April 2008, Pages 278-287.

purse, you've got yours. I've got my keys, you've got yours. Coats—check. Shoes—check. And *you're* even wearing matching socks!" Sometimes I would point out that we had both remembered to put on pants; sometimes it would be that we both had two shoes on or that neither of us had forgotten our socks. My tone was always playful and light. It wasn't important what words I included in my narration as we prepared to leave her house. What lowered my client's anxiety was my intonation: it told her there was nothing to worry about.

The modulation of our voices—their inflection and pitch— and our elocution also have a major impact. People who are now in their seventies, eighties and nineties were very likely taught modulation and elocution while in school. These skills are no longer taught in our public schools, having disappeared just like cursive writing and public-speaking classes. However, to the ears of someone who was taught these skills, an unmodulated voice and the lack of elocution can sound uncaring and harsh. I have seen seniors withdraw or seem to feel insulted when a young caregiver walks into the room and addresses them in a loud voice, even when it is clear to me that the young person is kind and well intentioned. Simply by using speech mannerisms that our elders were taught to avoid, we may unconsciously be suggesting to them that we don't respect them. The best remedy for this is awareness, and then to try to soften our speech with intonation and elocution. And—to smile.

We are not always aware of what expressions are on our faces; if we are spending time with someone who has dementia, though, we need to be. A great example of this comes from my own experience a few years ago. I needed to have a professional photograph taken for my website. A friend urged me to get Botox injections in my forehead and I resisted, thinking that it was an unnecessary expense. However, I eventually gave in and experienced a result I hadn't anticipated. During those next few months, once it became difficult for me to crinkle my forehead when I wanted to frown, I discovered just how much time I spent frowning. I had thought I spent most of my time smiling. Getting the Botox injection taught me to smile as much as I'd thought I was. When I commented to my dermatologist about my discovery, she told me that another patient of hers, who was a salesman, had become a regular when he realized the same thing. He began coming in for Botox injections every time he saw his sales drop. Most interesting of all, though, was that once it became harder for me to frown, I felt as if I was happier in general. Since the act of smiling releases dopamine, serotonin, and endorphins, this makes sense.[32]

Research tells us that we accurately interpret tiny changes in expression in milliseconds and that our gestures precipitate and are truer than our words.[33] A shrug, a careful drawing in of the breath, the slow tightening of fingers into a fist, a slight raise of the shoulders, an almost imperceptible tilt of the head or drawing in of the chin, and even a momentary stillness before speaking—each gesture is interpreted easily even when we have dementia. Touch is a gesture too. Being a caregiver and providing for someone's emotional and physical needs is a particularly intimate act. Often, caregivers become very close to their clients, almost to the point of becoming family. Here at DAWN, we are very careful that any touch is gentle, and only within the limits of the client's comfort zone. Not everyone is a hugger. For some, even a squeeze of the shoulder or the offer of hand when getting out of the car is too much. One of my clients snaps at me every time I offer my arm for support ("I'm perfectly able to walk by myself, thank you!"), and another is hurt if I don't come around and fully assist as she gets out of the car. However, we have found that even the most reserved clients eventually become hungry for the physical reassurance of touch as their dementia progresses and their intuitive abilities become their only means of communicating.

When we are taking care of someone who needs help with physical functions, such as eating, toileting or dressing, touch is

---

[32] See the article "There's Magic In Your Smile: How Smiling Affects Your Brain," by Sarah Stevenson: https://www.psychologytoday.com/blog/cutting-edge-leadership/201206/there-s-magic-in-your-smile.

[33] In *The Master and His Emissary*, McGilchrist explores the relationship between thought, language, and nonverbal communication in depth. See in particular chapters 2 and 3.

unavoidable. Always remember that your touch will communicate respect or disrespect, caring or indifference, concern or antipathy. If it were your responsibility to wake someone in the morning and you pulled off their covers without warning, your touch would have the same effect as a shove or a slap, and yet I have often seen this done by caregivers in institutions. Verbally offering a greeting first will only function as the introductory contact if the person hears you, and if he or she has first been given time to wake up and recognize your presence. In such circumstances, the first touch should instead be a gentle squeeze of the shoulder or hand, which brings the person gradually to wakefulness and gives him or her time to become aware of your presence.

One important gesture for many of our clients is a wave when we are leaving their homes. For several clients, the ritual requires three waves: one as we reach our cars, the second when we start the car's engine and put it in reverse, and the third after we've backed up and begun to drive away. I don't know why a wave is so important. It could be that a wave is simply an affirming gesture and communicates caring—a contact that extends beyond our immediate presence. Or maybe a wave is a kind of visual melody, something interpreted by the intuitive person like music. Whatever the reason, a wave as you get in your car and as you drive away seems to communicate, "I am still thinking of you and I will be coming back." It is a powerful gesture for people who have dementia.

Posture is another nonverbal form of communication that becomes loaded with meaning for people experiencing dementia. We all have habitual ways of standing and sitting. Some positions are welcoming, some less so. Standing with our arms crossed in front of us is the classic example of a way to communicate distance and wariness. Similarly, talking over your shoulder while you are preparing lunch or stirring a pot on the stove will communicate that you are not really engaging with your loved one or client. We cannot always stop what we are doing and adopt a forward-facing and listening stance with them, because there are times when there's too much to do and too little time. However, we can pause, look over our shoulder, and make eye contact. The more often we use our posture to communicate that we are listening and available, the sooner they will come to trust us as being readily available, as well as ready sources of information. We need to be careful our posture does not communicate impatience, frustration, or anger.

One of the most valuable truths that I have learned regarding posture came from an undergraduate language class on genderlect. Genderlect is the study of the differences between how men and women communicate, both verbally and nonverbally. One of its core concepts is that when women stand face to face, they communicate listening, openness, and acceptance—heart to heart sharing. Men, however, tend to interpret standing face to face (chest to chest) as suggesting aggression rather than openness. When two men are sharing something and want to be heard, they are more likely to stand shoulder to shoulder. I enjoyed putting this to use when working as a law clerk at the Oregon courts. I found my words and concerns were more likely to be received by male judges when I delivered them standing shoulder to shoulder or walking down a hall, whereas they were likely to resist me and react as if I was being pushy or "in their faces" when I stood directly in front of them to communicate.

This phenomenon is vital to consider when we are working with people who have dementia. If our loved one or client is a woman, we should stand in front of her to communicate—heart to heart—and offer hugs from the front. If our loved one or client is a man, we should stand beside him to communicate and offer a hug from the side. (Of course, these are general trends; there can be individual differences. Further, we should always choose the approach that fits best with the person's gender orientation.)

When Less Becomes More

When information is readily available, it doesn't seem as necessary to have it. This is the same principle as what hospitals have found is true with patient-controlled morphine infusion pumps. When post-operative patients are able to dose themselves with pain medication, rather than wait for a nurse or for the dose to be administered at a scheduled time, they use less. As caregivers of people who are losing the ability to use rational thought and retain information, we can impart a sense of control and security by making sure that we always respond when they ask, and happily. When we do this, the person experiencing dementia will become comfortable with *not* knowing—and ask for information less often. When they come to believe that their questions do not cause irritation or impatience, they will not feel embarrassed or afraid to ask. Once that happens, a profound transformation occurs. We often see even the most uptight, anxious, and goal-driven clients gradually become comfortable living in confusion.

Ronda, whom we met earlier in this chapter, will even now strike up a conversation readily with anyone she meets. She was not an extrovert to begin with, so this was quite a change when she developed dementia. She will now say, with a bright smile: "Hi, I'm Ronda. What's your name? You don't have to tell me because I won't remember it anyways. I'm really good at forgetting." After spending so much time with caregivers who never made her feel guilty about asking or feel worried that information might not be there when she needed it, Ronda learned that being forgetful was nothing to be embarrassed about, and asking questions was always acceptable.

■ ■ ■

When I first began working with one of our clients, Esther, she would stop me every time we got out of the car, and say, "Judy—wait—look at the sky. Isn't it beautiful? Look at those fluffy white clouds! Aren't they amazing? And that blue over there. It's so blue!" The years passed and her impairment progressed, but she still noticed the sky. I learned from Esther to stop and notice the beauty around us, too. One day, Esther pointed but couldn't remember the word for clouds. She called them "fluffies" or "those white things." But she still knew they were beautiful. Then she lost the word "sky." Eventually she had lost adjectives, too, but she would still stop each time and look up and exclaim, "Oh, look! *Look!*"

Now that Esther is even more impaired, we are the ones to stop her when we get out of the car and point out the lovely skyscapes and landscapes of the Palouse. She is no longer able to remember to look up on her own. Her vocabulary is very limited.

But when we point and Esther looks up, her face still fills with wonder and joy. Esther's intuitive functions are just as vibrant—her enjoyment just as apparent—even though her ability to express her appreciation is gone.

As dementia caregivers, we can take care of identifying things and reciting any needed facts—without being directive or authoritative—and encourage our companions to enjoy beauty, feelings and their senses, using their intuitive thought processes, which they can still successfully do. Then, as they become more comfortable, despite experiencing memory loss and confusion, we will experience more peace as their caregivers, too.

CHAPTER EIGHT

Security in Care

Margaret

Margaret sat down carefully at the kitchen table. She could feel blood pounding in her temples and her heart beating erratically. Sunshine was streaming in the window, brightening the piles of papers on her kitchen table with irregular rectangles of glare. Dust motes danced in the rays. Margaret knew she needed to sit quietly for a minute or two or it would become hard to breathe. And she knew that she was no closer to finding what she was looking for than when she'd started searching. *What on earth was I looking for?* she thought. *Oh goodness. I'm losing my mind. I am truly losing my mind.* She covered her face with her hands and took a deep breath. *Now, what* was *it I was so worried about finding? Oh, for goodness' sake.* She rubbed her temples.

Margaret looked up through her fingers and then reached out to flick a crumb from the placemat. She had been a model housekeeper and a devoted mother and wife. Her friends had admired her spotless home, and the ease with which she had managed not only the house but also her husband's busy travel schedule, their children, and her own teaching position in the English Department at Washington State University. Now papers seemed to collect almost as fast as the dust and, no matter how many times she sat down to deal with them, she never managed to finish the task.

Margaret glanced down at the piles of opened and unopened mail and asked herself, "Now, what was I doing just now? What should I be doing on a…a…what day is it today?" She looked up from the mess on her table to the cluttered countertop, and then over at the large calendar that hung at the end of the cabinet, where it was surrounded by thumbtacked scraps of paper, newspaper clippings, and faded photographs. *I'd better go look,* she thought.

Margaret stood slowly and walked over to the calendar. She saw that her purse lay on the counter below it and her checkbook was spread open on top of it, but empty of checks. *That's it—I've been looking for new checks!* Margaret sighed deeply. *Oh, how silly. Why can't I remember what I'm doing from one minute to the next? Now, where did I put that box of blank checks?* Margaret picked up the empty checkbook and then put it down again. She turned around and went back to the piles of papers on the kitchen table. *I'm sure I had it out earlier.*

"Margaret! Hello, Margaret?"

Margaret looked up to see a smiling face looking in through the screen door at the far end of the kitchen.

"Hi! It's me, Erica. How are you this morning?"

Erica? She searched her memory. *Erica. Oh, that's right—my new personal helper!* "Oh, Erica! I'm fine. I'm just looking for...something. Now I can't think of what it was." Margaret looked back down at the papers in her hand with a frown.

Erica walked into the kitchen, noting the open checkbook on top of Margaret's purse. "Do you have trouble finding things, too? I sure do. This morning I looked everywhere for my keys. I was almost late for my appointment with you! But I knew they'd show up, and they did." Erica gave Margaret a gentle hug.

"So let's see," she continued. "It looks like you're searching for your new checks. We know they're here somewhere. I remember helping you order them last month, and when they came last week, I think we put them away together. So let's look one place at a time. Let's start with your desk. She pointed to Margaret's desk, in the corner of the dining room. "Top drawers first. We know we'll find them. They're here somewhere safe. We just have to look one place at a time."

· · ·

Having dementia means experiencing increasing confusion and repeated failures. It means never feeling truly safe. At any moment, you might need to know something you cannot recall or need to find something in your own home that you used to lay your

142

hands on without a moment's thought. You might find yourself at the grocery store but have no idea how you arrived or how to get home. Our clients feel frustrated by their increasing forgetfulness in the early stages of dementia, but soon find themselves in endless loops of confusion, attempting to complete some small task only to repeatedly lose track of what they were doing and be forced to start again. Even determining what day of the week or month it is, or trying to figure out where their shoes are, can become an impossible task. Finding that you are unable to complete tasks that once were easy is scary. Realizing that you will become completely dependent on others is terrifying. The dementia caregiver's job is to overcome these negative emotions and impart a sense of security to the person who is experiencing dementia—an apparently daunting task, yet possible if you follow a few key guidelines.

Feeling safe with dementia does not come easily, yet it is something that we, as caregivers, must help our companions to learn as early as possible. We need to ensure that they feel secure often enough when with us that they learn experientially that they can trust others for their care needs. First, let's look at three simple but essential guidelines, and then consider the techniques we've found to be so successful here at DAWN for increasing our clients' trust that they will be cared for properly. When our clients learn during the early stages of dementia to trust their caregivers, they are more relaxed and willing to let others take over their personal needs later on, when dementia makes them more helpless.

Be Punctual

I think one of the unkindest things we can do to people who have dementia is to keep them waiting. Dementia takes away the ability to comprehend the passage of time—to imagine how long a minute will take, or an hour will last. Although at a young age we come to understand the difference between when Mom says lunch will be in five minutes and when she says half an hour, once someone begins to experience dementia, a minute has no more meaning than an hour. Both can feel eternal.

This may seem counterintuitive: that not being able to track time might free us from trying. However, people who have

143

dementia go through a stage in which they can interpret the position of the hands on the face of a clock and know that "1:00" means "one o'clock," yet are unable to comprehend how long it will take for the hands to move from 12:55 p.m. to 1:00 p.m. to 1:03 p.m. This leads to their intense worry over being late and missing appointments. It also means that they will be nervous if they have two appointments on the same day. For example, we find that when a client knows she has a hair appointment at 2:00 p.m., she might refuse to go out for breakfast at 10:00 a.m. because she cannot comprehend how much time lies between 10:00 a.m. and 2:00 p.m. and is afraid of missing the second appointment. Dementia caregivers need to respect this inability to comprehend the passage of time by being punctual. (We should also consider scheduling just one activity per day, or refrain from telling our companion about the second event until after the first one has happened.) Of course, there are times when unforeseeable events prevent a caregiver from arriving on time. In these situations, it is best to call ahead and alert your client or loved one, even if you will only be a minute or two late. A phone call when you should have been arriving, in effect, confirms the existing appointment you'd agreed with them, and creates a new one. When you arrive, they will still be in a relaxed state of mind.

Think about your own thought processes when someone is late for an appointment. Suppose you look at your watch and realize that you've already been waiting for ten minutes. Your rational mind jumps into action and you begin a fact-check using your long-term memory (*last Sunday we agreed we'd meet here today; we were standing on the church lawn after the service; he said only today would work*). Then you might turn to a calendar for verification, but once again it is rational thought that helps you to interpret the calendar, and memory or verification that helps you identify today's date. You might relive the original conversation once more, and recheck the facts you can recall for something you might have missed. Each of these actions requires rational thought. People experiencing dementia cannot take these rational steps. Instead, they can only look at the clock or calendar and worry, not knowing how much time has passed, or what has gone wrong. When we are late and our loved ones or clients are forced to try to decide whether they are waiting in error, we set them up to lose faith not only in themselves but in us as well. When we are caring for people who have dementia, we want the opposite to occur: we want their faith in us to grow stronger every day.

Provide Continuity in Caregivers

The second key factor to helping people with dementia develop trust in their caregivers is for them to have a consistent group of caregivers, because dementia makes it difficult to learn new information or cope well with change. However, it is typical in the senior care industry for workers to be paid little more than minimum wage with few, if any, employee benefits. The inevitable result in the senior care workforce is constant turnover. To me, this is the bedrock problem in how we provide dementia care in the United States. Because people who have dementia are not able to cope with change, introducing them to a rotating cast of caregivers is not only confusing and upsetting but also detrimental to their ability to learn to trust others for care.

When we are caring for someone with dementia, we should try to remain in his or her life for as long as possible. In addition, we should plan to gradually introduce additional caregivers, because, as mentioned in chapter 4, it is unworkable and detrimental, for clients and caregivers alike, for one person to provide dementia care day in and day out. At first, when the symptoms of the condition are just beginning to become apparent, a solo caregiver can do a great job on his or her own. But as the dementia deepens, a caregiver who is on top of things is gradually reduced to a caregiver who is coping, and then to someone who is just trying to survive. One day, survival almost inevitably disintegrates into a full-blown crisis. It is grueling to care for someone who has dementia, because the cognitive losses are sometimes gradual and sometimes sudden, with no lasting improvements. Here at DAWN, we always begin to provide care using a case manager (sometimes a family member) and one dementia care specialist. As the client's impairment progresses, we add a second caregiver, although not more hours of care. This means that early on our client has a team of three people whom he or she is learning to depend on. From the beginning, we strive to teach our clients that it is safe to trust others for their care. Once they believe this, we can add additional caregivers without causing them distress, because the ability to trust others for care has been learned by experience. This works best when family members are using the DAWN method too. As dementia progresses, we see our clients become less bothered by or aware of changes; but for the early and middle stages of the condition, the kindest and most successful strategy is to strive to keep the same people in their lives, and to introduce as few strangers as possible.

Respect Dementia Time

We first mentioned *dementia time* in chapter 6, while discussing mood management. As I explained there, this phrase refers to the fact that, since the person with dementia is unable to track time, maintain a train of thought, or plan ahead, caregivers often find themselves unable to accomplish their agenda or important tasks when with them. In order to help people with dementia begin to feel safe in our care, we must recognize when dementia time is affecting the situation. It's crucial that, particularly during such moments, our demeanor is kind and attentive rather than hurried and impatient; we must remember that, if our loved one or client didn't have dementia, he or she would understand the urgency just as well as we do. For when something must be done and we continue to focus on our companions' emotional needs rather than on the impending deadline, their trust in us as caregivers will grow. Respecting dementia time means accepting that our plans are just that—plans. When dementia is involved, accomplishing those plans must be balanced with the immediate needs of our clients or loved ones.

Respecting these three guidelines—punctuality, consistency in caregiving, and remembering *dementia time*—will take us a long way toward teaching our companions that they can safely trust others for care. Now let's look at a few techniques which, when used, will result in less distress for both parties to the care relationship because so many negative behaviors arise from insecurity. Avoiding insecurity requires building trust in three main areas:

1. Making the person feel safe even when they cannot remember;
2. Making them feel safe when they are unable to accomplish a task; and
3. Making them feel safe even though they see reality differently.

Make It Safe to Forget

In the previous chapter, we discussed in detail how we can help people with dementia feel comfortable in either asking questions or remaining in confusion. When we make information readily available, without fear of penalty, we allow them to become comfortable being confused when with us. However, for them truly to feel secure in our care, we must take an additional step: we must also stop putting them on the spot. We need to stop testing their increasingly defective ability to use memory and recall. Not testing memory is another core tenet of the DAWN approach, one equally as important as accepting our loved ones' growing inability to comprehend reality as we do. When we stop testing memory skills that are fading or gone (and avoid using reality orientation), we are simply recognizing their changing skillsets. We are being respectful and kind.

Margaret was deeply and repeatedly upset by her inability to locate her blank checks, which could have become a debilitating problem for her. She was at the point in her dementia where her anxiety over being confused was great and her ability to accomplish tasks was rapidly diminishing. Fortunately, her caregiver, Erica, knew she needed to make this experience end in a positive way for Margaret. She suspected Margaret had been going in circles for quite a while before she arrived that day and did not want her to start associating fear and embarrassment with her checkbook. She needed to remold the experience into a pleasant one, one resolved easily with her help and followed by something rewarding. That morning she delayed their usual grocery shopping trip. She helped Margaret find her checkbook and then took her for hot chocolate and a companionable chat before going for groceries. Erica also made sure that Margaret successfully used her checkbook at the coffee shop and again at the grocery store.

But imagine if she had taken a different approach. What if she had said to Margaret: "Well, we just put those checks away last week. You decided where you would keep them. Think. *Think carefully.* You chose the spot. Where did you put them? I know you can remember!" This combination of encouragement and prompting might be successful with a child learning a new skill, with an employee or student, or even with ourselves. But with someone whose memory skills and rational thinking skills are fading, never to improve, this testing of memory causes anxiety, which in turn increases forgetfulness. Let *us* not forget: people experiencing dementia are losing the skill of using memory, not just their memories.

We worked with one couple in which the wife had been diagnosed with younger-onset Alzheimer's disease. She was gradually becoming more impaired but could still drive if she had someone with her to remind her of the purpose of the errand and her destination. However, her husband, out of love and concern that she continue to function at her best for as long as possible, would test her memory while they drove. Each time she came to a stop sign or corner, he would ask her which way they should turn. His reasoning was that, just as you might help a child gain skills and better judgment through testing, he was helping her maintain her skills by putting her on the spot. Yet this approach proved counterproductive, even catastrophic. His wife felt ever more challenged and incompetent, and soon refused to drive at all, preferring to avoid the failures she had inevitably suffered. Their relationship was damaged, as her anger and indignation grew at being set up to fail in such memory "pop quizzes." Rather than learning that she was safe to continue using her vanishing skills while she was with her husband, she learned that she was safer to refuse to go along with his plans, avoid him, and isolate herself. Eventually, her fear of failure was so all-consuming that it was difficult to get her out of the house.

Testing the memory of a person experiencing dementia prevents rather than promotes the building of a trusting relationship. When someone has dementia, the feeling of being safe and in good hands despite his or her diminishing skills and memory comes, in part, from never being required to demonstrate those disappearing functions. If our loved ones and clients know they are safe from memory tests, they will feel safer with us and experience less anxiety about their growing forgetfulness.

Make It Safe to Fail

One of the most frustrating things about having dementia is waking up one day and finding yourself unable to perform a task or use a skill that has been effortless since you were a child. Remember how good it felt to drive a car for the first time alone, to make and serve your first meal to your family, or to catch a bus without the aid of your parents. Imagine, then, how humiliating it must feel to forget how to unlock your car door. One morning I walked into a client's home to find her at the kitchen sink drinking tap water from her hand because she had forgotten where to find cups in the house she had lived in for more than forty years. Such things happen time after time for people with dementia. As caregivers, we need to constantly join our companions in doing simple tasks, without being upset or critical, or even seeming surprised, so that they learn it is safe to fail—and safe then to turn to us for help.

One of the easiest ways to help someone with dementia feel successful at tasks is to verbalize the steps of the task as you perform them. This is another way in which chatter becomes essential. Think of Erica's response to Margaret. Margaret was focused on the end result—finding her replacement checks—and had found the task distressing and impossible to complete. Erica brought her focus from *finding* her checks to *looking* for her checks, by focusing on the steps they would take to locate them. When our companions are experiencing dementia, we should help them replace the distress of failure with the comfort of following a process. Erica verbalized her own rational thought processes for finding something lost. When we regularly break down the process of finding something or completing a task into an orderly series of single steps—and provide a cheerful narrative—we become companions on a mission together. We build our loved one's or client's faith in us as teammates. This is an important first step in helping them move from expecting to be able to solve a problem or do a task independently to feeling a sense of accomplishment even though they must work with someone else to succeed. When Margaret began looking for her replacement checks with her caregiver, she moved from playing the role of master to that of assistant. When someone internalizes being a team member or assistant, he or she can avoid exchanging autonomy for passivity. The dementia caregiver's goal is to communicate "let's solve this together" rather than "you should know how to do that" or "let me do that for you (because I can do it faster)."

Several of our clients have been quilters or seamstresses. Often their manual dexterity is too far gone for us to help them continue sewing, but one of our clients, Ingrid, was still physically able to sew by hand. Although she lacked the ability to identify the necessary steps, remain focused, or visualize the final product, her daughter Margot found that working on a quilt together was a pleasant and fulfilling activity for the two of them. Margot broke down the process of making a quilt into small, repetitive steps and said out loud what needed to be done as each step unfolded. With direction, Ingrid could complete a single task, such as appliqueing leaves, and needed less direction each time she repeated the steps. Ingrid eventually appliqued all the tiny leaves on an intricate quilt she and Margot were creating. Margot did everything else. Margot, however, did such a good job of helping Ingrid feel successful that once they had completed the quilt and hung it on a wall at Ingrid's, whenever Margot dropped by Ingrid would show it to her with great pride, claiming it as her own handiwork. Margot had given her mother a sense of mastery and success, and, more importantly, had strengthened her mother's trust in her as a partner and caregiver.

Another of our clients, Tasha, had a long-standing habit of assigning herself chores to complete each day. Some were indoor tasks; others were outside tasks, such as gardening, which she loathed. But Tasha knew the fresh air and outdoor activity helped keep her body and mind fit, so during the growing season she assigned herself half an hour each day to be spent weeding and watering. As her dementia progressed, Tasha became more and more frustrated with gardening. Each day brought a new roadblock: one day she couldn't remember where to find the trowel and before too long she couldn't remember how to make water come out of the hose. She began wandering from back yard to front yard, angry with herself, and we started to worry that Tasha might leave her property in an attempt to find a tool or water source.

Because she had been assigning herself gardening tasks for so many years, it would have been difficult to help Tasha unlearn the behavior and discourage her from attempting to garden. It was also good for her to be active and outdoors. Our response was to join her and model the tasks for her. Modeling is a natural addition to verbalizing each step. We would begin by verbalizing what we were looking for. "My, those flowers look thirsty," we might say. "Let's look for the hose. We'll use the hose to give them water. Oh, here's the hose." We chattered away with a companionable narration of the steps in each task, as we pulled weeds and watered plants with her, or joined her in search of gardening gloves or a trowel.

It doesn't matter whether we are helping someone find a toothbrush, comb his or her hair, or water the lawn—we can model doing each step of the task and narrate what we are doing as we go. This allows someone whose rational functions are becoming increasingly impaired to still take part in solving problems or completing tasks, and to feel the little burst of satisfaction that accompanies completion. Our goal should be to help our companions continue to be active participants in daily activities, to take over a task entirely only when they can no longer take part in it at all.

Make It Safe to Disagree

The third area in which people with dementia need to become able to trust their caregivers is with regard to what's real and true. Once again I am reminding us that, as companions of people who have dementia, it is critically important that we not use reality orientation. Nothing makes people feel more unsafe than having their companions disagree with what they think is real or has happened. Imagine how disorienting and disempowering it must feel to call for help in what you think is an emergency, only to have everyone around you refuse to help you.[34]

People who have dementia need to develop enough trust in their caregivers so that they feel safe expressing their beliefs about what has just occurred or is currently happening. Dementia affects people's memories in different ways. The hallmark of Alzheimer's disease is a consistent melting away of a person's short-term memory, which gradually extends further into the past. One of our clients has now forgotten her entire past back to the time when she was a young child. When her caregivers ready her for bed at night, she wants her mother and father to come tuck her in and is distressed that they are not available. Her caregivers distract her with headphones and music from her childhood, which she falls asleep with. This woman is completely unable to recall what someone has said from one moment to the next, and must entirely rely upon what her caregivers say and do.

Other forms of dementia can cause more inconsistent memory loss—making it harder to determine whether what the person reports is true. This type of memory loss also makes it harder to be understanding. We need to develop the habit of assuming that everything they say may be true, but not accepting it as such until we can verify it. Another of our clients, for example, routinely remembered that I had called him the day before to say I would be late for our appointment, and that I had been exactly seven minutes late. Yet he would just as adamantly insist that he had walked downtown and eaten dinner in a restaurant the previous evening—which was sometimes true, and other times simply false.

---

[34] It is difficult for those of us whose rational thought and memory skills are intact to truly imagine how distressing it is when our sense of reality differs from that of our companions. Several recent movies and stories realistically suggest what it must be like to have dementia and be without short-term memory. My current favorites are Anthony Doerr's short story titled "Memory Wall" and the book *Still Alice*, which became famous in 2014 as the movie of the same name, with Julianne Moore's award-winning portrayal of a woman experiencing younger-onset Alzheimer's disease. See *Memory Wall, Stories* by Anthony Doerr, and *Still Alice* by Lisa Genova.

Trying to determine which of someone's statements are true can be not only frustrating but dangerous as well. It can be dangerous when you are trying to determine whether your loved one or client has taken medications, turned off the stove, or taken their car for a drive they really shouldn't have taken. One of the most common unsafe situations occurs when we take clients to medical appointments. Typically, the doctor will turn first to the client for details about the symptoms, with a question such as: "Have you had the pain in your stomach recently?" The client, of course, will search her incomplete and spotty memory and then look the doctor in the eye and very honestly reply, "No, I haven't," even if we are there in the exam room because she was in pain just an hour earlier. If the doctor accepts her statements as true, she will not get the care she needs.

We are very careful to preserve our clients' dignity and belief in themselves while setting the facts right. We might gently interject: "Oh, but, Mrs. Jones, I know you don't recall it right now, but this morning you called me before seven o'clock because you had such a pain in your side. I remember because I was so worried about you. You said it was on the left side. I think it's the same pain that's been getting worse all week." We try to voice the pertinent details for the doctor and model respect for our clients' dignity at the same time. We are very careful to minimize any implication that we are correcting the client, and avoid putting them on the spot by saying something like, *"Don't you remember…?"* How we respond to our loved ones' or clients' memory errors is crucial. To develop their trust, it's important that we keep in mind that although their memories may be wrong, their reality is based upon what memories are available to them. What they believe reality to be is the only reality at their disposal, and feels entirely correct to them. There are three broad categories in which I see my clients experience changes to memory.

First, let's consider the most obvious: memories that are lost—those that are no longer available. Remember Nathaniel in chapter 6, who would wake in the night and reach out to caress his wife lying next to him in bed, whom in fact had died years earlier. Nathaniel remembered the many years he and his wife had lived together in their home, but his memories of his more recent years spent alone—those of his immediate past—more often than not had been erased, especially at night. All memories of her illness and death were completely lost. And since he could not recall his solitary life after her death, Nathaniel's version of reality was altered. He expected her to be there in bed beside him when he awoke in the night, and naturally became upset by her absence.

If, after he'd called the sheriffs and they contacted me, I had tried to tell Nathaniel that his wife had died three years earlier, I would have been asking him to change his sense of what was happening into something not supported by his own memory. Either I would have failed and then been dealing with an even more frantic man, or I would have succeeded and been dealing with a man overcome with grief. A better response was to figure out what Nathaniel's sense of reality was and add facts out of his own experience and continuing memories that would make his reality more comfortable for him.[35]

Often family members or caregivers at facilities express frustration to me about what happens when they try to use reality orientation. One day I was visiting a client who resided in a care facility. I had stepped outside his room to wait for aides to assist him with changing. Another resident hurried past me to the nurse who was standing beside a medication cart. This resident was physically able, so I assumed he was a resident of the facility due to dementia. Sure enough, he was confused and needed help. He explained to the nurse with great urgency that his six-year-old daughter had arrived alone on the train and he had to get to the station, but the front door of the facility was locked. The nurse's first response was to say that there is no train station in Moscow and so no daughter could be there. He continued to beg her to help him with the door and became increasingly upset. The nurse's responses got ruder. She seemed to feel that her intelligence was

---

[35] As I discussed in chapter 4, when someone is unable to perceive our reality, there is no common truth we can preserve. The kindest and most respectful approach we can take is to recognize that fading cognitive skills are the problem—not lack of integrity—and work with the person's individualized version of reality by shaping their perceptions rather than correcting them.

being insulted and her time wasted. When he clutched at her forearm, she pulled away and sharply insisted he forget about the train station and go back to his room. He continued to plead with the nurse, and now was waving his hands and hopping from one foot to another.

At that moment, the nursing director walked by. The nurse at the cart turned to her and said, "Mr. Smith is getting agitated. Can I give him an injection to calm him?" The director didn't even hesitate, just nodded and continued walking. Yet this man wasn't having a psychotic episode. He was simply experiencing a lack of memory, perhaps triggered by a dream about his earlier life in which his little girl was coming to see him. The nurse's responses antagonized him rather than helped him cope with his impaired memory. Medicating him was, at the very least, adding injury to insult. Neither of these professionals did anything to help this man develop a sense of safety or trust in his caregivers.

As with Nathaniel, a far kinder and more effective response would have been to work with this resident's version of reality, as caused by his missing memories, and to help him feel more comfortable with what he thought was real and happening. Overall, this approach would probably have taken far less time and effort than confronting him with "the Truth," and would have produced no hostility (much less the need for medication). The nurse could have offered to go back to his room with him to help him get his jacket and wallet. If that distraction didn't result with him forgetting about the train, she could have suggested that the bus would take him to the train station and that he could wait for the bus in the dining room with a cup of coffee or cocoa. Lost memories were the problem, not his "wrong" version of reality.

If we are providing care for people who have dementia, attempting to persuade them to agree that our version of reality is correct and theirs incorrect will only create fear or anger, and distress and conflict will result. Instead, we want and need our companions to gain trust in our ability and desire to take care of them. We can achieve that by accepting and supporting the realities their brains create for them in their memory loss, and then, if needed, help shift their realities to a more peaceful place.

What do we do when a loved one says, "You haven't visited in years! I've missed you so much—why don't you ever come see me?" or your client says, "You know I love cocoa. Why don't you ever bring me cocoa?" Of course, you've been making daily visits to see your mother or have been bringing your client hot chocolate daily because you know he loves it so much. It hurts to be accused wrongly of being uncaring, and it is frustrating when we put so much effort into doing things on someone's behalf yet he or she doesn't remember our kindnesses. But we must remember: whatever their response is, it is entirely valid to them, given their loss of memory. We too respond emotionally to what we experience. We need to recognize that whether someone's emotion is the result of something that really happened, or due to a memory added or removed by cognitive impairment, the emotional reaction is valid. Our response as caregivers should be to validate the emotions our companions are feeling, rather than to correct or reprove them, or to express feelings of being hurt or insulted.

One of my clients, Jasmine, had an only daughter who was a very successful businesswoman and who for most of her adult life had lived in distant cities. During her working years, her time with Jasmine had always been limited to a visit or two each year, but when it became clear that Jasmine's dementia was progressing, this devoted daughter retired early and returned home to live next door to her mother. Jasmine, however, was never able to replace the memory of her daughter's life far away with the more recent knowledge that she lived nearby. Jasmine continued to feel the pain of separation and distance, even if her daughter had just stepped out of the room for a moment. It was heartbreaking to watch Jasmine's tears and hear her talk of what was for her an ongoing separation from her daughter, but we would sympathize with her, validating her grief, and tell her that her daughter was currently visiting and would be there any minute. When her daughter reappeared minutes later, we shared her joy. We were careful to be empathetic when Jasmine believed her daughter was gone and joyful when she was present. Because Jasmine's reality was that her daughter lived far away, we accepted that, then gave her the good news of her daughter's imminent arrival whenever necessary.

Memories not only go missing, but are also altered by cognitive impairment, often reshaped into a version of an event that is less painful than the true one. When Jacob returned from his brother's funeral convinced that the two of them had just spent the weekend together at a reunion, for example, he was experiencing an altered memory. Memories can also change spontaneously for no apparent reason. Jacob became convinced that his son was his brother, which, in this case, was not a flattering comparison for the son. A parent might suddenly begin to insist that the wrong child is guilty of some past familial faux pas or create a memory of something unkind that no child had done. The wrong sibling becomes the one who earned a professional degree and made Mom so proud, or ruined Dad's business with his spendthrift ways. Again, though it is hurtful or frustrating to be wrongly accused by a parent or loved one in this way, as caregivers we need to overcome our frustration and hurt, and recognize that they are unable to choose to correct their distorted memories. When we do this, we will experience less stress in caregiving—and spare our loved ones or clients the inevitably painful clash with their emotions and their versions of reality.

Our realities are affected not only by memories that are lost or have become twisted but also by the spontaneous creation of false memories. Most of our clients go through a period during which their brains seem to be creating memories out of things or events that cannot possibly be memories, something like déjà vu. For example, I once had a client in the car who, when we pulled up at a stoplight and watched a pedestrian cross the street, turned to me and exclaimed in wonder, "Look! There's that woman again, the one with the green hat—she's *always* crossing the street when we stop here!" Another time I introduced a client to a friend of mine from Canada whom he had never met before, yet my client was convinced that he had known my friend well for years. These are clearly false memories, but it would have been counterproductive as well as unkind to correct my clients. My response is always to join them in enjoying such incredible coincidences: "Wow, you're right! How strange—how could we possibly end up here at this light whenever *she's* crossing the street!" or "You know Janet, too? Isn't she great! She's one of my dearest friends." Instead of ruining the mood with a pointless attempt to make my companions accept *my* reality, I joined them in a moment of whimsy and joy.

I accept my clients' distorted memories and realities as a part of their dementia—as an indication that they are unable to use rational thought to detect and reject what we, with our broader cognitive skillsets, find unbelievable. I am respectful and accept their false assertions as if they were true, however mistaken, because in doing so I am being kind and respectful. We all have varying memory skills and, as we age, what skills we have will begin to fade. I like to tell my clients that our brains are less like computers (at which they invariably interject that their brains are computers that no longer work) than libraries: the older we get and the more books fill our library shelves, the harder it becomes to find and retrieve the specific information we're looking for. But we need to remember that memory formation and recall is not only impaired by aging; it is affected by other factors all the time. Throughout our lives, how well a memory is recorded or recalled is affected by sleep loss, the stress or emotion of the moment, and other factors such as alcohol or medication. No one at any age has an absolutely reliable memory. We all experience creative memory, and each of us has a personal perspective and interpretation for any mutual experience. We should all be able to empathize with memory problems.

Here, as DAWN caregivers, we continuously own up to our own forgetfulness and creative memory with our clients. Sometimes we even fabricate forgetfulness, when this is helpful for our companion. If someone needs prompting to take her medications, for example, I lightheartedly relate how often my husband must remind me to take my own pills (which is true). And when someone becomes anxious about where they've left the house keys or a checkbook, like Erica and Margaret, we ruefully admit how often we find ourselves in a room wondering what we've come for, or can't find our keys when in our own homes. Demonstrating that faulty memory is a normal part of living, not just the result of aging and cognitive impairment, destigmatizes in a small way the experience of dementia.

■ ■ ■

In sum, we can and should help our companions with dementia learn to trust others to care for them, because their ability to care for themselves is diminishing every day. We do this by not testing their failing memory skills, partnering with them to accomplish tasks and solve problems, and accepting their altered versions of reality with kindness and respect. If we do these three things consistently, our loved ones and clients will learn that they can safely trust us, and their insecurities and distress will lessen.

Once a sense of security in confusion and care has been established, there are other critical steps we should take as well. Recently Heike exclaimed to me, "Our clients are just so *happy*." And they are. While we are working to help our clients develop a sense of security, we are also giving them doses of wellbeing whenever we are with them. We make sure that small delights and successes come their way every time we are with them, using the tools I will describe in the coming chapters. As our clients experience these little daily joys, we see them relax into an enduring sense that all is well in their lives. The behaviors caused by fear, confusion and anger diminish, and new behaviors arise out of their abiding sense of peace.

So in the next four chapters, let's look at the ways we can help someone with dementia experience happiness and wellbeing each day.

PART THREE

DAWN Tools to Develop Wellbeing

CHAPTER NINE

Social Success

Vivian

"Vivian, how *are* you? We missed you last Sunday. How have you been?"

Vivian turned slowly to face the voice. She found herself looking at an older man about her own age; he was short and slightly built, well dressed, and had close-cropped gray hair. Beside him stood a woman who looked to be a little younger than he, with a beaming smile as warm as his. *Oh my, I knew I shouldn't have come to church! It's always like this. So confusing. So many people. Everyone knows* me, *but I can never remember anyone's name,* Vivian thought to herself.

She gripped her purse a little tighter and leaned forward slightly, straining to focus all her attention on the man and his wife. *I know them,* she thought, as she smiled brightly in return. *I know that I know them, and clearly they know me. Now, I just need to figure out who they are.*

Vivian straightened and extended her hand. "Hello there! So nice to see you." But she saw that the woman was a little taken aback by the offer of her hand and quickly withdrew it.

The man spoke again, "Yes, you too, dear. But why haven't you called? We've been back a week already and you haven't given us a chance to tell you how things are down at the condo. Millie says she called and left a message for you Tuesday, and you haven't called back yet. How are you? How's Doris? Was the operation a success?"

Vivian stiffened. *Doris. Millie. Doris, my neighbor Doris. Left me a message? Oh my, I haven't been checking for messages lately, have I…. Millie? This must be Millie. Millie and….*

"Well, I'm fine. I've just been busy, that's all," Vivian responded quickly, realizing she'd been lost in thought too long.

"Now, you've been away, haven't you? I'm sorry; things have just been hectic, I'm afraid." She tried to sound unconcerned and as if she was speaking to close friends, because she was sure they must be. *Just don't let them realize I have no idea who they are,* she thought.

"Away? Vivian? Of course we've been away," Millie said. "We're always gone through March. You know that." Vivian watched Millie shoot a worried glance at her husband and then turn back to her. "Vivian, are you okay? How's your daughter? Has she been here to visit lately?"

Vivian said nothing. Her mind was blank. She knew they were concerned. Why could she not bring a single fact to mind about this couple who seemed to know her so well? Vivian's heart sank. All she could think was: *Oh my, oh my…. I really am losing my mind.*

• • •

In the previous three chapters, we discussed how to use the first three DAWN tools to help someone who's experiencing dementia develop a sense of security, so they can experience less of the fear and frustration that usually accompanies dementia—and exhibit fewer of the destructive behaviors that usually result. If you have been putting these tools to use, you will already have found that your loved one or client is becoming more comfortable and peaceful, and hopefully you will be experiencing less of the cumulative stress associated with being a caregiver.

If you were to stop reading right now and apply just the first three tools, both you and your companion would already be able to cope better with the condition. However, we can do more than achieve comfort. We can also help our companions experience wellbeing, living happy, even joyful lives with dementia.

What is wellbeing? In essence, it is happiness—the feelings of optimism, fulfillment, and purpose that amount to a general sense of all being as it should be. To feel this, as Abraham Maslow pointed out, we must already feel secure. If our safety needs have been met, however, we still risk feeling restless and unfulfilled, unless we find outlets for our energies and success in our interactions with others. Our need for a sense of wellbeing exists whether we are experiencing dementia or not, but dementia takes away the ability to meet our emotional needs on our own. As I explained in chapter 5, I have watched my clients develop a sense of wellbeing when they enjoy the following four emotions:

- Feeling socially successful
- Feeling some degree of control over self and life
- Feeling valued and respected
- Feeling that the future is secure

Given fulfillment in these four areas—each of which can be imparted in just a few moments by a thoughtful caregiver—our companions with dementia will experience wellbeing, just as we will experience less stress while spending time with them. We'll explore these four factors of wellbeing one by one, in this and the next three chapters.

Feeling Socially Successful

We need to think about social success in broad terms when applying it to people who are experiencing dementia. Instead of merely meaning someone with many friends or a high social standing, we should remember that social success can be perceived in even the most casual interactions in our homes, workplaces and communities, as can social failure. Having dementia means feeling like a failure most of the time. You find yourself in a room and cannot remember why you came; you look up from a task and then cannot remember beginning it or how to complete it; you answer the phone and are so busy trying to figure out who you are talking to that you can't keep track of what is being said. This is because having dementia means not having one of the most essential tools required for completing a task or holding a conversation: recall.

In the opening scenario of this chapter, when Vivian bumped into old friends and failed to remember them, she experienced social failure. If she were to attempt to buy stamps at the post office the next morning and became confused by the clerk's questions, she would again experience social failure. If she begins to find that she is often confused, always the slowest person in conversations—making comments out of turn or needing additional explanations—she will start to insulate herself from interactions with people and the resulting social failures. Once she begins isolating, her confusion will snowball and her social failure will be compounded.

In the scenario, Millie and her husband, George, are old friends of Vivian's and assume she can remember not only who they are but also that several years ago they began going to their second home in Arizona during the winter months. They assume Vivian knows that it is now March, so they have just returned; that they are also friends with her neighbor, Doris, who has just had cancer surgery; and that they would naturally be wondering about Doris's recovery. For Vivian, however, the conversation is completely impossible to take part in because she is unable to recall these facts from the near past. She is destined to be embarrassed and confused, and to cause her friends bewilderment and concern. Everyone, including Vivian herself, is likely to wonder: is she losing her mind? No, but she is losing parts of it: specifically, the ability to recall information at will. Has she stopped caring for these dear old friends? No, given the appropriate prompts she would be able to recognize them in her older memories and would feel just as much affection for them as she always has.

However, the need to repeat previously established facts and to add prompts in a conversation is not something we normally consider necessary when we bump into old friends. We expect them to have recall, not only of the immediate past but also of an extensive collection of supporting data: the content of all our recent conversations with them, as well as any relevant circumstances, people, or relationships that might have been mentioned. Providing prompts does not occur to Millie or George. Yet to talk with Vivian, who is developing dementia, they do need to do this—to repeat the relevant facts that a healthy person's memory supplies automatically. Failing to recognize close family and friends is particularly embarrassing, and makes us feel guilty as well. To isolate oneself is the natural result of constant embarrassment and being out of step in social situations.

My recent experience with a client illustrates how sensitive people who are experiencing dementia will become about being embarrassed in conversation. One afternoon, I met with Donna and her two sons to discuss plans for Donna's future. Her dementia had been progressing rapidly in the past months, and she was now also facing surgery for a hernia. The surgery would require a hospital stay followed by several weeks of rehabilitation in a care facility. I had asked that the four of us have this discussion so Donna would feel included in the decision-making process, although I knew she would be adamantly opposed to the idea of leaving her home, even temporarily. I began the conversation by stating that Donna needed surgery and then rehabilitation in a care facility. Donna understood my basic explanation, although she was not able to retain its details for more than a minute or two. Every few minutes, as we talked about the benefits of the therapy and various care facilities, I would restate her need for surgery and rehabilitation, and remind her that we were talking about which facility would have the best therapy team. Nevertheless, the discussion was clearly making her nervous. "What's going on? What are we talking about?" she began to ask repeatedly. After my third or fourth recital, Donna suddenly realized we were talking about her having to leave home for care. "Why should I leave home?" she said bluntly. "I won't move!"

Her younger son replied, "Mom, I'll explain that for you in a minute, but right now could you tell me how you would feel about doing therapy in a pool? Do you think you would like that?" He was using the technique of breaking the larger topic down into a single issue that she could hold in her mind for a moment or two and respond to. We continued the conversation with Donna still feeling that she was a valued part of it.

However, a few minutes later the older son lost his patience. He was worried and tired; he had driven late into the night to be in Moscow that day. When she asked yet again what was going on, he broke in and said, "Forget it, Mom. You won't understand. You don't need to know about this." At that, Donna sat back in her chair. Her shoulders drooped and her face fell. She looked dejected and overwhelmed. Even though she could not, on her own, retain the facts needed to take part in the conversation, she had felt like a participant when we recounted them for her and rephrased larger topics into smaller issues. Now she had been shut down and embarrassed. It would take days of mood management and encouragement after her sons left to renew her sense of wellbeing.

In this chapter I'll discuss techniques for enhancing your loved one's or client's social success. First, we need to think about how to foresee when failure is likely to occur, so we know when our help is necessary to avoid embarrassment and withdrawal. Then, we'll look at techniques for enhancing their ability to carry on conversations—such as restating facts, focusing the conversation on the present so that memory skills are less necessary, and finding ways to help them contribute successfully. Let's consider each of these techniques in turn.

When to Help

Our most common daily encounters are with friends and family, and it is in these interactions that the greatest amount of previous knowledge is assumed and the least expressed. Family members in particular assume that their loved ones know all the relevant facts, and are often indignant about having to supply and restate information they think the person already has in mind.

My caregivers and I are often out in this small community with our clients. In fact, we spend as much time as possible getting our clients out of their homes and involved in activities. We take them to the local swimming pools and fitness centers for exercise, to coffee shops and restaurants, and to shops and galleries to touch and see as many interesting things as possible. Our goal is to fill our clients' minds with as much sensory data as possible, to provide them with the greatest possible amount of physical exercise and movement, and to keep them as socially active as their personalities warrant. In short, we want them to experience life to the fullest and in the most familiar way possible. Naturally, we are constantly bumping into our clients' friends and family members, as well as our own.

Let's return to Vivian's encounter with George and Millie. If she had been with one of us at church that day, the conversation she had with her old friends would have been quite different. If I had been her companion, it might have gone something like this:

"Vivian, how *are* you? We missed you last Sunday—how have you been?"

A quick look at Vivian's face would have told me that she was unable to recall who was addressing her. Consequently, I would enter the conversation with a request for the facts she needs:

> "Hi. You must be friends of Vivian's. We haven't met—I'm Judy, her new friend. How do you know each other? Vivian hasn't had a chance to tell me yet."

> "Oh, well, nice to meet you, Judy. I'm George Turner, and this is my wife, Millie. Millie and I have known Vivian since our children were all in school together—quite a long time."

At this point, the couple would likely be looking back and forth between Vivian and me, waiting for an explanation of how I know her. I would need to identify myself in a way that was not embarrassing for Vivian, but that got more information from them:

> "Well, lovely to meet you, George and Millie. Vivian and I have been friends for just a few months. I know her daughter too. But have you been away? You look like you've been enjoying the sun somewhere."

(Living through a northern Idaho winter tends to make you notice even the slightest hint of a tan!)

> "Yes, we have. We've been at our condo in Tucson. Vivian, Millie called and left you a message when we got in on Tuesday, but you didn't call back. How have you been?"

> "Oh, really? Oh, I've just been so busy, I'm sorry about that."

Vivian would respond to the most recent thing said, and I know she would have already forgotten the clue regarding Tucson, so I'd interject that fact again:

> "In Tucson, George? You have a condo in Tucson? Oh, how nice, Millie—do you go every winter?"

I am consistently interjecting names (George, Millie) and relevant facts (condo in Tucson) so Vivian will be able to make sense of the conversation.

As our talk continues, with me supplying and reinserting facts as Vivian needs them, George and Millie are likely to begin to see the pattern in what I'm doing and realize that Vivian has developed memory problems. They'll probably begin to help her too. As a result, Vivian can enjoy their company, and they hers; she will feel good after the encounter with her dear friends, rather than embarrassed and lost. I want Vivian to feel empowered, capable, and safe to continue attending church; I don't want her to feel she must stay home and avoid her friends in order to escape embarrassing herself or slighting them. In addition, George and Millie will have gotten a useful lesson on how to talk with a friend or loved one who has dementia, and they will now have an inkling of how to keep their relationship with Vivian intact.

With her caregiver voicing the essential facts, Vivian can succeed in social situations. Helping your loved one or client succeed in a conversation with friends or family is as simple as voicing the relevant and supporting facts as they are needed. When we do this as caregivers, we make social situations a source of positive stimulation.

In daily life, we must also interact with people whom we are not acquainted with. We need to conduct business, such as asking a salesperson for assistance, paying for a purchase, or attempting to sort out a problem with an account. Once again, many questions are asked, and the ability to recall relevant facts is assumed. People who have dementia can easily become confused. A cashier might request their "ID." To respond, the customer needs to know the meaning of the word, assemble in her mind a list of what might constitute identification, narrow that list to what items she might have in her purse or wallet, and finally know where to look in her purse or wallet for the item. Answering a cashier's simple request for identification requires a great deal of memory and analysis. Each of these facts is simple and easily determinable for someone who has recall, but not simple at all for a person experiencing dementia.

We began working with one client, Kevin, during the early stages of his dementia. Kevin would have his seat belt off and be out the door a moment after the car was parked, because he was mortified to be seen with anyone who could possibly be identified as a caregiver. "I'll only be a minute!" and "You don't need to come in with me!" were his constant refrains. When his confusion became pronounced enough that we needed to accompany him into the grocery store to ensure that he wouldn't leave alone through another door, Kevin would insist that his caregiver, Megan, find a seat at the tables near the coffee stand, and then hurry away with a cart. During the first year, it took him about fifteen minutes to find the items on his list but, as the months passed, it took longer and longer.

However, being allowed to wander the aisles of a store alone will greatly enhance someone's sense of being capable and independent, so Megan would wait half an hour (while keeping an eye on both doors), and then take a basket and walk the aisles as if shopping on her own behalf. Megan actually did save some of her own shopping for when she was with Kevin, to make sure he didn't feel that she was supervising him. Upon seeing Kevin, she would unobtrusively help him locate what he needed while she found items for herself as well. Once at the checkout stand, it was time for her to guide his interaction with the cashier in a way that was cheerful and supportive, without being directive or critical. She wanted to ensure that he felt confident and capable of running errands and conducting business on his own behalf—for as long as possible. At the checkout stand, their conversation might sound something like this:

"Cash or credit?" the cashier asks.

"Uhhh…" Kevin replies.

Megan can see confusion on his face, so she quickly steps in to offer help, in a quiet, reassuring tone of voice:

"She means checkbook—you prefer to use your checkbook. You keep it in your jacket pocket. Yes, there. That's it. Okay, now we need to write a check for these groceries. Oh, *here's* a pen. Now, let's see. I think it's 9, 18,

2-0-1-6 today. Right, that's it. And 'Safeway,' we're in Safeway. That's right."

When I'm with a client in a store, I usually find that once the cashier and people behind us in line see how patient I am, and how graciously I provide information as it is needed, they become more considerate themselves. I've seen the mood change from exasperation to amiability so many times. My hope is that people are beginning to realize how prevalent dementia is and how possible it is that they too will experience it, either themselves or in someone they love.

Help with Beginnings and Transitions. When transitioning from one location to another, or from one activity to another, it is easy for a person experiencing dementia to become confused. When we are with our clients, we are careful to chatter about what is happening as we get out of the car, enter buildings or rooms, and begin or end activities. Think for a moment about how your own mind works. When you pull up at the grocery store, you have already unconsciously recognized the building as a place to buy groceries. You probably are going over your grocery list in your head as you walk in, or as much of it as you can recall. You will have decided what size cart or basket you need and may have chosen which door to enter according to habit or the items on your list. You'll have unconsciously noted where you have parked the car or, if you were truly preoccupied, you'll be able to find it when you leave the store because you'll recognize it.

Someone experiencing dementia is unlikely to perform any of these mental exercises. Although your loved one or client may have drawn up a grocery list with you and known that the two of you were headed for a grocery store when you got into the car, these facts will be long forgotten by the time you arrive. She may not recognize the building. She certainly is not mentally tabulating her list or deciding to use a basket because her items will be few and light. When we are with people who have dementia, we need to supply each of those pieces of information for them in a way that is natural and companionable rather than directive, condescending, or judgmental. Once again, it is the cheerful chattering of our own rational thought that is needed. Here's how we might begin an errand with one of our clients:

> "Well, here we are. I love buying groceries at the co-op. Everyone's so friendly here, and the vegetables seem fresher. Do I have my list—yes, here it is. And there's yours. Oh, good. We have our lists. How about a cart—you seem to have quite a few items on your list. Let's go in this door. I see your first item is tomatoes. This is the door nearest the produce section. Do you mind if I tag along? I know I brought my list, but I'm always forgetting something, and it helps me to remember when I walk up and down each aisle and look at everything."

By "narrating" what we are doing and about to do, we help our companions get emotionally prepared for the upcoming experience and help them feel in control of the situation. Think of every change of scene—going from home to car, driving, parking and walking in, being in the store—as its own activity or experience.

Help When Attention Wanders. People experiencing dementia will also increasingly forget where they are or lose their bearings without warning during an activity. Here's an example—drawn from another of Vivian's experiences while she was in the early stages of dementia:

> Vivian was worried. She drove at a snail's pace down Main Street, oblivious to the line of cars behind her. She needed to find a parking space close enough to walk to the Breakfast Club, and yet it needed to be head-in, not parallel. Lately she had found her neck was too stiff to turn and look over her shoulder when maneuvering into parking spots by the curb.

> *Ah, there's one,* she thought with relief. She jammed on the brakes and clicked on her turn signal, leaving just enough room for a car that began to back out from a spot in front of the bicycle shop. Vivian waited patiently until it had finished reversing and pulled away, and then eased her car into the spot. Once parked, it took her a minute to tuck her keys into the correct pocket of her purse, get her door opened, and then press and repress the

automatic lock button so she could be sure all the doors were locked. Before standing up, she checked again to make sure her keys were in her purse, not the ignition, and then scrambled out and slammed the door. Once standing beside the car, she couldn't help checking again. She reached into her bag to feel for her keys, pressed the automatic lock button on the key fob, and waited to hear the reassuring beep indicating the car was indeed locked. She was ready. She straightened her skirt and patted her hair and turned to look at the shop window in front of her. It held a display of bicycle clothing and helmets. *Now, where is the restaurant?* she thought. *The Breakfast Club*….

Vivian walked slowly up the block, passing the Chamber of Commerce and the print shop. *I know where it is*, she reassured herself. *They've never moved. I can almost picture the sign. It's close. I'll just keep walking this way.*

Vivian's lifelong friend Agnes was visiting from Seattle, back in town to attend Doris's funeral, and Vivian had been looking forward to this chance to have a quiet lunch alone with her. *We see each other so seldom, these days,* she mused. *We rarely get to chat alone together. Doris and I were always like sisters. Doris. No, I mean Agnes.* Vivian stopped short, gave her head a little shake, and moved her purse to her other arm. *What am I thinking? Agnes. I'm meeting Agnes.* She peered up at the sign over the door she stood beside. *Scott's Flowers*… she pictured the arrangement of yellow roses, daisies, and freesia she'd asked Scott's to deliver for the service tomorrow afternoon. *Doris would have loved them,* she thought. *Poor Doris, those last months were so terrible. She was in so much pain.*

Vivian moved on to the next storefront and found herself standing in front of the Breakfast Club. She entered and scanned the crowded tables for Agnes. There she was, at the second table by the window, looking as well put together and bright as ever. *My, she ages well, puts us all to shame*, Vivian thought as she sighed and unconsciously reached up to smooth her hair. Agnes got up and the two exchanged hugs. Soon they had settled themselves, placed their orders, and were deep in conversation. The room was noisy, filled with businessmen, young mothers with children, and students between classes. In the booth across from their table, a young couple was talking loudly to hear themselves over the commotion.

Soon their waitress returned with their orders—soup and salad for Agnes and a salad and sandwich for Vivian. They began to eat and were quickly engrossed in conversation again. Vivian found herself leaning forward and straining to hear Agnes's description of a depression-era glass decanter she'd found at the little espresso store at the Washtucna junction, the one that sold antiques along with coffee. Suddenly there was a crash and the sound of breaking dishes. Agnes stopped talking and Vivian turned in her seat to look. A waitress had dropped a tray of dirty dishes two tables away. A plate and a saucer had broken. The whole restaurant stilled momentarily; then the waitress laughed and the cheerful roar of conversation resumed as she began to gather up the pieces.

Vivian turned back to her companion. She froze. She was looking across the table at a woman who looked to be about seventy. The woman was carefully made up, with well-coifed hair, and was wearing a fitted gray tweed jacket. She was smiling pleasantly and her eyes were warm with friendship. *Who is this?* Vivian thought in alarm. She sat immobile, her fork poised over her salad. *What, what…who is this? Where am I?* She looked to her right, at a young couple deep in conversation, and then back at her plate. *I'm in a restaurant, with a plate of salad. It must be lunchtime.*

Vivian sat very still, her eyes downcast. The woman across from her was speaking again; her words broke into Vivian's thoughts abruptly. Vivian carefully arranged a polite smile on her face and looked up. She listened intently for clues as the woman expressed concern about someone named Doris. Suddenly the name "Doris" registered, and Doris's face popped up in Vivian's mind. *She's asking me about my friend Doris!* Vivian thought. *But Doris is gone. Oh my, who is this? What's wrong with me? I'm so embarrassed— who could this be?*

■ ■ ■

The ability to track time and events—to pay attention—is one of the functions typically lost in dementia. Normally, when something interrupts our train of thought, our brains quickly assess our surroundings and give us an almost imperceptive update; we have a "Now, where was I?" moment that is instantly followed by an "Oh, this is where" confirmation. People experiencing dementia seem to lose the ability to do this, which can be both disconcerting and frightening, as it was for Vivian. We need to help them by verbalizing how they came to be where they are, so they can recapture feeling at ease. If I had been sitting with Vivian and Agnes in the Breakfast Club that day, I'd have said something along these lines:

> "Wow, that was loud! Good thing the waitress was only carrying a few dishes. It's always so noisy in here, in the Breakfast Club, isn't it! But, Agnes, you'll have to excuse me—I've forgotten how you and Vivian and Doris came to be such good friends. Tell me again, please: where was it that you three first met?"

Help with Happy Endings. Helping people with dementia to keep track of what is about to happen and what is currently happening is necessary, but how we narrate and explain activities as they finish is critical, for even if the experience wasn't a completely pleasant one, our narration will influence the emotions and mood our companion retains. Behavioral psychologists have shown that people are inordinately influenced by how an experience ends—that when an experience has been mostly positive but ends in a negative way, we tend to recall the experience as a negative one. Conversely, a positive ending can strongly color a mostly negative experience and cause it to be recorded as a positive one.[36] This phenomenon is widespread among my clients. As we saw in chapter 6, although someone with dementia may no longer be able to use memory to recall the event or activity just experienced, the mood or feeling they were experiencing when the event ended can continue long after. As caregivers, we should aim

---

[36] See Kahneman's *Thinking, Fast and* Slow, Part 5, for citations and a complete discussion on how greatly an experience's ending affects our recollection of the entire event.

to ensure that events and activities end on a positive note, or our clients may have to deal with a negative mood, sometimes for days.

Here at DAWN, as we leave an event with a client, we choose the detail or aspect of the experience that will most positively affect mood, and chatter about that as we leave. This verbal recap will be our client's final and lasting experience of the event. As I exit a concert with a client, I might say, "Wasn't that violinist magnificent?" and continue talking about the music so that I can overlay any feelings of unease or confusion as we leave. In fact, leaving a crowded concert or theater can be distressing for someone who has dementia; as my client and I work our way through the crowd, find the right exit, and then cautiously walk arm and arm down icy steps or across a slushy parking lot in the dark to find my car, I will be chatting about the best part of the evening. I am very careful to forestall any possibility of confusion or uncertainty by talking about the music, the pretty concert hall, the lighting, or maybe a friend we met in the crowd.

One of our clients, Greta, was very much an introvert. She had been a stay-at-home mom married to a gregarious and domineering businessman. She was very comfortable being in a supportive role and never truly at ease in social situations. Her needs for social stimulation were met quite adequately in one-on-one situations, and one of the best ways to meet Greta's need for human interaction was to take her to an afternoon matinee. We chose positive, uplifting shows—movies about families, children, or animals. Upon leaving the theater she would inevitably need to use the restroom and, afterward, when we returned to the foyer, Greta would always look around and ask, "What's this place? What are we doing here?" Any recollection of having just seen a movie would be gone, and of course all knowledge of the movie itself. We could have gone back in and watched the same movie over again, and Greta would have been none the wiser and enjoyed it just as much. Instead, we would recount the experience for her, in a way calculated to give her the greatest sense of camaraderie and joy:

> "Oh, this is where we come to watch movies. We just saw this one—see the poster? It was so good. We both loved

it. It was about two dogs and a cat that got lost when their family moved, but they all found their way back home again entirely on their own. Just the cat and two dogs on their own, together. Isn't that amazing? It was such a happy story. You loved the cat especially—what a character. He looks just like your kitty. Shall we head home? Tabby will be waiting to see you, won't he, waiting for you to give him some dinner."

Helping people with dementia feel comfortable and successful in social situations requires that we stay alert to *when* they need our help, but there are also techniques that will enhance their ability to succeed in conversations.

How to Help (Managing Conversation)

Much of the time that we spend with our clients is spent chattering—providing a steady, low-key narration that helps them track events and direct their thoughts when they are finding it increasingly difficult to do so on their own. This is necessary. When we spend time with people who are experiencing dementia, we need to manage conversations as consciously as we manage mood.

Taking part in a conversation in a way that is not usual, like constantly restating facts as we saw with Millie and George, will earn you some quizzical looks from other people. Fortunately, most people rise to the occasion when they see someone else demonstrating patience and respectfulness. In addition to being kind and respectful about our loved ones' and clients' limitations, however, there are specific techniques that caregivers can use to help people with memory loss succeed in conversation.

Anchor Conversation in the Present. At first, it is difficult to hold a conversation without talking about the past or the future. When I first began working with my clients, I found our conversations stilted and disjointed. I kept catching myself saying such things as "How was your morning?" or "What are you doing for Thanksgiving?" and seeing their dismay. I began to realize that, in most conversations, both parties either exchange information about something that has already happened or consider something that is going to happen.

But having dementia means you will be increasingly uncomfortable discussing the past or the future, because talking about either is necessarily a memory- or reason-driven conversation. The safety zone for people with dementia is the present, and what our five senses can provide: what we are hearing, seeing, touching, tasting, or smelling in this moment. In fact, with some attention to what is around you at any given time, you will find there is much to talk about. And the more you do this, the better you will become at it. When you are out in the community doing errands and enjoying daily life, look for something to notice or comment on. Look up: the clouds are beautiful, even if framed by skyscrapers. Look down. There are flowers and footprints and bugs and gum wrappers—a world you might not have noticed since you were six years old and seeing it at a much closer distance. There is an abundance of sensory stimulation within reach at any moment, which will supply a ready source of conversation for you and your companion.

It is very important to supply stimulation for a brain that is losing functions. Here, we try to be sure our clients use and enjoy their senses for as long as possible. We take a chocolate-lover on an endless search for the best hot cocoa on the Palouse. We take another client who has an appreciation for foods from other cultures out for sushi, curry, or pad Thai. We take everyone out for an occasional breakfast at the Bloom Café, where breakfast arrives arranged on the plate in a particularly appealing and colorful manner. Whatever it is we are eating or sampling, we talk about the flavors, colors, textures, and presentation of the meal so that we can enhance our clients' enjoyment of the stimulation their senses are providing.

We often take clients to plays at our local universities and playhouses. Once I took a client, Martin, to see the Shakespeare play *The Tempest*, which was being staged in a huge, disused grain silo. It was an imaginative venue, providing a central stage and excellent visibility to everyone in the audience. The silo, however, was essentially a huge tin can which amplified and reverberated every sound; the players even seemed to have trouble hearing each other's lines. For many in the audience, the experience was deafening. Martin was not having any problem, though: his hearing was so bad that the actors seemed to be speaking just loud enough. In fact, he found this performance riveting. He was completely absorbed in the costumes and props, the sights and sounds before him—and he provided a constant narration of his enjoyment at a decibel level that matched the play.

"Will you look at that? That's a man, not a woman! That's a man in that dress. See—he has no chest at all. See, look! I think he's supposed to be a goddess. Oh, that one over there is a soldier. He must be, because he has a sword. Will you look at that sword! It's cardboard! That's no use! Now, what did you say this is about? A shipwreck? Really? I think that's a monster, and that's supposed to be their ship. Right? That's the ship, right?"

Martin was totally in the moment, completely absorbed and enjoying every minute, and he wanted me to join him in appreciating the panorama before him.

When the play finally ended, I tried to hurry Martin out, because I expected to be met with angry looks and probably a request to never return. But so many members of the audience came over to shake his hand that we were still there when the actors began coming out, and they began thanking him too. Everyone seemed to feel that he had added to the success of the performance and the imaginative venue, not detracted from it. That night, I learned that it is hard to find fault with the expression of pure and sincere enjoyment. Martin's experience of the play was total captivation—of complete absorption in the moment and the sensory stimulation it provided.

Another activity our clients find rewarding is peoplewatching. In a nearby town, there is a coffee shop with a shady patio and lots of seating right on the town's main street, which is also a regional highway. Even in winter, the Filling Station Café remains a regular destination because of its friendly proprietors, excellent espresso, homemade soups and sandwiches, and local Ferdinand's ice cream. Once seated at one of the outdoor tables (or indoors, during the cold months), our clients enjoy a never-ending parade of small-town life. Farmers drive by in tractors, pickups, four-wheelers, and combines. Highschool students rev past with music blaring and then turn around at the edge of town and return for another pass. The school bus chugs by with waving children and reappears again empty to park across the street. Housewives, students, and neighboring storekeepers drop in for their own coffees.

One day, while my client José and I sat there, an old yellow dog appeared, ambling right up the middle of the street. A car coming from the other direction slowed and stopped, waiting for the dog to choose a direction. The dog paused and then made a left in front of the car, using the turn lane. José and I got such a laugh from watching that dog nonchalantly navigate traffic—and the driver respectfully wait for him—that we had to explain ourselves to the couple sitting behind us. They had been having a normal conversation, not one focused on the present. They appeared to be very concerned. They were talking about the previous winter's snowpack and how it would affect the lentil crop, a subject that involved the past and the future. They hadn't noticed the dog obeying traffic rules or the patient motorist. The four of us were sitting in the same setting, at the same time, holding two separate conversations, but the one José and I were engrossed in brought us far more enjoyment.

Encourage Favorite Anecdotes. We are really very simple creatures. It doesn't take much to make us feel better about ourselves—or worse. For many of us, the slightest social gaff can start an internal litany of self-deprecation and ruin our day, while the smallest social success or affirmation can make it. Being able to add something to the conversation, and to have what we offer be appreciated or admired, is the essence of feeling socially successful. Because of this, when we are caring for someone experiencing dementia, we need to make sure that every day, in each conversation or social interaction, our companion is given the opportunity to recount a story, joke, or incident that we know he or she remembers well and likes to tell. Further, it is important that our reaction to the story be one of sincere and outright appreciation. Laugh like you have never heard the joke before; chuckle at the outcome of the anecdote you've heard a thousand times already. We need to savor with them the stories they tell repeatedly, because for them it is *always* the first time, and these are events that hold meaning for them. We are giving our loved ones and clients the gift of having added something valuable to the conversation and letting them delight in having provided a moment of pleasure to someone else. This is an essential part of their maintaining a feeling of wellbeing.

Of course, this goes against our aversion to hearing someone tell the same story or comment over and over. Why do we feel that way? It may come from boredom, or believing that our time is too precious for repetition, or feeling that our intelligence is being threatened. I suspect it comes from that same reflexive adherence to accuracy that prompts reality orientation. Our school system measures our intelligence in terms of how many facts we can memorize and recite, our achievement in comparison with our classmates'. As adults, we are competing for jobs, promotions, wealth, and status. One of the hidden treasures in spending time with someone who have dementia is that we can choose to set this all aside, to take a break from this constant striving to be the best, the smartest, and the most competent.

In fact, when we are talking with someone who's experiencing dementia, we can and should leave our need to demonstrate intelligence, knowledge, or superiority behind. Rather than being embarrassed by the failure of memory, we should accept it as immaterial, expected, universal...and just one more thing to joke about. When hearing repetitions, we can be forgetful and accepting. We can let our companions be the smarter ones or the funnier ones or tell the most interesting stories. And if you are like me and have difficulty remembering jokes anyway, you will now need only one joke and one anecdote, and every time you repeat it, your audience will enjoy it like they have never heard it before.

When we are with people experiencing dementia, we should be thinking about what topic we can introduce to enhance *their* sense of wellbeing, not our own. We want to use each conversation as an opportunity to create a sense of accomplishment and connectedness for them and to downplay the embarrassments we know they experience when with people who do not know how to be supportive in these ways.

Introduce Forgotten Memories. Though we keep conversation mostly in the present because people experiencing dementia are forgetting their pasts, we do not have to avoid their pasts completely. Instead of talking about the immediate past in conversation, we can introduce memories from their own deep pasts as stories. One evening I was sitting in a care facility with a client who had lost even her childhood memories. Ellie could not remember who I was for even a moment. However, she was greatly enjoying having someone sit and talk with her, because her fellow residents were unable to communicate at all, and the aides were busy with their duties.

I knew quite a bit about Ellie from working with her the previous four years. While she was living in her own home, she and I had spent a lot of time gardening and doing household chores together, and I had prompted her to tell me as many memories and stories of her earlier years as she could recall. I now had quite a repertoire. As we sat together that evening, I began telling her stories, just as I might to a child:

> "Oh, Ellie, I remember the story you told me about picking strawberries and blackberries for a big farm in the Willamette Valley near Portland each summer. You and your sister would pick berries to save money for school clothes. Her name was Nora. You two would walk home from school, past the drugstore where there was a soda fountain…."

Her face lit up a little more with each tale. As I told the stories, I think she could feel a sense of familiarity and comfort in the early-childhood storytelling pattern. I was very careful to present each account as a memory I was sharing with her. I was even able to use the same phrases and words she had used in telling them to me. At no time did she feel called upon to remember something herself or to add a detail; I was simply using her own life and her own stories to give her a sense of familiarity and to enjoy companionship with her.

When you find yourself feeling impatient about being told the same stories or anecdotes over and over again, remember that the time will come when you'll need to know those memories very well, so that you can use your own memory to replace what will otherwise become lost to your companion.

■ ■ ■

By paying attention to when our loved ones and clients need help and employing specific techniques to help them take part in conversations, we can enable them to continue to feel good about interacting socially and being with others. When we do this, we are also modeling the techniques for others in their lives so that they too can begin to use these tools. This is the first of the four essential areas in which someone experiencing dementia needs a sense of wellbeing.

Supporting our loved ones' and clients' ability to interact socially helps them develop a sense of wellbeing, but it will help ours too. If for at least a moment or two of every day, we stop and really look into our companion's eyes, pause, and truly be present with him or her, we will find ourselves reminded of what is truly important in life: people. Looking at a clean kitchen floor or folded laundry may bring a sense of accomplishment or satisfaction— even relief—but joy and laughter can be found in another person's eyes. The *New York Times* recently ran an article by Arthur Brooks about a wealthy and powerful emir and caliph, Abd Al-Rahman III, ruler of Cordoba in tenth-century Spain. This man had all the wealth and power a person could imagine, yet assessed his level of happiness as abysmal. "I have diligently numbered the days of pure and genuine happiness which have fallen to my lot: They amount to fourteen," he wrote. Brooks suggests that the problem with the emir's approach to life was that he loved things rather than people.[37] I think Brooks has a point: when we take the time to notice and love the people in our lives, happiness becomes more attainable.

---

[37] For the full article, see http://www.nytimes.com/2014/07/20/opinion/sunday/arthur-c-brooks-love-people-not-pleasure.html?_r=0.

CHAPTER TEN

Sense of Control

Wilson

Wilson woke in the night, needing to use the toilet. He pushed himself into a sitting position on the edge of the bed and rested for a moment, rubbing his eyes. Light from the streetlamp outside his bedroom window made a long, narrow oblong of light on the carpet at his feet, as if pointing the way to the bathroom. He rose and trudged along it, barely awake, and sat down heavily on the toilet. He sat there for some time, and used quite a bit of toilet paper, before standing and turning to flush. The water in the bowl rose slowly but steadily. He was more asleep than awake even as it overflowed onto the carpet around the toilet—until it wet his bare toes. The cold woke him up with a jolt. He tried flushing a second time, and a third. More water soaked into the carpet, and now waste and paper overflowed onto the carpet, as well. *Oh, for crying out loud! What a mess!* Wilson stood looking at his feet. Now they were not only wet, but, when he lifted his right foot, a piece of toilet paper dangled from his big toe.

What do I do? How do I fix this? Wilson frowned as he thought. *Let's see…the water isn't going down because something is too big. I just need to make the big things smaller. I need a tool that will cut.* A picture of the jumbled tool drawer in the kitchen popped into his mind, so Wilson headed for the kitchen. Between his bedroom and the kitchen was the laundry room, which also functioned as a mudroom, and he saw a pair of garden shears leaning against the wall beside the door to the backyard. Wilson paused and stooped to pick them up. *These cut very well—these will work!* He remembered his wife, Helen, using them to trim the back hedge. (He didn't recall that she had died decades earlier.) Back he went to the bathroom, shears in hand, where he proceeded to cut up the waste and paper that remained in the toilet bowl. He laid the shears on the soggy carpet beside the toilet and flushed again.

More water overflowed onto the now very soiled carpet around the toilet. Wilson struggled to think. He knew he had fixed such a problem before; he knew that he once could fix a toilet. It was just a matter of remembering how. *Oh, a tool!* Wilson straightened and rubbed his lower back when the quickness of the movement caused a twinge. *That's what I need—a tool, the right tool.* He headed once again to the kitchen tool drawer. This time he went through the laundry room, into the kitchen, and opened the tool drawer without getting distracted. He selected the largest screwdriver and returned.

Back in the bathroom, he took the lid off the tank and laid it on top of the shears. He could remember watching his father working on a toilet, and he began to poke about in the tank with the screwdriver. He flushed it again, sending more water onto the carpet. Now there was a great deal of water and waste on the carpet, enough that his toes squelched when he shifted his weight. His attention went from the toilet to his wet bare feet. He bent to lay the screwdriver on top of the tank lid. *What do I do about a wet floor? A wet floor,* he pondered, straightening slowly and pressing both hands against his lower back. *Towels! Ah, and I know where Helen keeps the towels!* Steadying himself with one dirty hand on the vanity, he began pulling bath towels from the closet beside it, and spreading them at his feet until he had completely covered the floor around the toilet and was standing on dry towels. However, as he stood there looking down at his mucky toes, the water gradually soaked up through the towels and Wilson found his feet wet again. Even the hems of his pajama pants had become sodden.

Now that the towels hid most the mess, Wilson forgot about the toilet and the soiled carpet. Instead, Wilson found himself looking at a great many wet towels. What should he do about wet towels? Once again, memories from the deep past told him how to proceed. He gathered up as many of the soaked towels as he could carry and dragged the sodden mass into the laundry room where he began to push them into the dryer. As he worked, memories floated through his mind. He had been a young father when he bought Helen their first clothes dryer. He had been proud of being able to give her such luxuries—of becoming a tenured professor in the University of Idaho's engineering department while still in his twenties. He so clearly recalled her delight when the Sears truck delivered a new washing machine and dryer to their first home. Now, as he closed the dryer door and reached to turn it on, he felt sure that he had solved his problems.

However, he had overloaded the dryer. It would not start. As he opened and closed the door, trying to figure out how to make it start, he saw that the towels had left dirty smears on both the outside and inside of the dryer. *Dirty things in the dryer? Dirty?* Wilson's heart sank. *Oh, won't Helen be angry! I'd better clean this up— what was I thinking?* He straightened slowly, rubbed the stubble on his cheeks, and ran his fingers through his hair. He steadied himself against the wall beside the machines, leaving a smudged handprint. *Of course! They need to be washed first,* Wilson told himself. *I've got to take care of this. I've got to fix the mess I've made.* Wilson began pulling towels back out of the dryer one by one and feeding them into the washing machine. The front of the washer was now streaked and filthy as well. He closed the lid and leaned on it, studying the control panel. How did Helen work this thing?

At this point, Wilson became overwhelmed with his inability to solve the problems he faced. He, the washer, and the dryer were smelly and streaked with feces. He had just as many soaked and filthy towels as when he had begun. Frustration and confusion surpassed determination. He returned to his bedroom to climb back into bed. However, as he plodded into his room, he discovered the water had seeped out of the bathroom, and the carpet was wet even at the edge of his bed.

This was too much. Wilson turned and went back through the laundry room and kitchen to climb the stairs to the guest room, where he collapsed onto the bed without even pulling the white satin comforter back. He lay on his back and tried to go to sleep. *How can I be so helpless?* Wilson thought. *How can I carry on?* His mind whirled with fragments of thoughts and images of the smelly, dripping towels. His feet felt icy. His back ached and throbbed as he tried to relax. *I'm a grown man, a very accomplished man,* he tried to reassure himself. *But I can't figure out* anything *anymore. Where's Helen? What on earth will I do?*

Creating a Sense of Control

In the previous chapter, we discussed how important it is for someone who's experiencing dementia to be able to feel successful in social situations, and how caregivers, friends and family can help their loved ones and clients thrive in the various activities and interactions they encounter in daily life. Feeling secure and able to take part in conversation is the first step for someone experiencing dementia to enjoy a sense of wellbeing.

Now, let's look at the second most important factor: helping people with dementia retain a sense of control over themselves and their worlds. For all of us, feeling that we have some control in our lives is vital to our wellbeing. Feeling out of control is a sure way to bring on negative behaviors—whether the person is a child, a healthy adult, or someone experiencing dementia.

Wilson, whom we met in the scenario above, had been a very capable man. He had been a widely published and respected professor who was also skilled at taking care of his and Helen's home and property. A plugged toilet was something that, in his earlier years, Wilson would have resolved in minutes. He would have recognized that the toilet was plugged, not broken, and grabbed a plunger, not garden shears or a screwdriver. And he would have recognized that the towels were dirty and needed washing before drying. But solving the problem of the overflowing toilet that night required many analytical processes, which at this stage in his dementia Wilson simply no longer possessed. As a result, he lost his sense of being in control—of being able to take care of himself and manage his world. He lost self-confidence and, with it, his sense of wellbeing. He was very distressed when I arrived later that morning. It didn't take me long to trace the smeared and smelly trail he had left and piece together the events that had followed his early-morning visit to the toilet, but it took several weeks for his team of caregivers to rebuild his sense of self. We had to repeatedly show Wilson that he did indeed have some control over his circumstances, which we did using the tools I will describe in this chapter.

When people have faulty memory and rational thinking skills, it is close to impossible for them to use good judgment and make safe decisions. If you have been caring for someone with cognitive impairment, you know the multitude of problems and hazards that impaired judgment can create. We deal with clients every day who insist they do not need a jacket even though it is snowing heavily, or refuse to take the pills in today's pillbox because they are convinced they did already, or who demand they be taken on errands that are expensive and unnecessary. Becoming increasingly unable to make rational decisions is a hallmark of dementia, and so those experiencing it frequently encounter hurdles in their lives, or caregivers who want to convince them to do (or not do) things against their will. Nevertheless, they still need to have a sense of control in order to feel comfortable and happy.

So how do we, as caregivers, provide this for our companions with dementia? The key to helping them retain a feeling of control over themselves and their lives is to make it easier for them to make decisions. We can present options in ways that help them feel that they have exercised choice. Also, we can look for methods to preserve their sense of independence. First, let's consider choice.

Enable Choice

Life constantly presents us with the need to make decisions. Each time we make a choice, we use a series of analytical processes—from calling up lists of items or facts, to grading those items and facts according to applicability, to evaluating possibilities and probabilities. Decision-making comes in two varieties: those decisions for which there are only two choices and those for which there are several options. If I were to say to you, "I have two gingersnap cookies here in my hand; would you like one?" I've given you an easy choice. The answer is either yes or no. Or, if you are looking at a plate of gingersnap cookies, it's a simple process to decide whether to reach out and take one. However, if I were to ask you, "What kind of cookie would you like?" or if you were looking at a variety of cookies on the plate, it would not be as easy. You would have to enlist your rational thought processes to analyze the options, use judgment and possibly memory, and choose from more than two possibilities. When we have both memory and rational thinking skills at our disposal, we are able to sort through options in moments, with little effort, but once those skills are no longer accessible, we try to take shortcuts—and often we find that our companions step in and make decisions for us, unless they understand how to support our independence.

Your loved one may begin wearing just a few pieces of clothing over and over—clothes kept on a chair or a few outfits at one end of the closet. He or she may begin purchasing and eating just a few grocery items, which are kept on the counter in sight. For the time comes when people experiencing dementia open a closet or drawer and discover an array of items they have no memory of, and then they forget where to look for sweaters or clean socks, and then they lose the idea of what a sweater is or why they might want to wear one. They seem to cease seeing stains and spills, maybe because they have lost the concept of cleanliness (how to use a washer or dryer is usually beyond them at this point). We see our clients forget that the closet or dresser is where they will find clothing, but even when we open the closet or drawer and show them their old, familiar items, they are unable to make a selection.

The best way to enable decision-making is to convert the decision from one with many possible options to one with only two. Instead of asking "What would you like to wear today?" we say, "It's cold out today. Do you feel like wearing your navy pants or the brown ones?" while holding up both. Instead of asking our clients what they would like for lunch, we ask whether they feel like having a sandwich or a bowl of soup. If they choose a sandwich, we give them two choices: "Would you prefer ham or turkey?" When we are in a coffee shop or restaurant, we consider the menu and its myriad choices, but select only one or two to say out loud—the one or two we know the client would enjoy most. If we do not change the array of information into either/or options, typically the client will say, "Oh, I'll just have what you're having." Having too many choices is overwhelming. When we convert decision-making into a selection between two choices, our clients are empowered by being able to choose between options they can retain and comprehend.

Remember Julia in chapter 6 and her daughter Jessie, who was so good about cooking and delivering meals to her mother? One afternoon I paid a visit to Julia in her home to see how much knowledge she still retained about how to use her kitchen appliances and prepare food for herself. I purposefully steered the conversation toward cooking and favorite foods. I commented on how my fridge often becomes so filled with leftovers that I can't find what I'm looking for. She took me over to her refrigerator, opening the door to display shelves laden with beverages, yogurts, fruit, and Tupperware containers of meals all carefully prepared and delivered by Jessie. She said, "See—my fridge is empty. It's always empty." Although it was actually full of food, Julia saw nothing to eat when she opened the door. There were too many options for her to process, so all became invisible. She was also losing the knowledge that a container could hold food. All of which showed me that Julia needed to have meals laid out for her, so that she wouldn't begin going hungry despite her well-stocked kitchen.

We are always watching our clients for the time when it becomes necessary to bring in or prepare and lay out meals for them. We make sure the kitchen or dining room table (whichever is their accustomed place to eat) is cleared of everything except a placemat. We set a place with everything needed—a beverage poured in a glass, finger foods and a sandwich on the plate under clear plastic wrap, and cutlery neatly arranged. When they feel hungry and walk toward the kitchen, they will notice the meal and can choose whether to sit down and eat. We use the same approach with clothing, laying out a complete outfit of clean clothes on the bed while our client is in the shower. This way, rather than being told what to do, our clients can walk by and see something; they can then feel that they are making the decision themselves. Being able to make small decisions on their own is empowering, especially now that the bigger decisions require more memory and rational thinking skills than they possess.

One of our clients would buy a carton of milk each week and pour it into pint jars, which she then lined up on the top shelf of her fridge. I asked her one day why she did this. "I do it so I can see how much milk I have," she said. This is a great example of the thinking flaws that occur with dementia: she was going to a tremendous amount of trouble to avoid having to lift the carton of milk to feel its weight. On the other hand, she had independently chosen to enhance her ability to decide whether she needed to buy more milk by creating her own visual cue. Likely, she had found herself opening the fridge and lifting the milk carton several times a day to see how much was left. I had to admire her ingenuity.

When this client stopped filling the jars in her fridge, we knew that more care was needed. Our clients eventually stop noticing things like clothes laid out or the meal carefully arranged and visible on the table. At that point, having someone present at mealtimes to join them in eating becomes necessary. They seem to be able to copy the actions of lifting food or drink to their mouths, but not able to initiate the actions on their own. With clothing, the caregiver now presents the needed item, such as a sweatshirt, and chatters about how cozy it will feel as she helps her client into it. We call this "cueing," and it applies to any behavior that can be encouraged with modeling by a caregiver.

Somehow, even though they are copying someone else's actions, it still feels voluntary. Seeing us put a cup to our lips or food in our mouths enables our clients to do the same, and we find that clients who will not eat otherwise will still mimic us when they reach this stage. I had one client who could only be enticed to eat breakfast if it was an apple fritter or raspberry jelly donut. Further, he would not lift the donut to his mouth unless I was lifting one to my mouth. (I put on a few pounds that year as I modeled eating donuts for him!) Another client loves ice cream and for years had gone on a weekly outing with friends to enjoy two scoops of extra creamy Ferdinand's ice cream at the Washington State University Creamery on campus. She always skipped lunch to make up for the indulgence (Ferdinand's ice cream is worth it). When we took on her care, we became her ice cream partners. Because she would only eat as much as her companion ate, and she needed the calories more than we did, two caregivers took turns sharing the responsibility of eating ice cream with her on alternate Wednesdays.

Eventually all our clients have problems retaining the information necessary to feel in control. Sometimes there's an imbedded behavior that is becoming increasingly problematic, or we may need to help someone accept a major change, such as a move or the loss of a companion. We have discovered a very valuable tool that helps empower a person to retain critical information or get through a necessary change. I am not sure why this tool works, but I have a hunch it is related to how we engage with music.

Use Catchphrases

In chapter 6, I described Dan Cohen's programming of iPod Shuffles with music for residents of care facilities, and his discovery that music unlocks something in the brain and allows people to communicate even in the latter stages of dementia. We have noticed something similar with our clients. A catchphrase— a distinctive string of words used repeatedly—also seems to facilitate communication, especially if it employs alliteration. When our clients need to be able to retain a piece of information, or we want to help them learn or accept something new, we turn a single word into a phrase that we use consistently to refer to the situation. This seems to change the information from a fact—something accessed using rational thought—into something accessible with intuitive thought, like a tune.

One of our clients, Jada, had been a very capable woman in her earlier years, the one in her family who always got things done. She was an organizer, leader, and accomplished dean and professor. When she developed dementia, Jada experienced a great deal of distress over her inability to accomplish tasks or keep track of the days of the week. Her calendar became more and more detailed. She turned to keeping additional detail on scraps of paper on the kitchen table; she then added a notebook in which she wrote down what she had done at the end of each day so that the following morning she could repeatedly reread her notes to confirm which day had just passed. However, the day inevitably came when Jada could not make sense of the calendar or decipher what day it was from her notes, and her level of anxiety skyrocketed. What we did then was take the name for each day of the week—a fact that she could not retain—and made it into a catchphrase. Each day became an expression of her usual activity for that day, such as "Tuesday Tea" or "Friday Errands." Because we had turned information into phrases, Jada once again became able to retain and make sense of them. These catchphrases gave Jada a sense of control over her day so that she could feel more at ease.

Another client had to move from her home of thirty-five years to an adult family home following a lengthy stay in a rehabilitation center. It was a terribly hard transition for her, and every time we got back in the car after an activity or outing, Ruth would say, "Wait, this isn't the way home. Take me home. I want to go home!" It would have broken her heart each time if we had told her that she could never go home again because her home had been sold, and that she now lived in a group home. Instead, I would respond:

> "Yes, it does look different—that's because we're headed to your *beautiful blue bedroom* right now. I just love your *beautiful blue bedroom*. You're so lucky to have Teresa for a daughter: she painted it your favorite color of blue and brought your blue chair and your blue cushions. It's right up here; we'll be there in a sec…."

This woman had had a lifelong love for the color blue, and we could talk about her kind daughter and her *beautiful blue bedroom* all the way to her new residence, where we joined her in admiring her bedroom, which truly was beautiful and blue. It didn't take many weeks before she had forgotten her former home and the way there, and became settled in the adult family home. Using a catchphrase enabled us to smooth the transition for her, helping her focus on something positive and avoid the heartache which the full truth would have caused her.

Another couple I worked with had a home with a narrow passageway between the kitchen counter and the cabinets on the other side. The husband had Parkinson's-related dementia and was a large man with other physical conditions that resulted in a very slow gait. His wife, on the other hand, was petite. Several times a day, they found themselves facing each other in just that spot, her hands full with dishes or food or laundry, he frozen in place and unsure what to do next. A healthy person would simply move out of the way, but he had lost not only coordination but also analysis, and had trouble imagining how to resolve this impasse. Like many people with dementia, though, he was quick to pick up the slightest hint of exasperation from his wife, and just as quick to mirror it back to her. Negative behaviors quickly followed the negative emotions. His wife and I decided to try a catchphrase: whenever she found herself stuck in that narrow opening facing her husband, this loving wife would exclaim, "Hug time!" and put down whatever she held to give him a hug. She used a catchphrase to redefine the experience as a positive one, and changed a frustrating moment into an opportunity to give him a dose of affection and acceptance.

Let Them Own the Moment

However, there are times when something comes up spur of the moment; we don't always have time to prepare a choice by making it visible or to come up with a catchphrase that will solve a behavioral problem. What can we do when our loved one or client insists on going for a walk in the snow barefoot, or refuses to bathe, or wants to put the indoor cat outside? One technique is to present the right choice as the "lesser of two evils," which gives the client a sense of control, and makes him or her more likely to choose the proper course of action. This tool is especially helpful with behaviors that threaten the person's health or safety. We often have problems helping our clients choose to maintain adequate personal hygiene. They may be convinced that they shower every evening before bed, although their shower stall is dusty and the hair we placed under the bar of soap weeks ago indicates that the soap has yet to be moved. A male client might be adamant that he changes his clothes every day, but his slacks are grease-spotted and his shirt grubby. A female client's hair might be hanging in unwashed strands, dandruff thick on her shoulders, while she insists that she washes it daily. Everyone else can see that they are not taking adequate care of themselves, while their memory loss and impaired judgment cause them to behave in ways they would find intensely embarrassing if they realized what other people could see.

Our first approach when one of our clients refuses to do something necessary for safety or health is to make it optional, by comparing it with another less desirable option. We might say, "Lynn, I know you don't like showers, so I brought you some of my favorite bath salts so you won't have to take one. Would you like to try my lavender bubble bath? I've filled the tub for you. Doesn't that look inviting?" Or we might suggest to Ned (who never wants to go to medical appointments) that we have arranged for him to see a new doctor because we know he didn't think much of the previous one. With Ned's memory loss and a little prepping of the doctor beforehand, it isn't even necessary to actually change doctors.

Often, we have clients who have been frugal throughout their lives and are now overdoing things, limiting the amount of food they eat or reducing their use of toothpaste or shampoo to a bare minimum. Sometimes they change their behavior when we suggest that swollen gums might lead to an expensive trip to the dentist, or a patch of dry skin may mean a doctor's visit, unless they begin using a certain toothpaste or shampoo. Sometimes telling a client that the doctor wants a prescription product purchased unless a cheaper version from the grocery store will work encourages a client to use the grocery store item. What we present as a comparative does not have to be logical or something we would carry through with, because our companions lack memory and analysis. Success and safety come from offering a choice—by presenting something we know is less desirable—so they can feel empowered when they choose to do what is actually in their own best interests.

Am I Being Manipulative?

Here on the Palouse, I teach classes to families and in the community about using the DAWN method. Invariably someone's hand will shoot up at this point in the lesson and, with a worried expression, he or she will say, "But if I do this, am I being manipulative? Isn't this sneaky?"

This is a valid question. The answer lies in who will benefit from the situation we are influencing—ourselves or the person we are inducing to behave or respond in a certain way. If we are influencing other people's behavior purely for our own benefit, we are being manipulative and should stop. However, when we influence someone else's behavior for *their* good—and at the same time spare them hurtful emotions and reactions that might emerge after a confrontation—we are doing something we can be proud of. The verb that better describes what we're doing in the latter case is *to motivate*—to give someone a reason for doing something. As the caregivers of people experiencing dementia, we should look for ways to motivate them to choose to do what they would have done on their own if not for their cognitive impairment. Because we are presenting information and arranging circumstances for their benefit rather than our own, we are not manipulating them.

Lawyers are very aware of the issue of respecting and preserving someone else's interests. A lawyer's duty is to act on behalf of his or her clients—to further their interests and theirs alone. When I was practicing divorce law, I had greater knowledge and experience than my clients about the likely outcomes of a given motion filing, negotiation stance, or demand. I would explain the law, the courtroom, and the likeliest outcomes to my client, but he or she made the choices regarding which motions to file and which issues mattered most. I could only pursue my client's stated interests. If I did not feel comfortable doing what my client wanted me to do, and I couldn't talk them out of it, my professional duty was to recommend another lawyer and resign.

However, this is not always true if a lawyer is appointed to represent a child, something that also sometimes happens in divorces. When a judge is concerned about whether a child's needs are being protected, the court will assign a lawyer to speak on the child's behalf. However, the lawyer who represents a child does not have a duty to present the child's wants or desires ("interests") to the court. Rather, the lawyer's duty is to identify and represent the child's "best interests," or needs. The assumption is that although children may know exactly what they want, they are not competent to know their needs, or what is truly best for them.[38]

When caregivers provide care for seniors who are competent, the relationship resembles that between attorneys and their adult clients. In the United States, anyone over the age of eighteen is competent unless a court has determined otherwise, so an elderly person can decide what his or her own interests are, and choose to accept care or not.[39] However, matters become more complicated when people develop dementia. Cognitive impairment results in faulty reasoning and bad decisions. Anosognosia can prevent people from realizing just how at-risk they are. Someone who was fastidious goes about with dirty hair and soiled clothing; others who were always careful about nutrition begin living on crackers and Oreos; a woman who never drank more than a glass of wine a day becomes an alcoholic or a man who quit smoking decades ago begins smoking two packs a day (not due to choice but lack of memory skills). People give away prized family heirlooms and wreck their cars and wander down the block at night in their pajamas—and their loved ones can only try to protect them. Confusion and memory loss cause people to behave in ways that are not only against what is in their best interests, but also contrary to what their family and friends know their preferences had been before dementia appeared.

Our duty in providing care to people who are experiencing dementia is twofold: we must protect both their *interests* (preferences) and their *best interests* (health and safety). This is the essence of person-directed care. Our focus is on them: we get to know who they really are, and were, and our care is shaped by their changing needs.

---

[38] Currently, this is a prevalent but not fully settled point of law; some states do grant children of certain ages the right to dictate what the lawyer presents to the court.

[39] A notable example of the exercise of competency occurred during the eruption of Mount St. Helens in May 1980. Harry Randall Truman, the eighty-four-year-old caretaker of the Mount St. Helens Lodge, refused to leave. His choice resulted in his death but, as a competent adult, the choice was his to make.

198

Silly Me—I Forgot Again

Another technique we use to give our clients a sense of control is to give them the upper hand in the interaction. Walter was rapidly failing physically and losing strength. It was exhausting for him even to move from his bed to the wheelchair, but he had a weekly appointment at a clinic downtown to help cure a pressure wound. As time progressed, convincing him to make this trip to the clinic, undeniably grueling for someone in his physical condition, became more and more of a battle. Walter would adamantly refuse to get out of bed and into his wheelchair, and became violent if we insisted. Even telling Walter that he could end up in a care facility if he missed the checkup had no effect, although during an earlier stay he had been despondent and inconsolable during his time there.

One afternoon, with inspiration born of desperation, I stumbled upon a solution. "Oh, Walter, I am *so* sorry," I told him. "This is my fault entirely—I've been forgetful. You asked me to take you to your doctor's appointment, and it's almost too late. I'm so very sorry. Can I help you get there now?" Walter's response to this statement was to be magnanimous, to rise to the occasion and accept my apology. Even though he hated the ordeal of the wheelchair ride, his ego was boosted by believing that he had made the appointment himself and that I had forgotten it. His physical need for rest was outweighed by his emotional embracing of this confidence boost. After that, whenever we needed him to cooperate with us in doing something that was necessary but uncomfortable, we first presented the activity or procedure as the lesser of two evils. If that didn't work, we presented the situation as something he had arranged and we had put at risk through our own carelessness or forgetfulness.

In care facilities, however, the staff's response when a client with dementia repeatedly refuses to cooperate is to use psychotropic drugs, which is both expensive and can create harmful side effects. But why do we expect someone who is constantly disempowered to *not* behave obstinately, to not attempt to take control in the few ways left to them? Why do we assume that people with dementia lose their need for autonomy? In reality, given a proper understanding of dementia, we should expect the condition to exacerbate a person's need for control. Walter's refusal to attend his doctors' appointments was actually a display of unmet emotional needs—his need for self-confidence and autonomy. When I put myself in an inferior position, by apologizing for committing an error, I gave Walter a sense of independence and control—a much-needed boost for his self-esteem.

Make Them the Instructor

Occasionally, we will find that a client has forgotten something overnight. A memory, with no warning, seems to have become dislodged or rearranged, or another memory has taken its place altogether. For example, one of my clients had, overnight, forgotten that she had children. Before this, we regularly discussed where her children lived, what they did for a living, and how much they cared for her. But one afternoon when I introduced the usual topic of her children, Cora looked at me with alarm in her eyes, froze, and asked, "My daughter? Do I have a daughter? When did I have a daughter?" I tried using the phrases I had always used in reciting details about each child and repeating the facts she typically told me regarding each of them, but nothing brought back to Cora her memories of having had children.

To lose the knowledge that she had loved and raised children was a great loss, for I knew that her children had always been the focus of her life. If I had reacted to her alarm with disbelief or amazement, I would have compounded her fear and distress about not remembering something important. Instead, I reintroduced the topic of her children as if this were a conversation we had been having for some time. From that day on, whenever I visited, I would say something like this:

> "Cora, you were telling me about how you and your husband used to take your children camping in the Gulf Islands each summer. Would you show me your photo album again? It's this one, right? I'd love to see pictures of you and your children again. Let's see, here's Andrea, and Scott, and there's little Jimmy. He's so young in that picture. Wow, now he's such a *tall* man."

With each visit, I would fill our conversation with facts and information about her children, just as Cora had previously recounted the stories to me. Cora didn't seem to notice that I was telling *her* about her memories and her children's lives. Her focus was on the happy times I described to her and the pictures I pointed out to support my stories, not the absence of her memories. (This is an important way we can help our loved ones and clients retain a sense of their earlier independent lives.)

At other times, the loss of a memory can be dangerous as well as sad. Remember Edna, whom we met in chapter 3? Edna has been a swimmer for decades, and still does a dozen laps three times a week, although she has long since lost her ability to retain information. Edna cannot undress or prepare to swim without direction, and doesn't know which pool to get into, so Megan changes in the changing room with her and swims in the lane beside her. When Edna wonders how many laps she has done, she just stands up and taps Megan on the head. However, one morning as they walked toward the edge of the pool, Edna grasped the ladder facing the water, rather than turning around to descend properly. Overnight, her memory of how to use a swim ladder had changed. Neither Megan nor the lifeguards, who quickly intervened, could change her mind, even though she ended up falling into the pool face first and getting water up her nose. "I've *always* done it this way," Edna insisted. "I'm not changing now." The lifeguard warned Megan that Edna would not be able to continue swimming if she couldn't get into the pool safely.

What we did was present the correct way of using the swim ladder as if it had been Edna's idea, to allow her to retain a sense of control and independence. On the next swim day, as they approached the edge of the pool, Megan turned to Edna and said:

> "Oh, Edna, thank you *so* much for telling me the right way to use the ladder. I've been doing it all wrong. You showed me how to do it—like this." And down the ladder Megan climbed, backward.

Edna stood, watching her, and said, "Did I say that?"

Megan said, "Oh yes, thank you so much for setting me straight!"

Edna responded with a smile of satisfaction and said, "You're welcome," and then proceeded to descend the ladder properly.

Periodically, Megan needs to replay the same scenario. Presenting the right way to use the pool ladder as Edna's idea has made it possible for Edna to continue swimming safely—an activity that is beneficial to her both physically and emotionally.

Hide the End Goal

There are times when we have tried every technique described above, and nothing has worked. Our client still refuses to go to a doctor's appointment or to stop doing something dangerous. We then turn to what we call our "9-1-1." This is the last resort and should only be tried when something must be done for someone's safety or a medical need must be met, and nothing else has worked. And be careful: use this only when a person's ability to use analysis or reason has disappeared completely.

The idea is to present no more than one step at a time—never identifying the true purpose or destination. To use an adage and stretch it a little, instead of leading the horse to water and saying, "This is water and you need a drink," we lead the horse on a circuitous route, in increments, never directly discussing the water, and hoping to arrive at the trough without the horse noticing it but feeling thirsty nevertheless. For example, Alma, who had a hot temper, resisted going to the dentist although her teeth badly needed attention, and she had a persistent toothache. But we had to get her to the dentist somehow. This time I said, "Alma, I have an errand to run. Would you like to join me?" She cheerfully got her things and came out to the car. Once in the car, I suggested picking up lattes at the drive-thru. She loved lattes and was happy to join me.

Coffees in hand, we then drove around a little, and I asked her if she would mind if we dropped by an office where I needed to talk to the doctor. She didn't mind. When we arrived in the parking lot at the dentist's office, I asked her if she wanted to come in or wait in the car during my errand, knowing she always enjoyed and welcomed the chance for a chat (she was blossoming under our careful management of conversation and had grown to love social interactions again). Into the dental office she came, smiling and cheerful. When I wanted to go down the hall to talk to the dentist, and I wondered if she would like to join me, she was again happy to go along. Soon she was sitting in the dentist chair ("Oh, Alma—you take the big comfy one!") and chatting with the "doctor" I had come to see. Without realizing that she had become the center of attention, or analyzing what was happening, she compliantly opened her mouth while I held her latte and let him give her a numbing shot as if it were a logical part of my errand. Less than an hour later, my chat with my doctor friend was finished, and she graciously joined me in stopping for protein shakes on the way home, with a brand-new filling.

This is a situation where lack of memory and the inability to analyze or use judgment can work with the caregiver's efforts and to the client's benefit. I believe it works because someone with dementia is losing the ability to recognize cause and effect (and because I'm making the most of my clients' increasing ability to live in the moment which, with the loss of past and future, is all that remains to them). I have used this approach several times successfully, although only once with something as prolonged and invasive as a dental appointment. The key is to only suggest the next step in the process, never mentioning or addressing the actual end goal, and to always let your companion make every choice on his or her own.

Give the Gift of Autonomy

In a small town like Moscow, we can do things that could not be done in a city. One of my clients was an avid walker. He had been doing his errands on foot for decades, because he believed that cars should be used only when truly necessary, due to their impact on the environment. His neighbors were well used to seeing him walk by, in the snow or under a blazing summer sun, on his way the few blocks from his home to the grocery store, the bank and the pharmacy. When he first became our client, we wanted to accompany him on his errands, but he often headed off alone. I would get phone calls and text messages from half a dozen neighbors along his route: "Judy, Richard sighting: headed west on Blaine." Off I would go, to ensure he was managing. I spent quite a bit of time during those first months coasting down side streets and idling on street corners to see if he could still successfully navigate a crossing or remember his route. Because of Moscow's small size and the interconnectedness and supportiveness of its residents, Richard could be allowed quite a bit of independence.

In a city, or in a rural setting with one or two watchful neighbors, independence can still be encouraged. Socks, shoes, and bracelets with GPS chips allow families to track a loved one's wanderings. Other technology enables people with dementia to function in their own homes longer; for example, researchers are developing a sensor no bigger than a smoke alarm that will track a person's movements inside the home, and alert family members via email or text messages when they deviate from their normal patterns.[40]

When we empower our loved ones and clients with the ability to make choices, we are giving them the greatest gift we can offer. We are giving them the ability to do the things they would have chosen to do for themselves without a second thought if they were not experiencing dementia.

---

[40] See Washington State University's Smart Home technology, at www.geekwire.com/2015/these-researchers-are-building-extra-brainy-smart-homes-to-monitor-aging-adults.

CHAPTER ELEVEN

Sense of Value

Who are we, who is each one of us, if not a combinatoria of experiences, information, books we have read, things imagined? Each life is an encyclopedia, a library, an inventory of objects, a series of styles, and everything can be constantly shuffled and reordered in every way conceivable.

—Italo Calvino,
*Six Memos for the Next
Millennium*

I remember coming across the above statement as part of my readings for a literature course and wholly agreeing with Calvino. I remember contemplating my own life and wondering how someone could possibly continue to be the same person without the array of memories and experiences that shape who we are. What if I forgot growing up in Alberta, or attending high school in Victoria, on Vancouver Island? Would I still feel a yearning for my childhood when I looked at glittering snow or wide expanses of table-flat prairie? Would the sound of rain on the roof still make me feel cozy, as it did in my tiny second-floor bedroom during my teenage years in rainy Victoria? Would losing knowledge of my years spent studying classical piano mean that I would no longer be drawn to attend symphonies and concerts?

If Calvino was right—if we are no more than an accumulation of knowledge, experience, and memory—what remains of us when we develop dementia? Must we anticipate the loss of our *selves* when we lose knowledge of our past? Does Calvino's precious "combinatoria" represent the whole of our personhood? In fact, after spending more than eight years working with people with dementia, I now think Calvino was completely wrong. Having seen what happens to my clients as their ability to recall the knowledge and experiences that shaped their personalities slips away, I no longer believe that we are merely a living library, a repository of memories. We do not become nonentities when we lose knowledge of our pasts. We are experiential as well as remembering beings: we continue on in the present, even if we become unmoored from our past. When I'm with a client now, looking into once-brighter eyes, I think of Tennyson's poem "Ulysses" rather than Calvino's *combinatoria*. Those faded eyes remind me of Tennyson's line "much have I seen and known." With the grip of that once-stronger hand comes a whisper of "I am a part of all I have known," to which my heart adds *and of all who have known you, too.* In the final couplet Tennyson pens:

> "Tho' much is taken, much abides; and tho'
> We are not now that strength which in old days
> Moved earth and heaven, that which we are, we are,"

Much is taken by dementia, but I hope in reading these chapters you now see more clearly the value of what is not taken—how our losses are not comprehensive. Other parts of us can flourish.

Is it a scary thought that we might lose our remembering selves? Certainly. I fear dementia as much as anyone. But it is not the thought of losing my memories that shapes my fear; it is whether there would be a caregiver who understood my needs and could help me function with my changed cognitive skillset. For even though my clients are experiencing the loss of memory that accompanies dementia, I have seen many of them gain something truly beautiful. I don't know whether this beauty is available to everyone—to all of us who lose rational thought and are forced to negotiate life with intuition only—because there are too many variables in the lives of the people I have worked with. But here in Moscow, when we have been able to put a protective circle of care around our clients, and they learn to trust that they will never be asked to do what their changing brains can no longer manage, we see a new way of life open up like a flower in spring. We have seen the men and women in our care become peaceful, attuned to beauty and to their senses, and adept at interpreting the emotions of those around them. We have seen autocratic and hardhearted businessmen become caring and aware individuals, and their relationships with family members be repaired and strengthened, even as dementia progresses.

Dementia will shuffle, reorder, and delete our memories. But we are more than a specific and carefully cataloged collection of past events. We are also experiencing life from one moment to the next, and those experiences should continue to give us a sense of value and purpose. We are shaped by our experiences, and the feelings that result from these experiences—not just our memories. When people experiencing dementia are fortunate enough to spend time with caregivers who help them maintain positive moods and feel safe—who will assist them in continuing to foster positive relationships and retain independence—they have experiences that are enjoyable and beneficial even though they cannot recall them moments later. As Thomas Merton observed, "no man is an island." Even when our reason is being eroded by dementia, we affect and are affected by those around us.

Giving our companions with dementia a sense that they are valued and respected, that they still have much to offer in their relationships with others, helps them maintain and develop their sense of self-worth. But consider the challenges of ensuring this, as captured in the following scenario:

Daryl

Daryl sat in his armchair in the living room, staring out over the frozen fields and rolling hills that flowed from the east side of his property to a line of blue mountains in the distance. The sun had just peeked over the horizon and thrown the landscape into sharply defined patches of sparkling white snow and deep blue shadows. The aspen tree just off the deck was rimed with frost, every twig lit and glittering. *We had a word for that,* Daryl thought. *When we lived in Alaska. What was it again? A layer of frost, looks like a dusting of sugar. Half frost. Hard frost? No—hoar frost!* Daryl smiled to himself. *That's it,* hoar frost. *How Bella would have loved this sunrise.* He shifted in his chair, stretching out his long legs and adjusting his weight to ease a twinge in his left hip. *She loved mornings.* His smile faded and his shoulders dropped. *Oh, Bella. Bella, Bella, I am so sorry.*

Daryl had been abusive to his wife and children, both verbally and physically. His daughters had grown up, gone off to college, and settled elsewhere—Gina in Spokane and Barb in Denver. Bella had gone to visit them often but they rarely came home, even after they had married and had children of their own. It wasn't ever said in so many words, but Daryl knew the reason as well as any of them: none of them trusted a grandchild within reach of his quick and heavy hand. Nevertheless, Daryl had always thought of himself as just a strict, but normal, parent—he treated his children no worse than his father treated him, and surely there was nothing wrong with that. Then, four years ago, Bella had died. Daryl found himself alone, with lots of time to think, and a phone that seldom rang. Bella had called their daughters regularly. They had called her. When they did and Bella offered him the phone, Daryl's response had always been, "Just say hi for me."

Now he found that his thoughts often went to Bella, Gina, and Barb. His thoughts were almost always with them, in fact. Yet, if he phoned one of the girls, he couldn't think of anything to say. When they were young, he didn't spend much time with them on weekends; he never attended their afterschool volleyball games or Irish dance lessons. He had certainly never attempted to share his thoughts or feelings with them. (*Why would a parent do that?* he often wondered. *Parents need to instill respect in their children, not explain themselves.*) Now he and his girls had nothing to reminisce about. If he mentioned how much he missed Bella, or commented on what a good cook she had been, or how quiet the house was without her cheerful humming, he was met with stony silence. As a result, Daryl had now spent four years almost entirely alone. And he had spent a lot of time remembering.

The memories would flood back in full detail, and he would see video-like reincarnation of his younger self from a spectator's view. There he would be, towering over Bella or one of the girls, raging and then swinging. *How could I do that? How could I hurt the people I loved so much?* Daryl slumped forward with his head in his hands, overcome by the memories that kept bubbling up. *An abuser. That's what I was; I was abusive. I was so cruel to them. Oh, little Gina, little Barb. I am so sorry.* He blinked back tears. *But, how can I ever tell you? How can I ever make it up to you?* Daryl stood up and headed for the kitchen, more as an attempt to escape his thoughts than to do anything. There, he stood in the middle of the room for a moment or two, looked at the table, the sink, the table again. He turned and walked slowly back to his armchair, and sat. He leaned back and closed his eyes, but felt restless. He stood again and walked back to the kitchen. Once more, he stood in the middle of the room and wondered what he should do next.

Lately Daryl had quite often found himself in places he didn't remember coming to. He would find himself standing someplace, feeling like he had just woken up. He would have no idea how long he had been there or what he'd been doing. Just the other day (*was it yesterday or last week?*), Daryl had walked out of the coffee shop downtown to get into his truck and found it gone. The shop's owner, Tom, who was used to Daryl's near-daily visits, had insisted that Daryl had walked up to the building—not driven— and that his truck must be at home, just a few blocks away. But Daryl didn't remember walking to the coffee shop; he always drove over in his truck. Regardless, Tom had driven him home, and there his truck was, in the driveway after all. Another time, Daryl had found himself in a strange kitchen with a young woman yelling "Go home!" and pointing out the window to his house across the street. He remembered looking out, seeing his house, and feeling like he was in a dream. He had no idea how he'd ended up in his neighbor's home. She was a young mother, balancing a baby on her hip. She'd been so upset; afraid, really. He remembered that so clearly—her fear.

Just a night or two ago, his neighbor to the west, Fiona, had been deeply upset. She had banged on the door late in the night and woken him, insisting he'd left his dog out barking in the cold. He'd looked at her in complete confusion. He remembered that moment and the feeling so clearly: the sense of having completely lost his bearings. He had been unable to recall any memory of even having a dog until he'd looked down at the shaggy form shivering at Fiona's side and recognized Bella's dog, Lucy. Seeing Lucy there at the door that night had felt like seeing something from the distant past dropped into the present. Now Daryl turned around to look for Lucy, and was relieved to see her asleep in a patch of sunlight by the table. He walked into the living room and sat down in his armchair. He suddenly realized he needed to urinate, but he felt too tired to get up and go just then.

Daryl turned back to the view and saw that the sun had jumped high up in the sky. *How can that be?* he thought. *Did I drift off? So strange. Time is so odd now,* he mused. *Sometimes hours disappear in a moment; other times a minute seems hours long.* The doorbell rang and startled him. He grabbed the arms of the chair to rise and then stopped to wait for his heart to steady. The door opened.

"Dad!"

Daryl looked up to see a plump, youngish woman standing arms akimbo just inside the door. Her clothes were neat and stylish and her handbag looked like a briefcase. He was too surprised to say anything.

"What are you doing? You're not ready." It was Gina, and she didn't seem happy.

"Gina? What—"

"We're supposed to be at the doctor's office in half an hour, and you look atrocious. Have you showered? You certainly haven't shaved. What's *wrong* with you?"

"The doctor? *Now?*" Daryl struggled to gather his thoughts. A moment ago, he was thinking about…well, it was something about Bella. He felt a very familiar sense of guilt and loss.

"Dad! You *knew* I was driving down this morning to get you to the specialist."

Daryl saw Gina look around and her expression change from frustration to disgust as she took in the living room's disorder and overall squalor. He felt another pang of guilt. His eyes welled up with tears. He didn't move.

"What now? Hurry up. We have to go."

Daryl looked up at the capable woman his oldest child had grown into and knew it wasn't because of anything he'd contributed to her life. "Gina, I am so sorry, *so* sorry. I wasn't a very good father. I am so *very* sorry."

But Gina just stood and looked at him. He saw her chin lift, her lips press into a thin line, and her face harden. She looked down at her watch and then back at him.

"Go put on a clean shirt. We have to be in the car within five minutes. You need to clean up."

Daryl held her gaze for a long moment. His sadness and remorse melted away before a surge of anger at her coldness. She was still his child. He was still the parent. She wasn't being respectful. His grip tightened again on the arms of his chair and he pulled himself up to his full height.

Give a Sense of Value

For any of us to have a sense of wellbeing, we need to feel that we are respected and are contributing something of value to the people in our lives. We need to have feelings of self-worth. For many of our seniors, maintaining this sense becomes increasingly difficult as they age. They are often segregated from the rest of society, in retirement communities available only to the elderly, often located far from city centers with their stores, clinics, theaters and parks. For all the assistance and additional care they provide, such facilities rarely enhance a senior's opportunities to continue to contribute to the community or society. The result, even without dementia, is an increasing sense of isolation and worthlessness as we age.

Having a functional role in a family and a community, a sense of being respected and loved there, is a basic human need, yet it can sometimes be difficult for families and caregivers to provide. Gina, in the scenario above, found it hard, and it's difficult to blame her. Not every parent or senior has been an admirable person. Yet a person who is experiencing dementia will make the caregiver's life more difficult unless he or she is given the sense of being valued in some manner. Daryl was experiencing remorse and sorrow when Gina came by to take him to his doctor's appointment. But she seemed unable to recognize his sorrow or respond with forgiveness, so his feelings of remorse turned into feelings of being disrespected. When we as caregivers cannot acknowledge the feelings our companions are expressing, the result is negative behaviors from feeling unloved or mistreated.

How, then, do we show our loved ones and clients that we respect and value them, even when they are not people we can easily admire? We can achieve this to some degree, regardless of how we feel about them, by focusing on little things said and done in the present moment. One of the quickest ways to communicate love and acceptance is by being respectful of the other person's statements and opinions. When that other person has dementia, however, you often find yourself faced with a statement that is fantastical or in error. As our companions' view of reality is progressively altered by missing and incorrect memories, their opinions and beliefs about what is real become more difficult for us to understand. We need not accept their statements as true, however. Instead, we can effectively communicate respect and acceptance by understanding the emotions that prompted what they are saying, and validating those underlying emotions.

One of my clients, Annmarie, had recently been moved into a memory care unit and her husband had moved into an apartment nearby. She was less and less communicative, but several staff members commented to me about how devoted Albert, her husband, was to her, visiting Annmarie every single afternoon. One morning when I came to check on her, I found her sitting upright in her wheelchair in the main room and looking extremely troubled. She beckoned to me, and confided, "Albert is seeing one of my girlfriends and doesn't come to visit me anymore." I had been working with the two of them for about a year and had not seen Albert demonstrate anything but devotion to Annmarie. I suspected that Annmarie was either reacting to having been moved into the facility and separated from Albert for the first time in a lengthy marriage, or she had dreamed that he had been unfaithful—images most likely prompted by her feelings of insecurity.

If I had disagreed with her or admonished her for saying such an unfair thing about Albert, Annmarie would have argued with me and felt that I hadn't taken her anguish seriously. I would have lowered her sense of self-worth. Instead, I needed to validate her feelings—without agreeing with her incorrect statements. My response, therefore, was to add details, giving her more information so that she could draw a new conclusion—one that was more favorable and accurate about her husband. I told her that I had come specifically because I had heard that Albert had come down with a cold, and that I knew she'd have been worried about him and would be feeling lonely when he didn't appear as usual. Tears welled up in her eyes, and she said, "Oh, my, poor Albert! I *did* miss him, but who will look after him while I'm in here?" I had validated her loneliness and feelings of loss, so her fears about him were easily turned to concern for his health. Now we could talk about the new scenario I had placed in her mind. We chatted about how miserable a cold could make someone, and how lucky it was that they never lasted long for dear Albert. That was one of the last days that Annmarie could sit up and hold a conversation. How fortunate it was that I had been there, and was able to validate her feelings of love for Albert and reaffirm his love for her.

When we are caring for people with cognitive impairment, grappling with their distorted beliefs about reality and truth is a constant challenge. Identifying the emotions which drive their statements allows us to work with their beliefs and still communicate our respect and acceptance.

Listen: Really *Listen*

Deciphering what is driving a statement or belief requires careful listening. When we are talking with someone who has dementia, it is important that we pay careful attention and use both our intuitive and rational thought processes. Eye contact becomes an extremely important tool: we can say with our eyes what they cannot decipher from our words. Allowing pauses is another important part of listening to someone experiencing dementia. Pausing while someone else gathers his or her thoughts communicates respect and equality. Earlier in dementia, our loved ones and clients will likely be able to find the word they are searching for; it will just take a little longer. Later, it becomes kinder to say the word for them, because when dementia takes away language words become irretrievable. Also, their words become more imprecise, less exact expressions of what they are trying to say.

In 2014, NPR ran a program they called *Improv for Alzheimer's: "A Sense of Accomplishment*," which detailed a study conducted at Northwestern University's Feinberg School of Medicine in which improvisation classes were provided for a group of people in the early stages of dementia. In the study, researchers found that the exercises used to teach actors the art of improvising provided a very positive social experience for people in the early stages of dementia. The participants played games in which any response that came to mind was correct, or any tune or sound was welcomed as an appropriate expression. This created an atmosphere of acceptance and equality in which each participant could provide something of value.[41] When people feel free to offer something to a group without concern for being censured, their feelings of personal worth are enhanced.

I love listening to this program and hearing the participants sounding so happy and uninhibited. They sound like our clients—people who are functioning successfully using the intuitive and creative parts of their brains. When a participant is asked what he thinks the music they've been creating in an exercise should be titled, his response is: "Chubby Chaos." What a creative use of language—an unusual but apt description of what he and his companions had just experienced. "Chubby" implies fullness, roundness, and a comfortable acceptance; "chaos" implies commotion and disorder, also unrestrained action. In the same way, we should listen with an open mind to our loved ones' and clients' use of language. There is wisdom and beauty in it, because it often comes straight from the intuitive processes of the mind, without censorship or the conventional constraints dictated by reason. At the end of the NPR program, we hear a researcher correct a participant's use of language. This participant wonders

---

[41] This study proved to be so successful that it is now available as a workshop; see www.in-themoment.com.

how he could describe "what we are celebrating" to a friend. The group leader responds with a gentle correction, but a correction nonetheless, saying, "What we're celebrating or what we're *doing?*"

There is value and beauty in the way someone experiencing dementia uses language. Look for those moments of inspiration— the poetry and genius that may accompany dementia.

Balance Safety and Selfhood

When we care for people who are cognitively impaired, we must constantly reconsider whether they can remain in their homes, continue to drive, persist in an activity, or attend an event. Yet being impaired does not make them any less mature or deserving of independence in their own eyes, nor should it in ours. Most people who are now living with dementia have earned the right to be treated with dignity and respect through their years of service to family, community, and often country. When we are dealing with small children, we might say, "I know best. Please do as I say." This doesn't work as well with teenagers and seldom works at all with those older than us, even when they are too impaired to maintain safety without assistance. I find that my clients are less likely to accept suggestions or direction from younger caregivers, for they view them as the equivalent of grandchildren; they often respond better when their caregivers are the age of their own children. Even so, we don't often say to a client, "You must do this," because it rarely succeeds. Instead, we try constantly to think creatively, pondering how to change a behavior from a negative or unsafe one into something positive— looking for ways to motivate our clients to do what they once would have done on their own.

For Angelina, one of our clients who was living in a care facility, mealtimes were becoming increasingly problematic. She grew up during the Great Depression, and knew firsthand the importance of the adage, "Waste not, want not." She could not stand to see food wasted. As her dementia progressed, she also became less able to foresee soon-to-occur events or imagine the passage of time. When her tablemates ate more slowly than she did during meals, Angelina imagined waste that was about to occur. She would announce that she wasn't going to let good food be thrown away, and then grab the remaining food from their plates and eat it herself. This was bad for Angelina, who was overeating, but worse for her companions, who weren't getting enough to eat!

If we were to evaluate Angelina's behavior without knowing its source—the belief system that prompted it—it would appear aggressive and out of control. But when we consider it in the context of a childhood of frugality bordering on deprivation, it becomes perfectly comprehensible. The typical response to such behaviors in a care facility would be to tell the person to stop, try to reason with them, then when that failed, use psychotropic medication or isolation during mealtimes—both of which are likely to cause harm. Instead, our suggestion was to place a small food storage container beside each person's plate at the beginning of the meal. Before each meal, the caregiver could say, "Angelina has had a wonderful idea that will help us not waste food. Now, if any of you can't finish something on your plate, you can put it in your own personal food container and enjoy it later as a snack."

Whether the food was saved or eaten later was immaterial. What was important was that during the meal there would be a visible reminder to Angelina that waste would not occur, and her sense of self-worth would be reinforced by being congratulated on her foresight in wanting to avoid it.

A client's beliefs are not always so easy to accommodate. Another of our clients was prejudiced against all non-Caucasians, and extremely intolerant of any lifestyle that differed from his own. As his dementia progressed, his inhibitions melted away, along with any sense of compassion or consideration for others. One day, while he and I waited in a café for the waiter to bring our lunch, an interracial couple walked in with two school-age children and sat down at a booth behind me in his direct line of sight. I knew immediately that there would be trouble. I did not want my client to make a comment or do anything that might make the family feel uncomfortable, especially the children. As I feared, though, my client began to eye them and become agitated. I decided to use distraction. I leaned forward and spoke in a voice so quiet that he had to lean in too. "Why don't we take our chicken teriyaki as takeout and go eat in the park?" My close eye contact and conspiratorial tone caught his attention, and he agreed. We stood and I took him out to my car. The café's staff knew us well enough that I could leave without explanation, and then go back in to pay and collect our meals to go.

The next time I had him out, it didn't work nearly as well, though. When we were leaving another restaurant, two very large women also got up to leave. Before I could distract him or get him out the door, he began making loud derogatory comments about their weight. The women, understandably angry, hounded us all the way to the car, berating both of us for his rudeness. After that, we began to bring meals in to this client's home so that we could limit situations where his bigotry would hurt or anger others. We can avoid these kinds of incidents when we take the time to get to know our loved one's or client's beliefs, and plan around them accordingly.

As you can see, it is not always necessary to accept or support our loved one's or client's beliefs. It is necessary, however, to be aware of them. Dementia prevents people from learning new things; people are not likely to become more accepting or change long-held attitudes—and trying to insist that they do will only accentuate their negative behaviors.[42]

Remember Raymond, the client at the beginning of chapter 7 who wouldn't stop building a fire in his fireplace each evening? Raymond had lived with his wife in that same home for decades before she died, and one of their most cherished rituals was to sit before a crackling fire late into the evening during the winter months. We and Raymond's family spent a lot of time thinking creatively about how to cure Raymond's love of a blazing fire. The prospect of him burning down his home was more than just possible—it was verging on probable. His memory loss was erratic, and he was unaware of his poor judgment. Yet we all knew that Raymond was too obstreperous to do well in a care facility. So we

---

[42] Daryl, at the beginning of the chapter, was an exception. He seemed to become increasingly aware that he had been abusive to his family. I have seen this twice, but there are too many factors involved to know exactly why we might see a client begin to see past behaviors differently and become remorseful.

had to come up with a way to make it safer for him to remain in his home despite the fireplace.

We began by canceling his subscription to the local paper and redirecting his mail to a son so that he had less paper at hand. He began burning any paper he could find and scavenging scraps when we had him out in restaurants and coffee shops. (Fortunately, at that point, he didn't recognize books as a source of paper or he would likely have burned his extensive library.) Next, we hauled away what remained of Raymond's woodpile and cleared the property of all windfall and brush, but he began picking up twigs and branches from his neighbors' yards after dark. In the end, we knew the best we could do was to make the fireplace as safe as possible. We had the chimney cleaned, and the flue and fireplace screen repaired, and moved all furnishings further away from the front of the fireplace. We crossed our fingers and hoped. Sometimes that is all you can do. When cognitive impairment is involved, it is often necessary to give up some amount of safety in order to preserve the sense of identity and self that comes from continuing long-standing habits.

Another of our clients, Pat, had always been very generous to family, church, and community, as well as to a number of charities. She was used to overseeing her own finances and could not feel safe without sorting the post and trying to understand each piece of mail, even after her ability to comprehend the written word had begun to fade rapidly. Every letter that arrived requesting a donation, however, resulted in her writing a small check, no matter how dubious the source. Her family allowed her to continue because the total amount she donated each month was low enough to not impact her financial health, and because she benefited from feeling generous and able to share her wealth. As Pat's confusion increased, she began spending more and more time sitting at the kitchen table, trying to decipher her mail. Unable to believe that we could understand her finances better than she did, she asked to be taken to the bank almost every day, so the tellers could explain account statements and notices to her. Whenever Pat's phone rang, she would answer immediately, and then spend a long time on the line, struggling to figure out who was calling and what they wanted.

One day, a caller claiming to be selling magazine subscriptions for charity convinced her to read out her checking account number. Within days, this fraudster was withdrawing increasingly large amounts from her account. Her family closed down the account and changed the address on all her mail to her son's address, whereupon Pat became frantic each morning when she found her mailbox empty. She knew bad things must be happening because she wasn't reading her mail or taking care of her business affairs. We wanted to respect her need to comprehend her own finances, while keeping her safe from criminals; somehow, we had to explain why the mail was missing, without bluntly reminding her of her own incompetence. We came up with a catchphrase: *bank fraud*.

> "Pat, it was the *bank fraud*. Someone was stealing money from people's bank accounts, but they've been caught. Now your son Andrew is dealing with the bank and the insurance company and making sure your money is safe. He needs to have your mail to do that. We just need to wait and let Andrew take care of the problem. You're so lucky to have a son who knows how to take care of a *bank fraud*."

We used a catchphrase to frame the situation as something her son could handle best, and we put the blame on a distant third party. Pat was able to rest easy in the knowledge that someone she trusted was taking care of her finances, until she eventually forgot that she had ever done so herself.

We often must talk with families about the balancing act between safety and selfhood. Together we come to an understanding as to whether a client may need to keep a rug with turned-up edges, even though it's a clear trip-and-fall hazard, or a rickety piece of furniture when something firmer would be safer. It's worth noting here that the assumption that a care facility is safer for someone with dementia than their own home is often false. When people are agitated by the loss of familiar surroundings and believe they are being prevented from returning home, they wander, fall, and get into arguments more frequently.[43] The

---

[43] For examples of risks in care facilities, take a look at the following articles: nursing-home residents fall frequently (http://www.cdc.gov/homeand

psychotropic medications often administered in care facilities will numb the emotions causing such behavior, but also cause dizziness and confusion. People who receive psychotropic medications become physically frail more quickly and need more oversight, increasing the overall cost of care. And, several times I have had families contact me in anguish, saying that a parent refuses to forgive them for having been forced to leave home and move into a care facility. Being compelled to leave home against one's will destroys a person's sense of self-worth; that the move was the family's attempt to preserve safety is rarely understood.

Bathing and selfcare are a safety area in which problems are often encountered. Our worst case was Sonya, a client who had been well dressed and perfectly groomed in earlier years. As Sonya's dementia progressed, however, she began to develop an unsightly case of dandruff that progressed into a skin condition that caused her doctor concern. Sonya was a very private woman and adamantly refused any interference in her daily grooming. She was also frugal and concerned about avoiding what she considered unnecessary costs. We were already using caregiving by stealth to keep her home clean (we often do this with female clients who in the past were responsible for their own housekeeping), so we could secretly lay a hair across the top of her shampoo bottle in her shower to see whether she was using it to wash her hair. Sure enough, a week later the shampoo bottle had not been touched, although the shower and bar of soap were still being used. We now suspected either that Sonya had forgotten the purpose of shampoo or decided not to wash her hair because she was concerned that it was falling out. Telling her that her doctor wanted her to wash her hair more often had no effect. To determine the root of the problem, we purchased the recommended antiseptic shampoo and presented it to her, saying that her doctor had prescribed it for thinning hair. This seemed a promising solution, because of her

---

recreationalsafety/falls/nursing.html), residents are attacked most often by other residents (http://newamericamedia.org/2015/02/elder-abuse-rising-in-care-facilities-mixing-the-frail-and-the-disturbed.php), and common nursing-home infections (http://www.thedoctorwillseeyounow.com/content/infections/art2748.html).

concern about her hair loss and her respect for her doctor. We waited and watched, but Sonya didn't use this shampoo either.

Now we felt sure that she no longer knew what shampoo was for, and that a more invasive step was called for. We asked her family to arrange for her to receive a shampoo and set every week at a nearby beauty salon, presenting this service to her as a gift. Sonya would have considered a weekly trip to the hairdresser to be an inexcusable extravagance, but when her children presented her with a year's worth of hairdos as a present, she was delighted. The result of this carefully crafted approach was both a healthy scalp and well-groomed hair again, and a weekly reminder that of her children's love. We had enhanced her sense of being valued, and at the same time preserved a personal value (good hygiene), one we knew she would hold dear if she were still able to, as well as helped her regain a healthy scalp.

Blame a Distant Third Party

None of us appreciate being told what to do all the time. Being ordered around will make us look for ways to push back and express our own will. People with dementia don't lose their lifelong desire to be independent; their initial resistance to orders from people they don't feel have authority over them—even when these are meant to keep them safe or healthy—can quickly become obstinacy, and eventually belligerence. As caregivers, we must avoid letting our loved ones or clients do things that may be unwise or dangerous, or develop bad habits simply because of the inability to use reasoning to select a better course of action. We need to address and redirect these behaviors before they become ingrained. One caregiver told me that after she asked her husband to not use so much toilet paper, he stopped putting paper into the toilet at all, and simply left it on the bathroom floor. His new behavior could have been an attempt to regain a sense of control in the bathroom, or it could have been the result of not being able to problem-solve on his own. In any event, behaviors—particularly when they involve hygiene—must be addressed, and we need to find ways to respond to them that allow our companions to retain their dignity and sense of self.

One very effective way to gain cooperation is to present the problem to your loved one as being caused by some distant third party, so that complying is something you both must do together. We have found that the idea of bending to the dictates of some distant authority is less troubling to our clients than being confronted with an immediate, face-to-face demand from someone they see as a peer or subordinate—and when everyone must follow the same rule together, compliance becomes easier still. Blaming such a requirement on an anonymous third party helps our loved ones and clients retain their sense of dignity and equality, even when it involves something they see as unnecessary or unpleasant.

We often invent remote "third parties" we can blame for a necessary change in our clients' behavior. For example, we suggested that the wife of the man with the toilet paper problem try introducing a "third party" expert:

> "My, this is a bother, isn't it, honey? But the plumber says we should only use two squares of paper each time and then put the paper in the toilet. He's the plumber; he would know."

She would demonstrate this new method for solving the problem, while chatting about how plumbers know best, are expensive, are very helpful—anything she can think of to make it seem that she is not the one giving the directive to her husband. This technique also allows her to include herself in complying with the plumber's directives, following the expert's advice just like her husband. If his reaction was due to a lack of problem-solving skills, she is providing a solution. And if the behavior was due to a feeling of obstinacy or loss of status, he will be able to retain his dignity and not feel threatened by his wife.

Sherri, in chapter 6, who picked up the cat poop and did not like to wash her hands, had never responded well to the simple observation that washing our hands after using the bathroom was customary and necessary. Very early in her dementia, she had lost the concepts of sanitation and contamination. During our early years with Sherri, she would wash her hands if we asked her to, but entirely for *our* benefit (she is a kindhearted soul!). But as her dementia progressed, she no longer washed even when we asked. So we reframed the act of handwashing from something she did to protect us from her dirty hands to something we did together to protect ourselves from other people's germs. I hadn't thought about it before, but to suggest that her hands were dirty was to imply that she was at fault for something—to subtly but surely lower her status. With the new approach, I would begin washing my own hands the moment she reappeared from the toilet stall and say:

> "Oh, Sherri, I always wash my hands very carefully in these public bathrooms because I don't want to catch the flu or a cold. Other people use this bathroom too. You never know what kind of germs *they* might be carrying."

As I spoke, I would turn on water for her, offer her the soap—and model and chatter about how to scrub thoroughly. This worked. Sherri would agreeably lather and rinse along with me in order to avoid catching someone else's flu or cold. This made handwashing something she did with us to solve a problem that had been created by other people.

As caregivers, we must strive to understand our companions' point of view. They face constant threats to their self-worth. It is demoralizing to never be in charge and to always be less able—particularly after a lifetime of competence and independence. As thoughtful and creative caregivers, we can change at least some of these negative situations into chances for camaraderie, by becoming their partners in forgetfulness and aging, pointing out how we are all walking the same path as we age, even laughing about this common plight. We routinely talk with our clients about life as a series of chapters—how people begin as infants who need their parents' help for everything, then mature into self-sufficiency, and then gradually need more and more help again, this time from their children. We comment on how nice it is to let someone else take charge and do the worrying. When we actively look for and find ways to show our clients that we value their input and do not judge them for their decreasing abilities, they almost always respond favorably, and enjoy an increased sense of value.

Give a Chance to Be Gracious

One of the kindest things we can do for our loved ones and clients is to give them the opportunity to exhibit their better natures. People derive great emotional rewards from being generous, kind, or forgiving. When we give people who are experiencing dementia the chance to show their nobility of spirit toward us, we can greatly enhance their sense of value.

One of our clients, Harriet, was in a memory care unit, wheelchair-bound and almost completely blind. Her family had hired us to provide the companionship and stimulation that she could not get in the facility. Sarah would read historical fiction and biographies to her in the afternoon, and I would join her each morning to read the *New York Times* and do the crossword together. (Although Harriet had been diagnosed with dementia, she had excellent recall. She would have me read several clues for the words down and across, and then she would tell me the answers.) She had no possessions and very few resources to display generosity with. But she did have time, and a kind heart. When we spent time with Harriet, we shared our worries and asked her advice. She became interested in our lives, our families, our heartbreaks, our concerns—and gave us her attention, empathy, and wisdom. Our goal was to respect her and love her, but I think Sarah would agree that we left her presence feeling that she had given us more than we'd given her.

Often, our clients go through a stage during which they want to express their gratitude to us by giving us gifts. Often, though, these gifts are of great value or they are treasured family heirlooms. At other times, our clients want to give away their possessions for reasons other than expressing gratitude. They may say they want to make it easier for their children to dispose of things after they are gone, or they feel the need to make their environments less cluttered and confusing. Whatever the case, it is important for us, as caregivers, to allow our companions to express their gratitude and to feel that we have recognized and accepted their gift. So my caregivers and I gratefully accept all gifts, then contact the family and quietly return the item. In this way, our clients' expressions of gratitude to us can be acknowledged—and their autonomy and ownership of their possessions be validated—while their heirlooms remain in the family.

And When We Can't Offer Love?

Although feeling valued and loved is a necessary component to having a sense of wellbeing, not every person who develops dementia is easy to value or love. Like Daryl in the scenario at the beginning of this chapter, some parents are callous or cruel. One of the cruelest women I ever met had angelic looks and a sweet smile, but also an unrelenting determination to let no kind deed go unpunished. If Daryl were my father, I probably wouldn't have heard his vague words of remorse and responded kindly any more than his daughter Gina did. He had inflicted great pain on her, her mother and her sister. Even as caregivers for people outside our family, we often meet clients who remind us of someone unpleasant in our past, who are less than lovable, or whose personality clashes with ours. How do we handle these situations? When possible, obviously, we should avoid being caregivers for people we cannot empathize with. But where this choice isn't possible, and we have to care for someone whom we cannot forgive or respect—to support his or her need to feel valued—we should not burden ourselves with guilt. Instead, we can try to be magnanimous ourselves, putting our past dealings with the person out of our mind, and concentrating on the present interaction. If we succeed, we will communicate tolerance, and through tolerance a measure of respect, the basis for a sense of value.

CHAPTER TWELVE

Secure Future

And the place we all thought was safe to stay
Was just a memory of yesterday.

—"Where Are We Going?"
by John Marquette

I have struggled with the name of this tool from the start, because it seems to imply a security need rather than one of happiness or wellbeing. But as I mentioned in chapter 5, I came to agree with Oliver James that feeling that your future is secure is a necessary component of having a sense of wellbeing, especially for people experiencing dementia. Each of my clients faces the future with trepidation; even those who have anosognosia seem to have an underlying unease about the future. As a result, I have thought a lot about how to instill in someone the sense that all is well and tomorrow will be too. Without this underlying sense of confidence in the future, contentment is short-lived. When tomorrow is scary or unknown, apprehension pervades all other areas of our lives.

In actuality, none of us has a secure future. But those of us whose reason is intact can plan and act in ways that at least give us the sense that things will be okay. People who have dementia feel greater risk, and for good reason, knowing that they are becoming ever more dependent on the attention and goodwill of others. Even normal aging—becoming less physically capable and slower to react—makes our futures less secure. So how do we give the feeling of future security to the people whose futures are the most unsure?

One morning I met with a woman and her husband who were in their late seventies. The husband had been showing signs

227

of dementia for several years, and his wife was ready to consider the possibility of getting help. He was beginning to unlock the front door and wander down the street at night. He could no longer sleep for more than an hour or so, and seemed to feel a constant sense of agitation, probably because he could not develop a sense of being at home in the condo they'd moved into after he had begun to decline. He was clearly in distress, and his wife was exhausted from watching him day and night. As I talked with them, I could tell he was still very aware that his cognitive abilities were diminishing. This man had been a medical doctor, someone whose rational mind was well developed and who had researched and learned all he could about dementia when he noticed that his memory and rational abilities were beginning to slip.

I turned to him and explained what I had discovered in caring for my clients—that although I saw them losing their rational functions, they retained a rich and often evolving intuition; that they seemed to begin enjoying life in entirely different ways when they received the right support and care. His eyes slowly came alive, with a blend of hope and desperation, as he processed what I had said. This man had been looking at the future and seeing only the complete loss of personal control (ultimately ending his life in an institution), and nothing but exhaustion, loss, and loneliness for his wife. I may have been the first person to offer him a sliver of hope. It broke my heart when his wife spoke up moments later, saying she had decided they didn't want to pay for outside help, and she would carry on as his sole caregiver. His heart appeared to break, too; as she said this his face fell, and the light went out of his eyes.

Everyone needs to feel that there is something in the future worth living for; people who are experiencing dementia are no different. So how, as caregivers, do we give our companions that assurance? There are several things we can do.

Apply Each Previous DAWN Tool

Let's look back for a moment at the first six DAWN tools. If you have already started applying them, you are well on your way to instilling a sense of safety and wellbeing in your loved one or client. You have laid the foundation. It will take time to build the walls and create the haven, but you have begun.

When we regularly use the first tool—understanding that we both can and must manage our companions' moods—they begin to absorb a sense of comfort from living with positive emotions rather than constantly being confronted with frustration and loss. When we, by using the second tool, help them learn through intuitive experience that they are safe even when they are confused, and, with the third tool, teach them that they can trust others for care, feeling secure becomes natural—almost something known by habit—and remains available to them when they so desperately need it in later phases of dementia. When a client turns to me and says something along these lines: "I won't remember, but that's okay, we always have fun," I know that I've succeeded in giving him or her an abiding sense of security—an invaluable gift for someone who will live the rest of their life with dementia. When we have consistently met our companions' emotional need for security, we have already taken a critical step toward reassuring them that their futures are safe.

Here, as time passes and our clients maintain lasting relationships, feel loved and valued, and are allowed to make choices and feel control over some areas of their lives, they regain a sense that all is well in their world—a sense that persists for some time. However, as their impairments progress, their faith in a secure future often is eroded, unless we find ways of reinforcing it.

Identify What Symbolizes Security

I think each of us has internalized a symbol—sometimes consciously, sometimes unconsciously—of what represents a secure future. Our childhood experiences may have convinced us that if we go to school and earn a certain degree, we will be able to achieve financial independence and, through this, true happiness. Or perhaps we desire the status of membership in a specific church or club, or the respect that comes from a certain job or career. One of our clients was convinced that all would be well in his world if he could just find a new wife. He knew that his wife had died some time before, a fact that remained in his awareness despite the loss of almost every other recent memory. All conversations with him would eventually turn to his primary concern: that every man needs a wife, that his wife had died, and that he needed to find another wife as soon as possible. As we began building a relationship with this man and helped him create a healthier life—getting exercise, eating regularly, being out in the community—he saw a potential new partner in every woman over the age of forty who crossed his path. "Wow, she's a looker! What about her? Do you think we could ask her if we can sit with her?" He would make these pronouncements in a loud voice that carried easily across a crowded restaurant. He had lost most of his inhibitions and any idea of what was appropriate to say in public but, fortunately, he was well known in the little town he lived in, and much loved. These announcements were often followed by invitations from the woman in question to sit at her table and her assurances that, but for the fact that she was married already, she would be honored to become his wife.

Because of his belief that a wife would solve all his problems, when we matched this gentleman with a caregiver, she had to be careful to remind him daily that she was already married. He was thrilled each day when she reappeared and took care of the household chores, saw that he ate, and took him on errands. He was overjoyed each afternoon when she laid out dinner for him at his usual place at the kitchen table. He began to refer to her as his girlfriend, though he continued to believe that he needed a wife. She was careful to support the latter belief, and to reiterate daily that he needed to find a wife and that she would help him do so. For him, having a caregiver who joined him in his search gradually gave him a sense that all would be well, even though she was not, of course, actually helping him find a new spouse at all.

Other clients needed to be convinced that their bank accounts and savings were safe, or that their children were financially independent. We helped each of them build a personal sense of a secure future by regularly remarking on the success of their approach. For the woman whose symbol was money, we would comment on how smart she was to choose such a safe bank, how wise she had been to invest her money so early in life, and how lucky she was to have married a man who was so good at saving money. For the client who worried about her children's welfare, we looked for ways to commend her on what great people they had grown up to be—how successful, mature, and attentive they were, both to her and to their own children. As our clients become less able to use their rational minds, they seem to pare their worries and lack of certainty down to a single item, which they begin to believe is the one thing they need to secure their futures.

Each of my clients has done this. What they select and become focused on may seem illogical or even nonsensical. However, we must take very seriously whatever symbol our loved ones or clients become fixated on, and seek out ways to reinforce their sense of security in that area by preemptively assuring them that their concern is valid. Actually meeting what they perceive to be their pressing needs—finding a wife or putting lots of money in the bank—is not necessary, but giving them the sense that their needs are being taken seriously is. During the earlier stages of dementia, when they are still able to identify and articulate their personal symbols, it is very important that we reinforce those daily, to improve the likelihood that their sense of security will remain intact as they enter the later stages of the condition. In fact, we consider identifying and reinforcing these personal symbols to be the most critical factor in fostering a sense of a secure future.

Be Present as Much as Needed

It is important to understand that spending time alone can be detrimental for people experiencing dementia once they have lost the ability to organize their thoughts and choose tasks or activities for themselves. People can lose their general sense of wellbeing in a moment of solitude, whether they live at home or in a care facility, once they no longer have a clear sense of time's passage. They can easily believe that they have been alone for many hours. They may leave home in search of someone to talk to, or become confused while trying to use the microwave to make breakfast, and still be pacing and agitated when their caregiver arrives at lunchtime. Even if the sensation of being lost or unsafe has only lasted a few minutes, it may take the caregiver hours or days to restore their positive mood and general sense of security.

Time takes on a different meaning for people who have dementia. My clients seem to revert to the sense of time I experienced as a child. I remember pondering time and eternity as a five-year-old, trying to envision time extending endlessly into the future. It made me feel very much at risk, almost dizzy, as if Earth's gravity had stopped working and everything from the chair I was sitting on to the planets far out in space was expanding incessantly. I was equally disturbed by trying to imagine time extending endlessly into the past. To my childish mind, it seemed that if it was true that time had no beginning or end, neither could I be assured that my little self lived only in the *now* that I perceived. For my clients, time seems to lose its limits in similar ways, producing something of the same sense of risk that I felt as a child. However, now when I see my clients' unease, I realize that time extends not only into the future and past but also into the present—that each moment holds an eternity within itself, because my companion and I have innumerable options for how we will fill the present.

Hence, it is vital to evaluate how much time our loved ones and clients are spending alone. When people are living with dementia and cannot track time, their minds often get stuck on a single thought, or take them in endless loops as they attempt the same task time after time, forgetting that they have attempted it just moments before. Although they may be resistant at first to having others around, or anxious to do things for themselves and keep their own schedules, this will change. As they become less able to fill their time with activities they like doing or believe to be necessary, they will both want and need to spend more time with other people, even if they have always been introverts. Recognizing these processes, we can monitor their changing needs and increase the time they spend with loved ones and caregivers. Be careful, however, to recognize the difference between the need to be with one other person and the need to be in a group, which are very different. When people reach this point in their dementia, they usually derive great comfort in knowing that another person is there to make the decisions they can no longer make. They are also reassured to have someone else identify what needs to be done in general. So we, as caregivers, must be careful that our companions continue to spend time alone for as long as solitude enhances their sense of independence, but not past that point.

One man we worked with was in the final months of his life, and spent much of his time dozing. He had lived a goal-driven life of widespread accomplishment, having reached a senior position at the local university, become a recognized writer in his field, and had a distinguished career in state politics. He had also been an officer in World War II. As he was now bedbound, we provided him with a television, and the movies, documentaries and programming that held his attention. He was fascinated by history and nature—in particular, accounts and re-creations of the events he'd lived through or had been involved with, and nature shows filmed in countries in which he'd lived. I believe we were seeing him—on some deep emotional level—resolve the experiences in his busy and often difficult life that he hadn't been able to come to grips with before. At one point, when his daughter came to visit, she asked him what he was doing to entertain himself. By that time his language skills were very limited. "I'm practicing sleeping," he said. He felt so safe and cared for that he could comfortably drift in and out of semi-somnolence. His family was giving him a priceless gift. Instead of making him live his final months in a care facility where routines are dictated by the convenience and legal liability of the staff and the billing procedures of insurance companies, they enabled us to create a safe space in his home where he could (on some level) recall and process his life in peace. We allowed him to determine how much interaction he had with other people, and met his needs as they arose. He slept and woke on his own schedule, and was never reminded of the passage of time, something that, in this late stage of his dementia, he no longer had the skills to comprehend.

Dementia is usually spoken of in terms of early, middle, and late stages. I have not found those terms at all helpful when designing a care plan, in deciding how much oversight or companionship someone might need. We do see our clients go through several clear emotional phases, however, as their capabilities change with their cognitive decline. The DAWN method recognizes the six stages we see our clients go through.

Since people with dementia can only feel their futures are secure when care is tailored to support their changing abilities and emotional needs, we carefully design our care plans around the behaviors and emotional states our clients experience in these six phases.

1. Independence

At first, people who have dementia want as little interference from their family and friends as possible. They are still able to read a clock, perceive the passage of time fairly accurately, and look at a calendar to determine what day it is so that they can attend appointments and activities. They wake up in the morning and understand that the events they dreamed the night before were just that—dreams. They can navigate the kitchen and take care of their homes more or less as well as they did earlier in life. If they have been diagnosed with dementia, they will be understandably distressed and afraid of what that diagnosis means. If they have not been diagnosed, they are likely to be frightened by ever more frequent moments when they cannot recall an event, find a word, or recapture their train of thought; typically, they are doing their best to pretend that nothing is wrong.

Those who do not have anosognosia prefer to do things for themselves but will be grateful and appreciative for help from others. When they do accept help from a caregiver, the common refrain is: "Thanks so much for the ride to the grocery store. But really, I'm managing just fine." Those with anosognosia will be less grateful for assistance. They may respond to offers of help with indignation, seeing them as subtle suggestions that they are needy or incapable. They often believe that any mistakes or confusion are caused by other people, and so may become paranoid or suspicious. However, in the earlier years of dementia, whether people have anosognosia or not, they will attempt to mask the true extent of their confusion and memory loss from others (and often avoid facing it themselves), so that they can preserve their independence for as long as possible.

At this stage—the beginning of the journey of dementia—it is best to provide as little help as possible. When our clients are still relatively independent, we arrange no more than a few appointments per week. We may take them out to do errands and then once or twice happen to stop by to say hello. In reality, we are verifying that all is well and monitoring their changing skills. At this point, families should try to make sure that all end-of-life documentation, both legal and medical, is in place. They should be putting together a plan for a long-term care team. And if a move must occur, they should think about ways to postpone it until the person is no longer able to recognize their familiar surroundings, so that their ability to use automatic thinking and muscle memory (the tools of mindlessness) is prolonged in a well-known environment.

2. Uncertainty

At some point, uncertainty will set in. The person with complete anosognosia will stubbornly persist in believing that their confusion and frustration are due to other people's mistakes, but even those with partial anosognosia will begin to doubt themselves. Now that they have so often found themselves unable to complete a simple task, or at a loss about what they were doing or should be doing, they know they need someone else to drop in regularly. They will find themselves staring at the calendar without being able to determine which day of the week it is, realizing that chunks of time have seemed to disappear, or standing somewhere with no idea how they got there.

At this stage, when we bring a client back to their home, rather than thanking us and telling us they are fine, they will ask, "Will I see you tomorrow?" or "Would you like to come in?" This indicates to us that our client has entered the phase of uncertainty and is ready for more assistance. Hence, we increase our number of contacts with them from a few times a week to one activity a day, whenever possible enlisting the help of family and friends to provide them with activities on weekends.

3. Follow the Leader

We know our clients have moved into the third stage, which we have nicknamed "Follow the Leader," if they start telling us, when faced with a decision they would previously have made for themselves: "Oh, I'll just have whatever you're having" or "It doesn't matter to me—you decide." They are no longer able to make decisions without assistance; they now cannot track time, read clocks, or interpret calendars consistently. The desire for independence has melted away unless anosognosia is present. Sometimes we see clients continue to function well inside their homes, remaining at the previous level (*Uncertainty*) so long as they remain there, but dropping into the *Follow the Leader* or subsequent stages when they leave familiar surroundings. This is when most people with dementia are moved into assisted living or care facilities—although this is also probably the most damaging time for a move. To be able to remain in a well-known place helps a person to continue using the mindlessness tools and intuitive processes—what he or she has learned through experience, habits, and muscle memory—and function as if on autopilot. To be removed from such surroundings is to be dropped in a foreign world, without the ability to learn the new contours of this world. The result is a marked loss of coping skills.

At the *Follow the Leader* phase, we again provide more support to our clients. We watch to see whether they are losing weight due to failure to recognize food, whether they are bathing properly (or have forgotten the purpose of soap), whether they have retained the concept of cleanliness in the home, and whether they have begun to lose the distinction between dreams and reality. Now we expect their judgment to be consistently impaired, and watch for misinterpreted realities that could become dangerous. Their daily activities with us are gradually lengthened to include meals, cleaning, and household chores—and maybe visits to our local wellness center for a supervised shower and soak in the hot tub.

4. Clinginess

Our clients slip into this stage—becoming clingy—when they are experiencing confusion to such a degree that they are commonly unable to do simple tasks when alone, or understand whether it is morning or afternoon, Tuesday or Saturday, October or May. They might signal their arrival at this stage by saying, "I'd feel better if I could hold your arm." They may not be able to verbalize this need and just reach out and take their caregiver's arm.

In a crowd, even in a small group, these clients sidle closer or lean toward their caregivers. They seek and hold eye contact with them more often. At this point most people have become strangers to them—even their family members and dear friends—although they do their best to conceal this fact. Memories can be recalled and faces placed, but only when they are carefully led through a series of related memories to get there.

We typically see these clients twice daily, seven days a week, unless their friends or family members are making regular visits too. Routine and familiarity are now essential. The smallest change can bring on a crisis of fear and confusion. When our clients are in this stage, we are vigilantly watching for the moment when they reach the next level of need. They are still safe without an overnight caregiver, provided they continue to sleep at night and do not feel agitated about being alone (which may cause them to wander or have accidents). This stage requires a very careful balancing of independence and safety, as well as adequate social and sensory stimulation during the day.

This past year we have been carefully watching one of our clients as she moves back and forth between the stages of *Uncertainty*, *Follow the Leader*, and *Clinginess*. She is fine when in her home, but defers to her caregivers when out in the community. After a family member died, she became very clingy and stayed at that level for several months, but she then went back to *Follow the Leader*. We were ready with an overnight caregiver to move into her home on a day's notice, but she continued to say that she preferred living alone—and continued functioning within the realm of safety while there. If we had forced her to accept someone living in her home, we would have had negative behaviors to deal with as she sought to regain the privacy she desired. However, when our clients ask for someone to be with them, we respond immediately, for it means that overnight care is needed that very night and they will be at risk without it.

5. Overnight

This is a transition that cannot be ignored, and requires vigilance on the part of the family and caregivers. The change may be sudden or gradual, the result of a crisis or merely a response to the accumulation of daily failures and irritations. Eventually, clients who have been living alone and do not have anosognosia will ask a caregiver, friend, or family member whether they would like to stay overnight with them. Wanting to have someone spend the night does not imply that they need full-time care, however. People at this point still enjoy the autonomy of being able to spend a few hours alone, but normally no more than that. Our response at this point is to immediately provide a caregiver who is present from dinnertime through breakfast, full-time on weekends, and off-duty during business hours. We have found this works very well as a part-time job for students studying nursing or social work. During the day, we arrange midday activities that provide the client with sensory and social stimulation, but allow them an hour or two each morning and afternoon to be alone.

6. Full-time

Eventually our clients become so unable to make sense of the world around them that they need to have someone present at all times to feel safe. Even people who have anosognosia will eventually welcome the full-time presence of other people. We know it is time for full-time care when our clients say, "Do you really have to go?" when we get ready to leave their homes. This will happen long before a person becomes bedridden or unable to communicate. At this point, we ensure that someone on the caregiving team is always present. We continue the same schedule of daily activities as before, and, as much as possible, use the same caregivers as companions for each activity or shift. Ideally, two or three caregivers are available to share morning and afternoon activities. Again, it is best to have the same person on duty for all overnights—and off duty during the daytime—and we try to have the overnight caregiver be the person who prepares the evening meal. Having a bedtime routine that never varies makes it possible for the client to fall into a rhythm of sleeping at night and through most of the night.

People who feel secure—whether or not they have dementia—are less agitated, which in turn determines how they behave. So the DAWN method stresses watching for and responding to our clients' changing emotional needs, and tailoring the level of care they receive accordingly, which ensures they do not resist our care or begin to engage in dangerous behaviors.

Verbalize Love and Caring

Finally, if we want to help people who are experiencing dementia trust that their futures are secure, we need to tell them, repeatedly and often, that they are loved and will always be cared for. We tell our clients every day that we enjoy spending time with them. Those who are aware that they have dementia constantly thank us for taking care of them, for being patient, and for spending time with them. We can reply truthfully—that we enjoy being with them, and that we are glad to help. And we make a point of telling our clients repeatedly that their children love them—and, in fact, that we have come to be in their lives because of their children's love.

We often begin working with our clients when their children decide it is no longer safe for them to drive. Remember Edna, the swimmer who lived alone with her cats? When I first started working with her, each time we got in the car, we'd have just gotten our seat belts on when she would turn to me and say, "That daughter of mine! She's always coming up here from Boise and meddling in my life, making changes. And now she's taken away my car!" I quickly learned that it did no good for me to remind her of the times she had lost her car or detail the ways in which a person with dementia could become distracted when driving. Besides, I wanted her to retain an understanding of her daughter's love and concern. So each time she erupted in anger and indignation when she got into my car, I responded using the same phrases, hoping that repetition would teach the necessary truth, despite her impairment. I would say:

> "Oh, but you're lucky your daughter loves you so much— she doesn't want you to get lost or have an accident. I hope my kids love me enough to take away my car when I get older. I sure wouldn't want to have an accident and hurt anyone. Right now, we have my car; let's just have fun doing errands together."

These phrases enabled me to turn her habitual response of indignation into a reminder of how lucky she was and how much her children loved her. I was so pleased when, a month later, she began saying, as she buckled up her seat belt: "Well, my kids took my car away. But that daughter of mine, she really loves me. She didn't want me to have an accident and hurt somebody. You'd better hope your kids take your car away when the time comes." And then we could laugh about forgetfulness and how we all become more forgetful as we get older.

It is important that the caregivers of people who have dementia repeatedly verbalize their love and caring. Often-repeated phrases will stick, like catchphrases, and negative attitudes can be changed into positive ones. Dementia takes away our loved ones' and clients' ability to look back into their memories and recall examples of their families' love and devotion, so their caregivers need to do it for them. When we do this regularly and repeatedly, we instill in them the sense that they are in caring hands and that their futures are safe.

■ ■ ■

This completes our discussion of how to look for the emotional needs that are affecting your loved one's or client's reactions and behavior—in other words, how to use the tools of the DAWN method. My purpose in creating the method and in writing this book was twofold. First and foremost, I wanted to help families enable their elders to age in place with as much dignity and autonomy as possible, for as long as possible—especially when they are experiencing the progressive cognitive impairment that is dementia. Second, I wanted to bring us back to an understanding of elderhood and what it can represent, if we recognize it as a singular and potentially delightful stage of life—one of *being* rather than *doing*, one of sharing rather than accomplishing. I truly believe that dementia does not necessarily have to rob us of the joys of elderhood. It can become a path to experiencing life in a manner we couldn't have imagined previously, due to our accomplishment-focused modern society.

CHAPTER THIRTEEN

Life's Final Chapter

I slept and dreamt that life was joy.
I awoke and saw that life was service.
I acted—and behold, service was joy.

—Rabindranath Tagore
(1861–1941)

As it turns out, it takes a long time to write a book, and this book has taken even longer to publish than it took to write. It's been more than four years since I sat down to describe this journey into the world of dementia that I unwittingly began back in 2010—to try to explain what I've learned from my friends and neighbors along the way. Many of the people I describe in these pages are gone now. My heart has been broken many times, when I could only stand by and watch as families made fateful errors regarding my clients. I've watched many cruelties carried out since I began writing, some unintentional, others not. And I have seen kindnesses where none could have been anticipated. What comes to my mind when I look back, however, are the innumerable gifts my clients have bestowed on their families, on my staff, and on me—spiritual gifts of grace, kindness, wonder, and service—as we walked the path of dementia with them. This is a book about how to create more comfort for both you and your loved one when dementia is present, but I hope I have hinted at another truth: that the essence of family life is care, or serving each other; and that there is joy in service: a joy that enriches both those who serve and those served.

Hazel, my tablemate at the Thanksgiving dinner I described in the Introduction, is much older now, and her life has changed dramatically. When she and I sat side by side at her daughter's dinner table that fall, she lived in an assisted living facility nearby. Now she lives in her daughter's home, where her family is experiencing benefits none of us expected. "I had no idea how much stress was added to my life by having Mom live in a facility," my friend tells me. "Finding time to spend with her was yet another appointment to fit into my overly-busy days. Working with the staff and management of the facility took time and interfered with what should have been simply *us*, as a family, caring for each other." My friend admits that moving her mother home created certain problems, especially the loss of privacy with caregivers in and out of the home daily, but says the benefits have outweighed the disadvantages. "Having Mom at home is much better," she tells me. "Now I can just pop upstairs in a moment to give her a hug. And I always know what's going on."

A frequent concern when a loved one lives in a facility is not knowing for sure what is happening there, given that the source of most information is someone who has dementia. "I was always trying to find an aide who could explain why Mom was upset about something," says my friend. Now, with Hazel at home, she knows; and she can stop what she's doing at any moment to answer a question, change the music or start a nature video, share a hug, or put together a snack to be enjoyed on the front porch together. They now have impromptu moments of companionship that could only occur within the home. And perhaps most important of all, my friend is able to provide care personally—to serve her mother in the way she now does. "Like many in the Great Depression, my mom had a difficult childhood," she told me once. "Now I'm able to give her the childhood she never had." Caring for her mother in her home allows my friend to complete a circle, to give back to the woman who cared for her when she was a child and needed supervision herself. This continuous cycle of caring is the essence of being a family.

My friend's twenty-eight-year-old daughter also reports a benefit from her grandmother's move into the family home. She reports that she's getting to know her grandmother for the first time now that she lives nearby rather than in a distant state—despite the effect dementia has had on her grandmother's ability to communicate and interact. "When Grandma was in the facility, I could only be an infrequent visitor," she said. "Now we can visit for a few minutes, or longer, whenever I drop by my parents' home. You never know when it will happen, but sometimes Grandma is fully aware and present with me, just as if there was no dementia at all." When I asked her about her experience with her grandmother's move home, she told me, with wisdom beyond her years, just what I'd been pondering since I started writing this book. She said: "I really like being able to help my family. Now I'm a help to Mom, Dad, and Grandma. By simply dropping by and spending time with Grandma, I am supporting my family." This young woman already recognizes the reward in being able to contribute, to serve.

I believe that, in our accomplishment-driven, productivity-focused, and technology-distracted society, many of us have lost sight of the value of family and service. We have lost the knowledge that when we care for people who cannot care for themselves, we are exercising kindness and generosity, even if our actions are initially prompted by duty alone. In serving, we are expressing and fostering our very humanity. Most of us pursue an increasingly-elusive perception of happiness and fulfilment, while failing to see that these things lie within easy reach, and always have, within our families and homes. We find it there when we pause, and spend time with someone who is walking life's road ahead of us, and do for them what they can no longer do for themselves.

These past eight years of learning about dementia and how to help those experiencing it have brought this lesson home to me with remarkable power. During the first four, I spent most of my time with people who were experiencing dementia; since then I've spent most of my time learning to write, teach, and use technology to share with others (family members, caregivers) what my clients with dementia taught me. Yet while I was absorbed in learning how to help others, my own unhappiness and yearnings somehow faded away. I'm a different person now than the one you read about in chapter 2. Contentment has found me. I have been awakened to what Rabindranath Tagore called "joy in service."

As a friend and visitor in Hazel's home, I'm an unofficial member of her care team. While I'm writing these paragraphs, her family have left her in my care while they work and run errands. I'm sitting at that same dining room table where Hazel and I were tablemates last Thanksgiving. A video baby monitor is propped next to my laptop, so I can see her upstairs in her sitting room, enjoying breakfast to the sounds of her favorite big band playlist while watching a YouTube video of an aquarium which she especially likes. I can see her holding a sprig of tiny champagne grapes in one hand and eating them with great concentration, one by one, her head nodding to the music. Sometimes the movement of the tray on her lap tells me that her feet are keeping time too. Every minute or so she glances down and notices the little bowls on her tray; then, when she picks up the spoon to sample the yogurt or minced apricots, her expression of discovery and delight is unmistakable even on the tiny screen of the monitor. If Hazel begins to look concerned, or starts to put her tray down, I'll go up and help her, but I won't interrupt her enjoyment of these sensory-rich moments unless I see that she needs my help. She doesn't want or require constant companionship. Her delight in her own space, surrounded by the things her daughter knows she likes and enjoys, is a pleasure to watch.

This is Hazel's last chapter in life; the final stage of her dementia is approaching rapidly. She no longer knows who most of us are, even close relatives or friends, but that doesn't worry her: we all introduce ourselves each time we enter her presence. She is having trouble putting words together in sentences, and understands little of what we say to her, but that doesn't cause her concern: we listen for meaning in her intonation and fill our conversations with the information we know she can't recall on her own. She spends more and more time sleeping, but we expect that and entice her to stay awake by tempting her with what we know she enjoys: her big band tunes and the "Sound of Music" soundtrack, flowers from the garden, anything blue, old M*A*S*H episodes, ice cream of every flavor, and endless cups of good strong tea. At her core she is still the same person she always was, although a little more fully herself now that the habits, inhibitions, and restraints of her upbringing and culture have faded away. I can see, as I sit here typing and watching her enjoy her breakfast, that Hazel is happy and filled with peace in her sunny bedroom upstairs. She is living this final, important chapter of her life at her own pace—without the restrictions or demands of a facility's schedules or staff—even though she has dementia.

Supporting someone's needs and dignity at the end of life is a profound kindness, but it is also a duty we cannot ignore. "What I do for my Mom now is what I will leave as my legacy—my example to my children," my friend told me one evening. She's right: how we care for our elders will shape and affect our culture for generations, for we are modeling the role and duties of adulthood for our children.

I worry that we have forgotten that life has three distinct roles. The first is childhood, the time for being and growing. We recognize childhood as a valuable stage that prepares and enables us to live fulfilled and happy adult lives, and we accept that children need to gather the skills and knowledge necessary to be successful adults through play and exploration. We understand that when children are properly cared for, they arrive in adulthood better equipped to take on the role of being providers and caretakers themselves. In addition, we understand that adulthood is the time for mastery and accomplishment, for putting our skills to good use. We expect adults to be responsible, to work and provide for their families, to gather resources and accumulate assets, to fulfil community responsibilities. As adults, many of us struggle to carve out time from all this achievement simply to be.

Yet, although we recognize childhood and adulthood, we seem to have forgotten that there is a third role: elderhood. We speak of our elders as if they are people who are failing at adulthood—in terms of what they can or can no longer do. "Dad can *still* drive" or "Mom can't keep track of her purse or keys anymore." But our elders are not broken adults, nor is elderhood an extension of adulthood. Elderhood is a distinct role, the time for being and sharing, for an end to mastery and accomplishment. I think that as a nation we have become so focused on action that we have forgotten that there is more to life. I wonder, as Socrates did, whether there can be value in a life that leaves no time to consider what has been learned along the way. Aging and waning capabilities naturally bring inactivity; elderhood is the time to stop being doers and become thinkers, looking back and considering what has gone before. Our elders have much to share with those of us who are still in adulthood (and childhood), if we allow them to embrace their role of being and sharing, and we assume our role as their caretakers. When Hazel moved into her daughter's home, her family discovered that providing for her needs gave them the opportunity to watch her thrive in elderhood, in dementia—through simply *being*—even as she taught them the joy of service.

Caring for our elders is as much the role of adults as is caring for our children, but it is also an opportunity to heal wounds that are sometimes generations-old within our families, to break cycles of inadequate care and start a new pattern, one of kindness and service. Another friend explained to me that when she and her husband moved her mother into their home, all three generations experienced benefits. She and her husband added another dimension to their already strong partnership, through caring for her mother together. Their adult sons were able to get to know their grandmother (she had lived in another state throughout their childhood) and they became enthusiastic and active members of her care team. "My sons have both acknowledged that they'll be better husbands and men for this experience," my friend told me. But their grandmother reaped a benefit too: when she began living with her daughter's family, she saw their closeness and was able to acknowledge that she'd been less available to her children when they were young, an awareness that is bringing healing to her relationships with each of them.

Unfortunately, multigenerational American families who live together are comparatively rare nowadays, as are caregiving at home and the idea of service. In her book *Cultivating Conscience*, Cornell law professor Lynn Stout points out that unselfish prosocial behavior and passive altruism have been on the decline in the United States since the 1960s, changes not caused by fading religious faith or diminished prosperity. Stout ultimately concludes that this loss of our basic human kindness has been caused not only by the fact that we now spend more time interacting with technology than with our fellow humans, but also due to the conviction, which has emerged since WWII, that material incentives shape behavior more effectively than conscience and should be relied upon to modify behavior.

Stout makes two points that are particularly relevant to this book. First, she details the great neurological rewards we derive from cooperative behavior and service to others. Second, she demonstrates that asocial behavior is a self-fulfilling prophesy—that when a society treats its citizens as if they were greedy and suspicious of others, they end up behaving in precisely this way. I see very good news in these two statements. The first implies that, when we behave in a more humane way with our own family members, the emotional rewards we will receive have been proven by science. In the second I see an inverse truth, that when society assumes a positive, altruistic model of human nature around which to write laws and shape norms, people treat each other more kindly.

And yet, the joy of service is not all that we gain when we become caretakers of those who are less able. When we take time to be with our elders, especially if they have dementia, we are forced to slow down and (sometimes quite literally) smell the roses. You will find yourself becoming more aware of what is beautiful in life, and more willing to mindfully pause and contemplate it. You will find yourself more able to wrest your attention away from that device in your hand, to curb your mind's inclination to leap into the past or future so that the wonders of the present fill your awareness.

The theme of this book, in brief, is the immense value of kindness, not only to its recipient but to its giver. Caring for someone awakens our intuitive thinking skills and our right brain functions; it activates our humanity and leads us to engage more empathetically with the world around us. When we become teammates in care with someone, we really are just walking each other home.

■ ■ ■

Bibliography

Books to Help You Understand:

DeBaggio, Thomas. *Losing My Mind.* New York: The Free Press, 2002.

Genova, Lisa. *Still Alice.* New York: Simon & Schuster, Inc., 2007. (fiction)

Kahneman, Daniel. *Thinking, Fast and Slow.* New York: Farrar, Straus and Giroux, 2011.

Koenig Coste, Joanne. *Learning to Speak Alzheimer's.* New York: Houghton Mifflin Harcourt Publishing Co., 2003.

Langer, Ellen. *Mindfulness.* Philadelphia: Da Capa Press, 2014.

McGilchrist, Iain. *The Master and His Emissary.* Totten: Hobbs, 2012.

Power, Allen. *Dementia Beyond Drugs.* Baltimore, MD: Health Professions Press, 2010.

Books/Movies to Broaden your Perspective:

Aubrey, Sarah; Cameron, John; and Sidney Kimmel (Producers) & Gillespie, C. (Director). (2007). *Lars and the Real Girl* [Motion Picture]. Canada, United States: Metro-Goldwyn-Mayer.

Doerr, Anthony. *Memory Wall, Stories.* New York: Scribner, 2010. (fiction)

Gawande, Atul. *Being Mortal.* London: Profile Books Ltd., 2014.

Murat, Júlia (Writer, Director). (2011). *Found Memories* [Motion Picture]. Brazil: Vitrine Filmes.

Sacks, Oliver. *The Man Who Mistook His Wife for a Hat.* New York: Touchstone, 1970.

Tolle, Eckhart. *The Power of Now.* Vancouver: Namaste Publishing, 1999.

Books to Help You Cope:

Brackey, Jolene. *Creating Moments of Joy.* West Lafayette, IN: Purdue University Press, 2007.

James, Oliver. *Contented Dementia.* Croydon: Vermilion, 2009.

Lamott, Anne. *Help Thanks Wow, the Three Essential Prayers.* New York: Penguin Group (USA) Inc., 2012.

Merton, Thomas. *No Man Is an Island.* Orlando: Harcourt, Inc., 1955.

Thomas, Abigail. *A Three Dog Life, a Memoir.* Orlando: Harcourt, Inc., 2006.

Index

Made in the USA
Columbia, SC
09 June 2022

61555779R00153